STUDIES IN JUDAISM, HUMANITIES, AND THE SOCIAL SCIENCES

Vol 1.1, Fall 2017

Studies in Judaism, Humanities, and the Social Sciences

Published bi-annually, beginning Fall 2017

ISSN 2473-2605 (Print)
ISSN 2473-2613 (Online)

EDITOR-IN-CHIEF
Simcha Fishbane (Touro College)

MANAGING EDITOR
Eric Levine (Touro College)

REVIEWS EDITOR
Herbert Basser (Queen's University)

Studies in Judaism, Humanities and the Social Sciences is an interdisciplinary peer-reviewed academic journal published by Academic Studies Press. The mission of the journal is to publish original works of interest on Judaism through the "eyes" of the humanities and the social sciences. Its goal is to advance the systematic, scholarly, and social scientific study of Jews and Judaism, and to provide a forum for the discussion of methodologies, theories, and conceptual approaches across the many disciplines. Articles may be contemporary or historical in nature and can include case studies, historical studies, articles on new theoretical developments, results of research that advance our understanding of Jews and Judaism, and works on innovations in methodology. Studies in Judaism, Humanities and the Social Sciences encourages contributions from the global community of scholars. All articles in this journal will undergo rigorous peer review, based on initial editor screening and refereeing by anonymous reviewers. The journal will also publish book reviews of important new scholarship.

All inquiries may be directed to sjhss@academicstudiespress.com.

EDITORIAL BOARD
Ira Bedzow (New York Medical College, US)
Jonathan Boyarin (Cornell University, US)
Benny Brown (Hebrew University, Israel)
Rachel Einwohner (Purdue University, US)
David Elcott (New York University, US)
Roberta Farber (Yeshiva University, US)
Rebecca Golbert (University of California at Berkeley, US)
Calvin Goldscheider (Brown University, US)
Klaus Hermann (Free University of Berlin, Germany)
Steven Huberman (Touro College, US)
Elazar Hurvitz (Yeshiva University, Israel)
Norma Joseph (Concordia University, Canada)
Shaul Kelner (Vanderbilt University, US)
Daniel Maoz (Waterloo Lutheran Seminary/Wilfrid Laurier University, Canada)
Tirzah Meacham (University of Toronto, Canada)
Ira Robinson (Concordia University, Canada)
Nissan Rubin (Bar Ilan University, Israel)
William Shaffir (McMaster University, Canada)
Michael Shmidman (Touro College, US)
Arik Tayeb (Sapir Academic College, Israel)
Donald Sylvan (Ohio State University, US)
Mervin Verbit (Touro College, US; Brooklyn College, US)
Lynn Visson (Middlebury Institute of International Studies at Monterey, US)
Laura Wiseman (York University, Canada)
Jeffrey Woolf (Bar Ilan University, Israel)

Table of Contents

From the Editors
Simcha Fishbane, Eric Levine, Herbert Basser ... 1

ESSAYS

Inclusion and Exclusion in the Mishnah: Non-Jews, Converts, and the Nazir
Calvin Goldscheider ... 3

Textual Study and Social Formation: The Case of Mishnah
Jack N. Lightstone ... 21

Genealogies of the Future
Jonathan Boyarin ... 45

The Role of Life Motifs in Commitment Journeys of *Ba'alei Teshuvah*
Roberta Rosenberg Farber ... 57

Mipnei Darkei Shalom: The Promotion of Harmonious Relationships in the Mishnah's Social Order
Simcha Fishbane ... 73

On the Unknown Soldier Symbol in Israeli Culture
Irit Dekel ... 85

Why Religious Discourse Has a Place in Medical Ethics: An Example from Jewish Medical Ethics
Ira Bedzow ... 101

החופה בספרות חז"ל – סמל בתהליך שינוי
Nisan Rubin ... 113

BOOK REVIEWS

Jon D. Levenson, *The Love of God: Divine Gift, Human Gratitude, and Mutual Faithfulness in Judaism.* Princeton, NJ, Princeton University Press, 2016.
Review by James A. Diamond ... 125

Todd M. Endelman, *Leaving the Jewish Fold: Conversion and Radical Assimilation in Modern Jewish History.* Princeton, NJ: Princeton University Press, 2015.
Review by Sylvia Barack Fishman ... 129

Moshe Halbertal, *On Sacrifice.* Princeton, NJ: Princeton University Press, 2012.
Review by Zev Garber ... 133

From the Editors

Simcha Fishbane, Eric Levine, Herbert Basser

Producing a scholarly journal is truly a labor of love. We are honored to serve as editors of the new journal *Studies in Judaism, Humanities, and the Social Sciences*. In presenting this inaugural issue of the journal, we anticipate many years of offering the highest level of scholarship in the broad field of Judaic studies. It is, furthermore, a privilege to be working with Academic Studies Press, an outstanding publisher of fine scholarship and an emerging force in the field.

Studies in Judaism, Humanities, and the Social Sciences is envisioned to be an interdisciplinary, peer-reviewed academic journal published bi-annually. The mission of the journal is to publish original works of interest on Judaism through the "eyes" of the humanities and the social sciences. Its goal is to advance the systematic, scholarly, and social scientific study of Jews and Judaism, and to provide a forum for the discussion of methodologies, theories, and conceptual approaches across the many disciplines. Articles will be both contemporary and historical in nature and will feature case studies, historical studies, articles on new theoretical developments, results of research that advance our understanding of Jews and Judaism, and works on innovations in methodology. *Studies in Judaism, Humanities, and the Social Sciences* encourages contributions from the global community of scholars. All articles in this journal will undergo rigorous peer review, based on initial editor screening and refereeing by anonymous reviewers. Under the editorial leadership of Professor Herb Basser, the journal will also publish book reviews of important new scholarship. Importantly, in an age marked by partisan views inside and outside the halls of academia, we voice our pledge to academic freedom and to upholding and respecting contrasting views, creating a vital and vibrant platform for dialogue and debate.

The journal will present challenging, informative, and provocative reading, and will pursue cutting-edge inquiry that will feature work spanning the range of academic, professional, communal, and scholarly interest. Indeed, this first issue features articles reflecting the range of academic fields in Jewish studies, primarily sociological and social-anthropological methodologies for the analysis of Judaism and Jewish texts.

As a new undertaking, your feedback as readers and as key stakeholders in this venture is essential. We welcome your suggestions and comments. Your help would be invaluable in still other ways. We view this journal as a shared journey and seek colleagues willing and eager to submit articles and book reviews and to serve as referees for submitted work. We hope you will join us in our excitement for the journal and will share that enthusiasm within your academic and professional circles, encouraging agencies, universities, libraries, and individuals to become avid readers of the journal and to consider subscribing and recommending the journal to libraries.

We also welcome an outstanding journal editorial board, composed of scholars from North America, Israel, and Europe, who come from a wide range of disciplines. With the inaugural issue, they assume responsibility for envisioning the future of the journal with us, and we look forward to their guidance. We are confident that the journal will make a significant contribution to the intellectual development of the historical and contemporary study of Judaism, the humanities, and the social sciences. We invite you to become part of our new journal community.

Welcome to *Studies in Judaism, Humanities and the Social Sciences.*

Inclusion and Exclusion in the Mishnah: Non-Jews, Converts, and the Nazir

Calvin Goldscheider

Abstract

Exclusion from a community almost always implies the continuity of both cultural preservation and social inequalities within that community. In Judaism, exclusion and inclusion as constructed by the Mishnah reinforces the distinctiveness of the Jewish community. The Mishnah imagines a community that is not homogeneous, by not being exclusively Jewish and by not being completely "holy." Is it relevant to understanding the community to know who is included and excluded in the community that the Mishnah constructs? To help in addressing cultural and inequalities issues, this study assesses how the groups that are included fit into the social class and communal hierarchy of the community. An outline is developed of the differential social and religious obligations of those who are included, the "in-group" and those excluded, the "out-group." In so doing, it is possible to highlight that exclusion for the out-group does not necessarily imply exclusion on all dimensions: some exclusions are temporary and others are more permanent; some deny access to resources and others do not. Understanding better the existing emphasis on inclusions and exclusions directs analytic questions to identify how generational continuities are conceptualized and what are the possibilities of transition to inclusion among those who had been excluded. Our illustrative focus is on two core "ideal typical" types—the Nazir and the Non-Jew—who are at opposite ends of the exclusion spectrum.

All communities have social and physical/geographic boundaries. They may be relatively open or closed, porous or rigid, and temporary or permanent. Some boundaries define a local community or region; still others control the continuity of castes, social classes, or religious/ethnic groups by structuring social interaction and, in turn, acceptable marriages. Social boundaries protect and separate those inside from those outside and vice versa, defining groups that are included and groups that are excluded from the broader community. When community formation is studied, we seek to know how those groups who are in power within the community define both exclusion and inclusion relative to their community, and, thereby, reinforce community cohesion and solidify their social boundaries. The balance of exclusion and inclusion shapes continuity and influences cultural change from outside the community and from sub-communities inside.[1]

Who is included and who is excluded in the Jewish community, therefore, are questions whose answers help us to understand the shape and the boundaries of membership of that community. This paper explores some groups that are excluded from the community as constructed by the Mishnah.[2] Exclusion almost always implies social inequalities within a total community as well as cultural preservation. How included groups fit into the social class and communal hierarchy of the community will also be assessed. In exploring and making clear potential ways that exclusion matters, an outline of the differential social and religious obligations of the in- and out-groups is developed. As my study of the Mishnah on these topics progressed, it was evident that the exclusion of persons on some dimensions of social life did not necessarily imply exclusion on all dimensions: certain exclusions were identified as partial; others as more thorough/complete; some were temporary and some were more permanent; and, finally, some denied access to resources while others did not.

The study of inclusions and exclusions[3] directs analytic questions beyond *how* the Mishnah constructs social differentiation to identify *how* generational continuities are conceptualized—that is, who are the people that remain excluded over time, what are the possibilities of their transition to inclusion from a prior exclusion state, and how is exclusion transmitted generationally (these are basic micro-level questions). In addition, the dynamics of inequality are assessed as a consequence of exclusion—how differences between groups are projected to change over time and, more broadly, what are the changes in the openness of communal boundaries (these are macro-level questions). A focus in this essay is placed on a variety of exclusions that are explicitly discussed in the Mishnah, how some of those excluded are able to transition to the community and are (re-)integrated. In turn, the question of the implications of exclusion for the character of the community is addressed. The discussion of exclusion in the Mishnah is treated as part of the social construction of an ideal or imaginary community rather than a description of reality. One of the goals in this article is to infer some aspects of social and cultural cohesion (i.e., what binds members of the community together) through identifying the macro- and micro-parameters of exclusion.

In examining relevant Mishnah texts, there are many types of exclusion constructed and accompanying different degrees of exclusion described, as well as multiple ways in which those excluded can be re-integrated into the community. We begin with two core types—"ideal-typical" in the Weberian sense—each at opposite ends of the exclusion spectrum. The first major type of exclusion is voluntary as well as temporary and represents a minimum type of exclusion. We shall define this type as "voluntary self-exclusion" and illustrate it as among those who take a vow to abstain from wine and wine products, who refrain from cutting their hair (allowing their hair to grow long and wild), and who withdraw from having any contact with dead persons (so as to avoid impurity).[4] These Jewish persons are referred to as Nazirites (Hebrew: *Nazir* [male, sing.], *Nezirim* [male, pl.]; *Nezirah* [female, sing.], *Nezirot* [female, pl.]). They exclude themselves voluntarily, and, often temporarily, from selected activities in the community, perhaps as an attempt to express a greater sense of the sacred. By inference, the community as a whole includes, all other things being equal, individuals who do not abstain from wine or who do trim their hair or are not constrained in their contact with deceased persons (and in general with impurities). Also, becoming a Nazir requires intention, thus, a subjective element to the process; it does not occur automatically nor is it defined only by external and behavioral criteria.

At the other extreme, the second type of exclusion is more obvious and is involuntary—these are non-Jews or non-Israelites (often referred to as *Nochrim* or *Goyim*), who are excluded from various but not all aspects of Jewish community life. Unlike the Nazir, they are excluded from almost all religious or ritual activities that signify Jewishness. We will explore the variation within each of these categories and how members of excluded groups can become part of and participate in the community. It is important to note here that there are other kinds of exclusion impacted by particular contexts: women, children, the disabled, those whose gender is indeterminate, and servants. While excluded from some religious and social activities, these excluded persons remain fully functional parts of the diversity of social roles in the general community. The Mishnah views these "contextual exclusions" (excluded only for particular and specified activities vis-à-vis the aforementioned societal position or gender) as integral to the ongoing activities of the community, even if they are not involved in all the obligations (and privileges) of communal membership. They are mainly excluded from selective rituals and religious activities, often for lengthy parts of their life course.

VOLUNTARY SELF-EXCLUSION: NAZIRITES[5]

We begin at the minimal end of exclusion by focusing on these Nazirites: members of the community who, in various ways, exclude themselves from some activities, often for a limited period of time. These are Israelite men and women who take upon themselves vows of asceticism—or Nezirut. The moral position taken by the Mishnah that one should *not* separate oneself from the community (Avot 2, 4) refers by inference to "complete" separation. Those who exclude themselves in specific and limited ways with the goal of being more committed to achieving a life of greater holiness remain part of the community. Unlike the priests, who are viewed as more holy and of higher social status than non-priests (or more involved in activities that are defined as sacred) and have specific economic roles based on family inheritance (tribal origin or through marriage), the Nazir and Nezirah belong to a category of persons who voluntarily separate themselves out from some normal activities of communal life. They add another dimension to the social class hierarchy based on prestige, education, occupation, and economic resources.[6]

There is an entire Mishnah tractate (Nazir) devoted to a definition of Nezirut. Based, in part, on biblical references to the Nazir (see, in particular, the Book of Numbers, chapter 6), and in the Samson stories (see the Book of Judges, chapter 13), the Mishnah specifies what the biblical account omits: how one becomes a Nazir and a Nezirah in the context of vows or commitments taken orally.[7] In the Tractate Nazir, there is an emphasis on the process of taking a vow or verbal commitment to designate oneself a Nazir or Nezirah. There is almost nothing directly in the Mishnah that specifies *why* one makes such a vow or commitment. The Nazir is discussed mainly in terms of process and prohibition; that is, this is how one becomes a Nazir, specifying the prohibitions of that status and its various durations. There is no justification or rationale given for the status of Nezirut. The Mishnah does not ask why one becomes a Nazir or explain the goals of becoming Nezirut or detail whether by way of such a status the Nazir attains some new position within the social hierarchy of the community. Perhaps, at the time of the Mishnah, the motivation behind becoming a Nazir was so well understood that the Mishnah did not need to specify motivation or goals. In simpler words, a straightforward reading of the mishnaic text takes the motivation behind becoming a Nazir for granted.[8]

The Mishnah assumes that there are Israelites who make such vows and that abstention from three types of communal/social participation—drinking wine, hair cutting, and taking care of the deceased (with its associated ritual defilement)—are legitimate paths to greater holiness, a desideratum. Only indirectly does the Mishnah note the special "holiness" of the Nazir: the focus is on "becoming" a Nazir, the seriousness of making such a commitment (or a vow) and what that commitment entails in terms that imply some communal separation. The Mishnah spells out the length of time for self-exclusion that the Nazir status implies and for some, the temporary nature of the Nazirite status. It further specifies the ritual paths back to full engagement with the community. In addition, the Mishnah clarifies how the vow undertaken by the Nazir can be nullified. Therefore, the clear implication is that the status of the Nazir (and the Nezirah) is voluntary and not ascriptive, and for the most part temporary.

The key set of discussions in the Mishnah focuses on selective social restrictions of the Nazir and includes abstention from wine, grapes, and intoxicating liquors; refraining from cutting the hair on his or her head; avoiding contact with corpses and graves, even those of family members; and avoiding any structure that contains an impurity or contaminant. Of the three constraints imposed on the Nazir, the most problematic one is the restriction on defilement. For example, taking the vow of Nezirut in areas outside the Land of Israel would automatically result in a status of defilement, since it is assumed that non-Jews are not particular about burying their dead in marked places and, thus, anyone living there is assumed to be exposed to defilement (Nazir 3, 6).

There is no indication in the Mishnah that the Nazir abstains from marriage or intimate sexual relationships or lives in areas segregated from the community or performs religious ritual activities assigned specifically to the Nazir role, except when ending his period of Nezirut. The Nazir is not exempt from religious rituals that are the obligations of everyone in the community, nor is the Nazir enjoined to live without family or work obligations. Thus, there are narrow restrictions self-imposed by the Nazir and limited (but perhaps conspicuous) markers that differentiate the Nazir from other Israelites. For the most part, this voluntary and temporary status does not interfere with most of the personal and communal obligations and responsibilities of Israelites of the remaining community.

It is obvious from the Mishnah that self-exclusion for selected features of Jewish community social life was an acceptable practice among Jews, according to the Mishnah. The Nazir did not live in a separate community of other Nezirim, nor is the status of the Nazirite portrayed as an ideal. Some considered the Nazir a "sinner," since he/she was separated from some but certainly not all the normal pleasures of communal life (one of the animal sacrifices brought in the transition from the Nazir status is the sin or guilt offering—the Karbon Hatat). The Mishnah apparently could not eliminate or ignore the Nazir and Nezirah from its constructed community since both are mentioned explicitly in the Torah, along with the three rules of exclusion (abstention from wine, hair cutting, and ritual defilement). These self-imposed restrictions are temporary for a minimum of a month, and there are explicit rituals to reintegrate the person as a full functioning person in the community. The reentry of the Nazir into the community requires the bringing of animal sacrifices that at the time of the Mishnah (post-destruction of the Temple) were not possible. So, the discussion in the Mishnah is in large part academic and perhaps the actual extent of Nezirut was minimal. More likely, the category was limited to long-term Nezirut (well beyond the minimum of 30 days) since there were no obvious ways to make the transition back to full communal participation without the ritual of animal sacrifices in the Temple. Nevertheless, the constraints on the Nazir were not designed as a form of complete isolation, seclusion, or segregation from the broader community.

NEZIRUT IN THE MISHNAH

Let us examine more closely how the Mishnah proceeds to define and identify different Nazir types. The first mishnah in the first chapter of the Tractate Nazir deals with declarations about being a Nazir when a person does not actually say, "I want to be a Nazir" but says, "I want to be like that person who is a Nazir" (or like that person with a particularly long [wild] hair growth—a sign of Nezirut, a statement that is indicative of the intention to become a Nazir). With some exceptions noted in the Mishnah, becoming a Nazir requires the explicit intention of the individual. And the Nazir makes a *vow* indicative of a serious statement of intent.

Only by inference does the Nazir acquire a greater sense of holiness or a stronger commitment to God. The greater "holiness" associated with the Nazir status is noted in the biblical text (the word "kodesh," or holy, occurs four times in the 21-verse sequence dealing with the Nazir in the Book of Numbers). The significance of that holiness for activities or for ranking within the community is not elaborated on in the Mishnah except to note the prohibition against becoming impure (Tameh). It is unclear what the additional level of holiness means in the defining quality of the Nazir in the Mishnah.

There are three types of Nazirites (Nazir 1, 2–3): First, there is a temporary or a minimum time-based Nazir as someone who makes a declaration of being a Nazir for an unspecified time period or a limited period of time. The minimum period of time for being a Nazir would last for 30 days or for a longer period when specified by the Nazir. A second type of Nazir is based on a declaration of being a Nazir like Samson, a Nazir from birth—a lifelong Nazir. A final type of Nazir is a "Nazir Olam"—a Nazir forever—all his/her remaining life. The Mishnah deals with distinctions between the last two types. A Nazir like Samson (essentially designated by others from birth by God or an angel—but not self-designated) never cuts his/her hair and never drinks wine but can be in contact with the dead, a source of uncleanness (as the case with Samson). In contrast, a Nazir Olam designates him/herself a Nazir for the rest of his/her remaining life and can cut his/her hair every 12 months but does not drink wine or wine products. If that type of Nazir has contact with the dead, he/she must bring a special animal sacrifice, and must also bring a special sacrifice to the temple when trimming his/her hair. The point is that Samson was not a complete Nazir since he made no Nazir vow; the commitment was made for him. There was no intentionality in Samson's case. A complete lifelong Nazir requires intention. All these types relate to the way the commitment to Nezirut and to the process of becoming a Nazir is made along with the language that is used in the context of making a Nazir vow or a commitment. In the process of specification, the Mishnah modifies some of the biblical restrictions for some types of Nazirites.

The importance of intent and the self-definition of Nezirut are clear from the case of someone who said, "I will abstain from drinking wine." That person becomes a temporary Nazir, for the declaration is the formula for a Nazir vow. If, however, he was drunk, his statement can be dismissed since it did not imply that he consciously intended to become a Nazir. The same process applies equally for men and for women (Nazir 2, 3; 4, 1–3).

There are only indirect indications in the Mishnah that becoming a Nazir implies a commitment to greater than normal holiness. A Nazir is compared in his/her "holiness" to a Kohen (someone of the priest caste), as is picturesquely stated in Nazir 7, 1:

> A High Priest (Kohen Gadol) and a Nazir should not deal with the burial of deceased relatives so as to avoid uncleanness. But they may do so for a neglected corpse [which would be a special obligation requiring burial]. If the High Priest and a Nazir were traveling together along the road and found a neglected corpse—Rabbi Eliezer says, let the High Priest contract corpse uncleanness [because he does not have to bring an animal sacrifice on account of his uncleanness] but the Nazir should not [since he has to bring an animal sacrifice to transition from his uncleanness]. The Sages disagree with this position and suggest that the Nazir [will] contract corpse uncleanness [since his holiness is temporary] but not the High Priest [since his sanctity is permanent].

Thus, according to the Mishnah, both the Nazir and the High Priest have a special holiness, and there is a dispute as to who has a higher degree of holiness, at least as defined in terms of ritual uncleanliness. That is, they have different types of holiness that require different forms of transition from ritual uncleanliness. And in contrast to the Nazir, the Kohen has permanent holiness. Unlike a Nazir, a Kohen (even a regular—lower level—Kohen, not just the High Priest) is so designated from birth and conveys his status to his children generationally; a Nazir cannot convey his Nezirut status to his children (Nazir, 7, 1). By inference, the hierarchy in the community constructed by the Mishnah leaves the Kohen in the top position within the status system, and the Nazir is the next ranked status, but only on a temporary basis.

This comparison between the High Priest and the Nazir indirectly poses the question of whether a Kohen can become a Nazir. The Mishnah, in another tractate (Makkot 3, 7–8), refers to "Kohen V'Nazir"—a priest who is a Nazir—in the context of the multiple penalties for violating the rules of impurities. A person who has the status of both a Nazir and a Kohen violates separate rules of impurity; the question raised by the Mishnah is whether the penalties for such violations are combined and overlap or are additive. While the Mishnah does not elaborate on this particular status combination, it obviously considers being *both* a Nazir and a Kohen a theoretical possibility. There appears to be no special class or hierarchical status associated with this Kohen-Nazir combination. We do not know that such a person has a higher or different status than either a Kohen or a Nazir separately. The combination of priest and Nazir is parenthetical in the Mishnah, and the hierarchical ranking of the Nazir relative to priests remains disputed in the Mishnah.

Nazir status is not restricted to adult men. The general principle is laid out in summary form in the last chapter of the Tractate Nazir (9, 1): women and slaves can become Nazirites but non-Jews cannot. Women cannot be forced into Nezirut but servants can.[9] The Mishnah contrasts the Nazir context of women and slaves: a master can force his slave to take a Nazir vow, but a husband cannot force his wife to become a Nezirah (Nazir 9, 1). As with other vows, depending on the context, a husband can nullify the vow of Nezirut made by his wife when he first learns of her making such a vow. When the husband nullifies the Nazir vow of his wife, she is completely free from her vow to become a Nezirah. In contrast, a master cannot nullify the Nazir vow of his servant and the servant has to complete his Nezirut when he is freed.

The Mishnah also raises two issues associated with the Nazir: can others designate a Nazir and can others fulfill the obligation of Nezirut made by someone else? These questions are discussed in the context of generational issues. A son who is under age (less than 13 years and a day) can be made a Nazir by his father, so long as he or his relatives accept that status and do not protest. But a child's mother cannot designate her son to be a Nazir (Nazir 4, 6). The Mishnah does not provide any justification for this distinction by gender. Furthermore, a son can end the Nezirut vow of his deceased father (by bringing a sacrifice and cutting his hair in lieu of his father), but a daughter cannot substitute for her father or mother in this way. The generational substitution occurs only if both the son and father had been Nezirim and the father is deceased. A woman cannot carry out the Nezirut transition of her father (Nazir 4, 7), but it is unstated whether she can carry out the Nezirut obligations of her mother.

Despite the Mishnah's explicit position that a mother cannot designate her son as a Nazir, an example is presented of a mother (Hannah) who made her son (the prophet Samuel) a Nazir from birth (Nazir, 9, 5). Samson's Nezirut is also in this category. The question of who may nullify the Nazir vow (whether the court or a Rabbi or husbands or fathers, as in the case of a woman or a minor) is left ambiguous. According to one Mishnah text, a Hacham, a learned person, can nullify the vow of Nezirut if the original commitment was done by error or by ignorance. In that case, no animal sacrifice would be necessary to make the transition back to the community (Nazir 5, 3–4). The details of the transition back to full participation in the community, including shaving, drinking wine, and bringing three sacrifices for various components of Nezirut, are presented in chapter 6 of the Tractate Nazir.

A woman can become a Nezirah directly by self-designation (Nazir 4, 1–3). The Mishnah (Nazir 2, 6) reports a story about Queen Helena (d. 56 CE) who became a Nezirah for either

14 or 21 years (depending on two opinions cited in the Mishnah) from the time she began this period while living outside of the Land of Israel. The story does not report anything about her hair but does make clear that a woman cuts her hair when she has completed her time of Nezirut (Nazir 4, 5; 6, 11). The text also does not specify issues of impurity, perhaps given that she, like all women, was impure during menstruation. From Nazir 2, 3, it is understood that she is obligated not to drink wine.

The story of Helena raises directly the question of how one becomes a Nazir outside the Land of Israel, but it is likely that one would have to re-start the timing of Nezirut when returning to the Land of Israel. Being outside the Land of Israel always assumes that there is contact with defilement of dead persons; only in the Land of Israel can one be in a state of purity (Nazir, 3, 6) and be able to bring the necessary animal sacrifices to return back to the community upon the conclusion of the Nezirut period. So, one cannot become a Nazir or begin the time of Nezirut outside of the Land of Israel.

Overall, the actual extent of Nezirut is unknown; in many ways, the Mishnah must deal with the possibility of Nezirut and the process of becoming a Nazir, since the Torah text is so explicit. Two features of the mishnaic discussion need emphasis: (1) So long as the Torah notes the role of the Nazir, the Mishnah has to unpack the various processes associated with what is not explicit in the Torah; and (2) The discussion in the Mishnah appears to be mostly theoretical, as the particular roles of the Nazir (and for that matter the role of the priest) at the time of the writing of the Mishnah is mainly "imagined" rather than being an obvious presence in the society. Reinforcing this view is the reality of the difficulty of transition from the status of Nazir in the absence of the Temple and its related sacrificial system. Perhaps there is a general reluctance of the Mishnah to reinforce the role and status of ascetics, given that they were a more common feature of Christian than Jewish society.

In summary, the sociologically interesting themes about the self-exclusion of the Nazir in the Mishnah are as follows: The process of becoming a Nazir is the same for men and women, but there are gender differences in power that men may nullify the Nazir vow of their wives but women cannot nullify the vow of their husbands. Similarly, mothers cannot designate their sons to be a Nazir but fathers can. A Hacham (a learned man) has the power to nullify the Nazir vow of women, substituting for husbands and fathers. The rules of Nezirut vary by whether the vow takes place in or outside the Land of Israel. The text of the Mishnah does not clearly specify why anyone becomes a Nazir but, instead, focuses only on the process of becoming a Nazir. Implicit in the Mishnah is that the Nazir and the Kohen are in high-status positions in the community, and it appears that the Kohen has a somewhat higher status than a Nazir. Only Jews can take on becoming a Nazir. Intention to become a Nazir is critical, with some obvious exceptions. There are processes of transition back from being a Nazir, but without animal sacrifices (in the absence of the Temple), the transition back to normal status is problematic. Together, these characteristics suggest that the Nazir role as constructed by the Mishnah remains for the most part a regular participant in the community. The boundaries of the constructed community in the Mishnah are flexible enough to allow temporary, self-imposed restrictions accepted by Nazirites and the inclusion of persons previously excluded from some communal activities. Except for the prohibitions of Nezirut, there are no stated positive religious rituals that the Nazir is obligated to carry out.

THE EXCLUSION OF NON-JEWS

In contrast to the various types of Nezirim that are rather marginal in their influence on the social organization of the community that the Mishnah constructs, the exclusion of non-Jews is critical for positive cohesion of the community. Some specific non-Jewish groups are excluded based, in part, on biblical injunctions. Members of specific non-Jewish (or non-Israelite) ethnic groups—Amoni and Moabite males—are never permitted to enter the community; female Amonites and Moabites (after conversion), however, may enter the Jewish community (Yevamot 8, 3). Male and female Egyptians and Edomites are restricted from entering the Kahal (community) for three generations. (Some communities permit women, Egyptians or Edonites, to enter immediately). Netinim (defined as Samaritans) and Mamzerim (usually defined as the children of adulterous or prohibited sexual unions) are also excluded from the community.

These exclusions involve entire ethnic groups rather than designated individuals as in the case of Nezirim. The social system conceptualized by the Mishnah specifies the nature of these more complex exclusions: These are more or less permanent exclusions, from which it is difficult to transition into the Jewish community, and are not a consequence of individual intent. They are what social scientists would designate as "group exclusion based on ascription or ethnic origin." The sharpest, most defined exclusion is that of the subset of non-Jews who are defined as *Ovdei Avodah Zarah*—idol worshippers, or pagans.

The Mishnah expounds on the biblical prohibition against Avodah Zarah—idol worship—by focusing both on issues of worship and on social and economic relationships/interactions of Jews and non-Jews. Idolatry is one of the most severe prohibitions in the Torah, repeated in the Ten Commandments and many times throughout the Torah. The prohibition includes the belief and worship of all deities except the One God, whether on their own or in concert with God, whether the "items" of worship are perceived as spiritual, as natural forces, or as animals. Any worship of these deities, whether worshiping the concept, the thing itself, or a representative object, is forbidden as *idolatry*. The severity of this prohibition reflects the conflict between idolatry and the core Judaic belief in a single God who rules over all things. The Torah intensely emphasizes refraining from idol worship and the need to destroy idols, to distance oneself from them and from their adherents in a variety of ways (Lev. 18:3). The Mishnah adds further limitations whose purpose is to discourage interaction with those who are involved in idolatry or with objects, or both, that may be used in worshiping idols.

The severe penalty for idol worship is spelled out in the Mishnah (Sanhedrin 7, 4 and 7, 6–7) including the specification of what "worship" encompasses. For a variety of types of worship, for example, a person who brings an animal sacrifice to an idol or offers incense commits a capital crime and is liable to receive a punishment of death by stoning. But when one is "involved" with an idol, even to the extent of kissing the idol or washing/cleaning it, that person transgresses a negative commandment—but is not liable for the death penalty, since that is not how idols are worshiped (Sanhedrin 7, 6). Thus, the Mishnah indicates a range of practices that is included in the definition of worship, suggesting that some of these lesser practices were, in fact, carried out. Some worship violates the core prohibition against idolatry and deserves by mishnaic decree the severest penalty; other forms of interaction do not. Our interest here is to examine the ways in which the Mishnah constructs the idolater (one type of "non-Jew"), so as to exclude him/her from the Jewish community.

NON-JEWS IN THE MISHNAH

There is an entire tractate devoted to Avodah Zarah, including five chapters and 50 mishnayot.[10] Technically, there is no specific tractate on the broader category "non-Jews," but the tractate on idolatry and idolaters reveals a great deal on the topic of the exclusion of non-Jews. In large part, we argue that understanding the type of exclusion associated with idolaters (a subset of non-Jews), allows assumptions of some aspects of *inclusion* for the broader category of non-Jews, many or most who are not idolaters. This is particularly the case for those persons of the community who themselves are not part of the specific religious or ritual dimensions of its social life.

Along with women, slaves, and some persons defined as socially vulnerable—the deaf, the mute, and minors—non-Jews were excluded from the rights and obligations of full participation in the Jewish community constructed in the Mishnah. The status of the non-Jew in the Jewish community is complicated by the specification of types of non-Jews, their relative segregation, and their transition through conversion to the Jewish community. While the entire tractate of Avodah Zarah deals with the non-Jew in the context of idolatry, the rules of exclusion of non-Jews appear in many other tractates of the Mishnah. The category "non-Jews" is multi-dimensional, with various types of non-Jews specified in the Mishnah. There are "Goyim," "Nochrim," and a general category of non-Jews and idol worshipers. The Mishnah specifies somewhat different laws for each category, although not always clearly. Most important is the social distance or segregation that the Mishnah describes as a basis for controlling the interactions of Jews and non-Jews, so as to retain the integrity of the community as Jewish and to avoid a more severe violation of the Torah prohibition of worshiping idols.

The focus of the Tractate Avodah Zarah is on the need to distance oneself from idol worship and all things connected with it. It is forbidden to derive benefit from the idols themselves, their ornaments, and donations made to them. The Mishnah decreed a severe level of ritual defilement for coming in contact with idols. Similarly, participating in pagan holidays and festivals is forbidden, even if direct idol worship is not involved. Much of this tractate on idolatry defines the boundaries of what would be forbidden and whether indirect benefit from idolatry or passive participation in religious ceremonies of non-Jews would be permitted.

In the process of dealing with avoidance of interaction with idolaters, inferences may be made about the nature of acceptable interactions between Jews and non-Jews and, hence, the variety of forms of inclusion of non-Jews in the Jewish community. It seems that worship is mainly the issue at hand, not thoughts about or discussions with non-Jews or other forms of social interactions.

Part of the prohibition against benefitting from idolatry is the prohibition of eating food that has been used as part of a pagan ritual. One core aspect of these laws revolves around prohibition of wine, specifically, wine that was used as libation on an altar during worship to a deity. It was common practice, as described in the Mishnah, to prohibit the consumption of that wine; the practice among non-Jews was so widespread that it was reasonable for the Mishnah to assume that any wine that had been touched by a non-Jew was likely to have been offered in some ceremony to a pagan deity. This led to the establishment of a mishnaic position that even ordinary wine of non-Jews that had not been used for religious purposes was forbidden. This ruling was made, primarily, because of the concern with wine that served as libation to a deity on an altar and, secondarily, because of a general interest in limiting the social interaction between Jews and pagans.[11]

Since the Mishnah teaches about the need to remove oneself from idol worship and associated practices, it is necessary for the Mishnah to describe the details of some of the common activities that were carried out as idolatry. In this tractate, we find descriptions of Greco-Roman pagan practices as they were known in Israel and surrounding countries during the mishnaic period. Again, our interest is to infer from mishnaic text the nature of exclusion and inclusion of non-Jews from the community of Jews.

In one context, the Mishnah lists a number of categories of persons who are excluded when making a particular kind of vow, essentially one of disavowal: (1) If one vows not to have any benefit from Noachites, Israelites are permitted, but all other nations of the world are forbidden; (2) if one vows not to have any benefit from the Children of Abraham, Israelites are forbidden but all other nations of the world are permitted; (3) if one vows not to have any benefit from Israelites, Israelites are forbidden but Nochrim (non-Jews) are permitted; (4) if one vows not to have any benefit from the uncircumcised, Israelites who are uncircumcised are permitted but circumcised non-Jews are forbidden; (5) if one vows not to have any benefit from the circumcised, Israelites who are uncircumcised are forbidden but uncircumcised among other nations are permitted.

Thus, the categories of the hierarchy (from low to high) appear to be: Noachites, Children of Abraham, Nochrim, the uncircumcised non-Jew, the uncircumcised Jew, and the circumcised Jew (Nedarim 3, 11). In an adjacent mishnah, another category of Jew/non-Jew is established, Kutim (Samaritans). If one vows not to have any benefit from Sabbath observers, both Israelites and Samaritans are included in the vow (but not Gentiles). But if one vows not to have any benefit from those who make pilgrimages to Jerusalem, only Israelites are included but not Samaritans (since they are not included among those who go to Jerusalem, the latter having established an alternative central worship area). These categories do not exhaust all the possibilities, but they do give one a sense of a wider range of subcategories than simply "Jew and non-Jew."[12]

There are dozens of places in the Mishnah where the non-Jew is exempt from various forms of participation in the community. For example, there is the obligation of Jews to care for the poor through agricultural practices in rural areas and by way of charity in non-farm areas. It is clear from the Mishnah (Peah 4, 6) that these obligations do not fall on non-Jews living in the Land of Israel. This is also obvious in the case of Judaic religious rituals but extends as well to rules about marriage, trade, business exchanges, and additional agricultural activities. We noted above how the non-Jew cannot make a commitment to become a Nazir. These exclusions are expected and not surprising and are a systematic part of the overall stratification pattern conceived by the Mishnah. The exclusions are part of the obligations and presumed character of the non-Jew. The critical issue of the Mishnah is the relationship of Jews to non-Jews from the point of view of the Jews and the Jewish community.[13]

The Mishnah presents several reasons for Jews to distance themselves from non-Jews. Primarily, the goal is to prevent interaction with non-Jews, so as not to be influenced by them religiously and culturally. Exclusion is also designed to discourage the Jew from any association with idolatry, even beyond that of worship per se, given the severe Torah-based prohibitions. Thus, Jews should not sell things to non-Jews that may be used by them for idolatry nor should Jews conduct business with pagans before the latter's holidays so that they will not be "thanking" pagan gods on a pagan holiday for business transacted successfully. Similarly, the Mishnah prohibits the use of wine produced, in general, by non-Jews (*S'tam Yenam*) to prevent the more severe restrictions associated with *Yayin-Neseh*—wine used in the context of idolatry. Even wine simply possessed by Jews that is touched by a non-Jew is deemed problematic, since the intention of the non-Jew might be to use the wine for idolatry. Other things are prohibited to the Jew so as not to derive any "hannah," or benefit, from interaction with non-Jews.

The details of the prohibition of *Yayin Nesech* are discussed in Avodah Zarah from 4, 8 through the end of the tractate. Crushed grapes are not included in forbidden wine until the juice from the grapes is in the vat; Jews may join non-Jews in grape pressing but not in gathering grapes; Jews may transport grapes to the vats with non-Jews. These actions jointly between Jews and non-Jews do not result in the prohibition of deriving some benefit from the wine. Wine belonging to non-Jews but made by a Jew and stored and located in a house open to the public in a city where Jews and non-Jews lived is permitted and is not considered *Yeyin Nesech* (Avodah Zarah 4, 11). The issue of Jews working for non-Jews in making wine is the subject of detailed discussions and whether not only the wine but the wages of the Jews would be prohibited (Avodah Zarah 5, 1). Other joint activities of Jews and non-Jews in the transport of wine or using sealed vats are discussed as well as eating food and drinking wine together with non-Jews at the same table, and mixtures of wine and water (Avodah Zarah 5, 3–8). These complications in the context of wine that is potentially associated with idolatry again point to the incidental fact that there was a considerable social and commercial activities among Jews and non-Jews together even involving forbidden wine.

SOME SPECIFICS IN THE MISHNAH

Let us review selected details and specifics in the Mishnah: The prohibitions to engage in selling to non-Jews three days before non-Jewish holidays or in lending money or exchanging goods or settling debts are explicitly designed to prevent non-Jews from using those monies or goods for idolatry (Avodah Zarah 1, 1–2). The objective is to prevent Jews from being involved indirectly with idolatry. These three-day prohibitions refer to public holidays; private pagan celebrations are different, and restrictions are then only for individuals, not the general public, and for a shorter period of time—one day (Avodah Zarah 1, 3). After the pagan holiday, it is permissible to do business with non-Jews, so the issue is strictly the prevention of idolatry, not economic activities. Similarly, the restrictions of doing business with Goyim (or non-Jews) are designated for cities that have local celebrations, but not for places outside the city (Avodah Zarah 1, 4). The prohibition for Jews extends to entering a city where the celebration of a non-Jewish holiday is taking place and it appears that Jews are going there to attend that celebration (Avodah Zarah 1, 4).

In places where some stores owned by non-Jews have pagan holiday decorations and other stores are not decorated for the holidays, those that are decorated are off limits for Jews, but the stores without decorations are accessible to Jews. The Mishnah, thus, limits the prohibition of business activities with non-Jews to public holiday celebrations and not to private celebrations of non-Jewish families or to local festivals (Avodah Zarah 1, 3–4). All of these circumlocutions and exceptions in the Mishnah are designed to prevent the public appearance of sharing a non-Jewish (pagan) holiday or contributing indirectly to idol worship.

Clearly, the conception of non-Jews and of distancing from them is not simply based on economic or social segregation. Jews are indeed presented in the Mishnah as actively engaged in business practices with non-Jews, living among non-Jews, and recognizing their holidays. The Mishnah goes far to point to ways to circumvent as well as limit the ban on commerce with non-Jews. There is no indication that Jews, as constructed in the Mishnah, are isolated economically and/or separated residentially from non-Jews. Nor is there any sense that may be inferred from the mishnah texts that it is inappropriate to do business with or to live together with non-Jews, except for the concern over idolatry and intimate (sexual) relationships. The Mishnah, in other words, does not construct a Jewish community that consists solely of Jews, is solely isolated from non-Jews, or one that is totally self-sufficient economically.

Extending the general prohibition of selling to non-Jews near their public holidays, the Mishnah goes so far as to list items that Jews should not sell to non-Jews or build with and it broadens constraints for non-Jews all year long if the objects could be used for idolatry (Avodah Zarah 1, 5–7). The ban on selling items to non-Jews because of the concern about their use for idolatry depends on local customs, not on the absolute prohibition against the sale of these specific items. For example, the Mishnah states that one is permitted to sell small cattle to non-Jews where it is a custom to do so but not in a place where the custom is *not to sell* these animals. Apparently, doing business with the small cattle of non-Jews is not the core issue—except for doing business when celebrating a business deal might involve some form of ritual thanks to an idol and that depends on local custom. So, we can imagine that selling small cattle to non-Jews in one community might be forbidden while in an adjacent community it would not be forbidden. Recognition of the *power of local custom* to determine whether objects sold are forbidden or permissible is a hallmark of the mishnaic discussion of non-Jews.

Beyond the concern with idolatry, there is a prohibition of selling large wild animals (bears or lions) or weapons that are a public danger (Avodah Zarah 1, 7). There even are restrictions on helping non-Jews build places that involve dangerous games or places of execution. In contrast, it is permissible to help non-Jews build public and private bathhouses. The making of jewelry for decorating idols is forbidden, but, according to one opinion, it is permitted when done for pay or wages (Avodah Zarah 1, 8). And according to another opinion, selling or renting fields or houses to non-Jews in Israel is forbidden; outside of Israel (e.g., in Syria) renting housing but not selling land is permitted. Selling houses and fields is permitted in areas outside of both the Land of Israel and Syria. The prohibition of land or housing sales is explicit, because the non-Jew may bring idols into the non-Jew's house (Avodah Zarah 1, 9). Hence, one can infer that Jews are engaged in real estate and land sales and, at times, are engaged in these practices with non-Jews. And the sale or rental is limited or prohibited to the extent of the association of these building activities with idolatry.

In a more severe set of injunctions, Jews are commanded not to bring their animals or women or even men into the confined and private space of non-Jews, since non-Jews, as presented in the Mishnah, are suspected of adultery, murder, and of having sexual relations with animals (Avodah Zarah 2, 1). Again, the concern is not a simple extension by the Mishnah of the original Torah prohibition but with the inference about how the Mishnah conceptualizes "the other" and impacts the interaction of Jews with non-Jews.

Concerns are expressed about Jewish midwives working for a Gentile woman, but non-Jewish women can act as midwives for Jewish women. The same asymmetry applies to nursemaids; non-Jewish nursemaids are permitted for Jewish infants in a Jewish household (Avodah Zarah 2, 1). There is a general caution about using non-Jewish healers (or barbers) because of the avoidance of placing oneself in a vulnerable position vis-a-vis non-Jews, especially in private places. That said, according to one opinion in the Mishnah, healing activities by non-Jews are permissible in public places (Avodah Zarah 2, 2). These mishnayot, in essence, list items that Jews should not engage with vis-à-vis non-Jews and names activities with non-Jews that Jews are forbidden to take pleasure in or gain benefit from. The activities range from concerns over pagan idolatry to indirectly participating in the celebrations of holidays of non-Jews to concern over their tendency toward adultery, sexual relations with cattle, and murder.

There are whole lists of food items that are forbidden in addition to wine and wine products (including restriction on the bags that hold the wine, some of the vines, and the grape skins). There is also a discussion of cheeses (those that are fermented in the stomachs of animals that are not kosher) or of animals used for idolatry. Jews are prohibited from using these items if they were made by non-Jews; other items prohibited are, among others: milk, bread, oil, small fish, some spices, and pickled or preserved items (Avodah Zarah 2, 5–7). Some of these items are prohibited for only eating but not for other types of benefits (e.g., selling) regarding them. There is an additional list of mixed items that are permitted, including milk prepared by a non-Jew under supervision of a Jew, honey, and grape clusters, as well as some other food items sold by non-Jews.

Throughout, the emphasis in the Mishnah is on separation from non-Jews to prevent idolatry, prohibited foods, and close interaction that would result in social or sexual intercourse. It is clear that non-Jews are on the bottom of the social and religious and cultural hierarchy in the Jewish community as conceptualized by the Mishnah and are to be excluded from some of the ongoing functions of its economic and social life. Unlike the self-excluded Nazir, non-Jewish exclusion is systematic, imposed, and extensive, and, of course, not voluntary or temporary although often significantly contextualized and limited.

There is a further delineation of statues or images that should be avoided if they are perceived to be part of idol worship. But there also is a serious attempt to differentiate those statues or images that are not used for idolatry from those that are and, hence, to allow Jews to be involved in commercial activities involving these items (Avodah Zarah 3, 2–4). As well, with buildings, the Mishnah differentiates between an edifice that was made as a place of worship for a god and the use of a symbol or an image of a god as an ornament in a general building, as is made clear in an anecdote involving Rabbi Gamliel in a bathhouse that included a figure of Aphrodite,. The principle here is that the prohibition of use is limited to when one treats the facility as a place of worship (Avodah Zarah 3, 4). So, Rabbi Gamliel did not hesitate to use the bathhouse that had an ornament of Aphrodite, since it was not being used as a place of worship.

The Mishnah also discusses a case where a Jew's house is adjacent to a place of idol worship, and the wall separating the two structures falls. The Jew is prohibited from rebuilding the wall except with a distance of four cubits between the structures so as to be physically separated from idol worship (Avodah Zarah 3, 6). The important point in our context is understanding Jews had housing next to places of idolatry but that was not considered problematic except when there were opportunities to create greater separation. In sum, there appears in the mishnaic conception of the community no absolute value, or assessment, on residential separation or economic exclusion of Jews from non-Jews.

The category of restriction of non-Jews in the conception of the Mishnah is not one of consciousness or intent but is like a "*sheretz*" (any low crawling creature, such as a worm) that automatically contaminates. In that context, the non-Jew automatically is a contaminant (Avodah Zarah 3, 6). There is a further discussion of the types of houses associated with idolatry, of stones used for an altar, and of ferns or trees (Asherah), and cloth and clothing (Avodah Zarah 3, 7). In each of these cases, if the houses, stones, or trees were designed initially for idolatry or decorated for idolatry then there is a prohibition of any commercial benefit from this form of idolatry. But if the designs were for other purposes and only were temporarily used for idolatry, then it is permitted to have some benefit from them when the practice of idolatry was removed. We can infer from these texts that Jews lived in close proximity to places of idol worship, and the Mishnah attempts to find ways for Jews to continue to live and conduct business with non-Jews and live near them rather than to encourage them to leave those places (Avodah Zarah 3, 8–9).

Perhaps even more importantly, there are discussions of the ways that the non-Jew can nullify or change the structure or object of idolatry. Several conclusions emerge from these discussions: First, intention on the part of non-Jews to use a building or stones or ferns as an object of ownership makes these, potentially, objects of idolatry. And it is the non-Jew who has the power to do so by his intention and by the meaning of his actions (especially in Avodah Zarah 4, 5). There are also circumstances where no act or action has to be taken in order to nullify the meaning of an idol. An idol that is left in the non-Jew's house in times of peace is permitted to be used for commercial purposes by

Jews since there is no indication of the desire on the part of the non-Jew to return and worship the idol. In times of war, it would be forbidden for the Jew to use the abandoned idol based on the assumption that the non-Jew would be returning from battle and using the idol for worship. Furthermore, the Mishnah notes that temporary platforms used to display idols can be used for limited purposes when abandoned (Avodah Zarah 4, 6).

There appears to be no inherent meaning of idolatry or absolute prohibition of any object unless it has been given meaning by the non-Jew for idolatry. It is the social construction of idolatry that is critical in the conception of the Mishnah and, hence, the ability of non-Jews to reverse the object so that it is no longer to be considered idolatrous in nature. In turn, this reversal by the non-Jew permits the Jews to have practical use of these objects that were formerly used for idolatry (Avodah Zarah 3, 10).

The Mishnah also specifies that the areas around buildings used for idolatry, a garden, or bath house, can be used for the benefit of Jews, as long as the objects around the idolatry are not an integral part of idol worship (Avodah Zarah 4, 3). This mishnah is explicit: an idol belonging to and made by a nochri (non-Jew) is forbidden to a Jew immediately (even before it is worshipped); an item made by a Jew that will eventually be used for idolatry is not forbidden to use for the benefit of the Jew until it has been used for worship by a non-Jew, in other words, prior, had been an idolatrous object. A non-Jew can nullify the idol he or any non-Jew has made; a Jew cannot nullify the idol of a non-Jew; nullifying the idol also nullifies all the attached accessories. Nullifying the accessories does not, in turn, nullify the idol, only the accessories (Avodah Zarah 4, 4). This appears completely consistent with the above argument about the absence of inherent value of (and, hence, the commercial benefit from) an idol until it has been used. What is noteworthy is that the Mishnah specifies that Jews were at times in the business of making objects that would eventually become idols for use by non-Jews.

There is an interesting story in the Mishnah addressing the question why God permitted idolatry to persist. The question is asked to the elders of the Jewish community of Rome. They responded that non-Jews were worshipping the sun, moon, and stars, asking how could *they* be nullified, being celestial bodies? The follow-up question is to why God did not nullify those objects of worship that could be nullified (such as concrete objects of gold, for example)? The answer is: to avoid the assumption that the sun, moon, and stars created these objects of earthly creation. The point is that God allows all of these symbols of idolatry to exist so that people will be able to distinguish between the Creator and God's creations (Avodah Zarah 4, 7). The critical point inherent in this mishnah text is that idolatry is defined (and nullified) by human beings and not objectively defined or eliminated by God.

In other contexts, the Mishnah body notes positive relationships between Jews and non-Jews in commercial activities. When leavened products are not permitted to Jews on Passover, the Mishnah notes that leavened food products owned by a non-Jew during Passover are permitted after Passover, while those owned by a Jew are forbidden (Pesahim 2, 2–3). There does not seem to be any concern about the potential contradictory nature of such arrangements or the use of products after Passover that were in the possession of non-Jews during the holiday when these products were hametz, hence forbidden to Jews during the Passover holiday.

If there are restrictions on some business-related activities involving idolatry with non-Jews, it is not surprising that intimate contact, meaning sexual relations, with non-Jews are not permitted. The Mishnah (Terumot 8, 12) is explicit that sexual intercourse of Israelite women with a non-Jew is condemned. In contrast, there is a puzzling Mishnah within the tractate Mikvaot (8, 4), dealing with ritual cleanliness, which states: "A Gentile woman who discharged semen from an Israelite is unclean; an Israelite woman who discharged semen from a Gentile is clean." It is strange in this particular mishnah that there is no condemnation about non-Jewish interaction of the most intimate kind.

CONVERTS AND CONVERSIONS TO JUDAISM

Perhaps no theme is more illustrative of the value (and limitations) of focusing on the Mishnah as a complete document than the issue of converts and conversion to Judaism. Overall, the Mishnah does not deal extensively with converts and does not specify the processes of conversion.[14] Why the Mishnah ignores the details of conversion has been extensively debated; however, it is not clear whether this is because there were few converts during the time of the Mishnah and, therefore, conversions were not an issue of great importance or because the authors of the Mishnah assumed that the details were well known or for other obscure reasons. Later texts deal extensively with conversions; indeed, sections of the Talmud on conversions have been viewed as a tractate within a tractate (Talmud Bavli, Yevamot 46–48).[15] The Mishnah, however, which is our specific focus, has only quite limited discussions of converts and conversions.

What then does the Mishnah report about converts and conversions? What about the transition from non-Jew to Jew and the issue of formal conversions? In particular, what inference can be drawn from the mishnaic conception of converts and conversions that inform us about the concepts of Israelite identity and community inclusions? Porton argues that converts are not fully Jewish, not "fully" Israelites but also are effectively distanced from their previous relatives if they were genealogically Jewish. In effect, they represent a distinct class of persons in the community. Unsurprisingly, Issues of marriage with a convert and the question of inheritance remain complex. That said, the Mishnah focuses on the convert as an individual and his or her status in the community. While converts are no longer treated as Gentiles, differences between them and ethnic native-born Israelites remain.[16] They essentially remain marginal to some extent in both communities. Hence, there is no full transition to Jewishness from this ascribed status. Non-Jewishness, therefore, retains a distinctive attribute of the Jewish community.

CONCLUDING OBSERVATIONS

We can draw some general conclusions from this studied review of the Mishnah about exclusion. First, it is clear that exclusion is multidimensional: one can be excluded from some community activities and not others. Some persons are permanently excluded and others are only excluded temporarily. It is also clear that exclusion does not always occur from a specific activity; context and often the intent of the person are the bases of exclusion. The two examples (Nezirim and idolaters) here are best conceptualized as "ideal types," representing the extremes of exclusion.

Second, exclusion of some Jews, for example, the Nazir, from the community and from some social activities is temporary, with the goal of separation being to increase his or her holiness. Gender is not a factor (men and women can be declared temporarily "distant" from the community) but often there can be gender differences in the details regarding how to make the transition back and who can nullify the Nazir status. In contrast, holiness and the exclusion of non-Jews is a concern primarily for idolatry with no differences explicit for men or women who are non-Jews. Thus, business with non-Jews is generally prohibited in the context of pagan holidays, but business is permitted when the celebration of the holiday of the non-Jew is local or private.

Third, exclusion does not mean isolation and geographic or economic segregation of a Jew from non-Jews or the Nazir from the rest of the Jewish community. Nor does the Mishnah always present the relationship between Jews and non-Jews as not involving intimate relationships. Exclusion status is primarily temporary among Jews and can be temporary between Jews and non-Jews. There is an element of "birth" or biology in the exclusion of non-Jews, an ascriptive status in the sociological sense. This is what some (Porton, for example) refer to as an ethnic consideration, in contrast to religious differences; however, that barrier is able to be nullified through marriage. The breaking of caste barriers between Jews and non-Jews through marriage parallels the marriages between those marriages between priest and non-priest families. Both the overall Jewish caste and the Kohen caste division can be broken. In addition, there does not seem to be a concern in the Mishnah of caste or Jewish community continuity in relationships between Jew and non-Jews. Therefore, conversions to Judaism appear to be hardly an issue and even not fully discussed in the Mishnah.[17] Yet the status of non-Jew as constructed by the Mishnah reinforces the distinctiveness of the Jewish community.

Issues of exclusion and inclusion in the Mishnah are illustrated by these extreme ideal types of the Nazir and the pagan. There is, of course, much more to the analysis of exclusion and inclusion that builds on these models, including the role of other groups such as Mamzerim, women, servants, and the disabled. Mostly, these groups fall between the extreme types and are connected to the cohesion of the community that the Mishnah constructs. The key point, it appears, is that the Mishnah constructs a community that takes into account the continued presence of non-Jews and the limited presence of those who refrain from selected social activities in order to express particular types of holiness. In this sense, the Mishnah envisions a community that is not homogeneous in a variety of ways: neither by being exclusively Jewish nor by being completely "holy," perhaps so to best serve itself as a continuing, thriving body. The recognition of religious heterogeneity in both ways is one of the fundamental social principles of the mishnaic orientation to community and, in turn, to its "Judaism."

REFERENCES

1. Compare the discussion of how rabbinic literature conceptualizes the "other" and the outsider in Christine Hayes, "The 'Other' in Rabbinic Literature," in *The Talmud and Rabbinic Literature*, ed. Charlotte Elisheva Fonrobert and Martin S. Jaffee (New York: Cambridge University Press, 2007) 243–69.

2. This paper is part of my current larger project on the social sciences and the Mishnah. The focus *here* is on social boundaries, where geographic boundaries are reviewed separately in the context of prohibitions of transporting objects on Shabbat outside of community boundaries; marriage boundaries are reviewed fully in the context of intermarriage. An earlier paper explores the relationship between social hierarchy and the Mishnah (see Calvin Goldscheider, "Inequality, Stratification, and Exclusion in the Mishnah: An Exploratory Social Science Analysis," in *Gazing on the Deep: Ancient Near Eastern and Other Studies in Honor of Tzvi Abusch*. eds. Jeffrey Stackert, Barbara Porter, and David P. Wright (Bethesda, MD: CDL Press, 2010), 565–84).

3. Simcha Fishbane, *Deviancy in Early Rabbinic Literature: A Collection of Socio-Anthropological Essays: Brill Reference Library of Judaism* (Boston: Brill, 2007) takes a different approach to the study of exclusion. He places the analysis in the context of deviancy of individuals who, for various reasons, appear to have no place in mainstream rabbinic Jewish society, or who may be perceived by that society as posing a threat to its norms and even to its very existence. Deviant groups studied include witches, prostitutes, Gentiles, bastards, Nazirites, soldiers, Kutites, the disabled, and the menstruate woman. His focus is also on the Mishnah. He has emphasized a framework of insiders and outsiders in the community. I tend to conceptualize the issue in terms of transitions from insider to outsider status and include the modifier "not always" and "not for all social activities" as qualifiers to the simpler dichotomy.

4. Some have argued that we should always look at apparently voluntary self-exclusion with skepticism. In general, an individual or the members of a group may withdraw from participation in the wider society in response to experiences of hostility and

discrimination. Our focus on this minimum exclusion in the Mishnah is "voluntary," but the context within which it occurs still makes it a case of social exclusion. For the Nazir, there is every reason to assume the voluntary nature of the act of self-exclusion. Compare Brian Barry's chapter in *Understanding Social Exclusion*, ed. John Hills, Julian Le Grand, and David Piachaud (Oxford: Oxford University Press 2002). An example of temporary but not voluntary exclusion is women who are in their period of menstruating (*nidda*) or after childbirth. For either status, a woman is in a state of impurity and, thereby, excluded from performing certain religious rituals and is limited in her relationship to men. However, there are specific ways for women to transition back to the community. An entire tractate of the Talmud (Niddah) is devoted to these temporary separations from the community.

5. As in other analysis on other topics, I treat the evidence as presented in the Mishnah as complete and do not include ancillary evidence or elaboration in the Talmudic materials. See my discussion in "Social Science and the Mishnah: Family Structure, Kinship, and Life Course Transitions." Paper presented at the European Association of Biblical Studies, Cordoba, Spain, July 2015 and compare to Jacob Neusner, *The Evidence of the Mishnah* (Chicago: University of Chicago Press, 1981).

6. Goldscheider, "Inequality, Stratification, and Exclusion in the Mishnah," 565–84.

7. In the Mishnah sequence of tractates, the Tractate Nazir follows the Tractate Nedarim; the latter deals extensively with vows. Both tractates are part of the Mishnah's limitations regarding women because of the special rules about vows made by women and how their vows may be nullified by husbands or scholars. The logic behind these three restrictions of hair, wine, and the deceased is not clear either from the Bible or the Mishnah. Wine consumption seems to symbolize joy, not cutting hair may symbolize distancing from the mundane and external beauty (also for war captives), and ritual defilement stands in contrast to holiness.

8. This may be a common feature of the Mishnah. The same characteristic of the Mishnah pertains to the presentation about the observance of the Sabbath, in particular, the lighting of Sabbath lights (Tractate Shabbat, chapter 2) and in the context of prohibitions and ritual activities of non-priests on Yom Kippur (Tractate Yoma, chapter 1). In these and other cases in the Mishnah, there is an assumption and description of an activity without a focus on motivation or a justification for it.

9. Although this rule violates the need for intentionality in Nezirut, since, in general, servants are treated as persons without intentionality.

10. The tractate is included in the Mishnah order of damages designed for judges and courts.

11. See Haym Soloveitchik on the development of this wine prohibition in *Collected Essays* (Oxford: Littman Library of Jewish Civilization, 2013), vol. 1: pt. 3. As a social historian, Jacob Katz exemplifies ways in which a social scientist can shed light on Talmudic and post-Talmudic Judaic texts. See, among others of his works, *Exclusiveness and Tolerance: Studies in Jewish-Gentile Relations in Medieval and Modern Times* (London: Oxford University Press, 1961) and *The Shabbes Goy: A Study in Halakhik Flexibility* (Philadelphia: Jewish Publication Society, 1989).

12. There are seven Noachite, or universal, rules that apply to all persons, including non-Jews, although these are all negatives with no religious ritual component, for example, not to murder, steal, or commit adultery.

13. Voluntary contributions are accepted from non-Jews but obligatory ritual sacrifices and contributions to the Temple are not (see Shekalim 1, 5).

14. See Gary Porton, *The Stranger within Your Gates* (Chicago: University of Chicago Press, 1994), chap. 2.

15. The *Toseftah* also has more details, and there are systematic differences between the Talmudic versions of conversions in the Talmud Yerushalmi and Bavli. See, by comparison, Porton, *The Stranger within Your Gates*, chaps. 5 and 6. See also the details in Shaye J. D. Cohen, *The Beginnings of Jewishness: Boundaries, Varieties, Uncertainties* (Berkeley: University of California Press, 1999, chaps. 5–7.

16. See details in Porton, *The Stranger within Your Gates*, chap. 2.

17. The process seems to be mostly Babylonian and not mishnaic. See Moshe Lavee, "The 'Tractate' of Conversion—BT Yeb. 46–48 and the Evolution of Conversion Procedure," *European Journal of Jewish Studies*, 4, no. 2 (2010): 169–213.

Textual Study and Social Formation: The Case of Mishnah

Jack N. Lightstone

Abstract

This paper examines, in context, the place of Mishnah study in the nascent rabbinic movement around the turn of the third century CE, a period of its social formation (or re-formation). The essay reviews two types of evidence: (1) attestations to Mishnah study and its mastery as a hallmark of being a rabbi and (2) Mishnah's most pervasive literary and rhetorical traits. In so doing, the paper addresses the question, "What type of occupational or sapiential expertise is engendered by intensive study of a document with these traits?" The paper argues that Mishnah study prepares the ancient rabbinic novice to recognize and parse finely differentiated circumstances, and reinforces and further hones the same in full-fledged rabbinic masters. Mishnah models, and its study demands, "high-grid" thinking (as defined in Mary Douglas's work) and analysis by its life-long students as an occupational set of skills, founded on knowledge of Scripture's law and, at times, on legal traditions that intervene between the "raw" dicta of Scripture and the starting point of a mishnaic treatment of matters.

In recognition of the inauguration of this journal, permit me to begin with several basic claims about the academic interests of the humanities and social sciences and their relation to the study of Judaism. The proper objects and subjects of the academic pursuit of the humanities and social sciences is to enlarge the critical understanding of what it is to be human, apart from or in addition to our physiological-biological makeup, and within the limits of the natural world.[1] Humans produce art and literature to entertain and give expression to thoughts and feelings, they make claims about the world in which we live, they define and validate forms of social organization and exchange, they posit the existence of unseen forces to make sense of our experiences and social institutions, and they make tools, and build infrastructure to support individual and collective lives and reinforce in material culture their social constructs. To study the Judaism (or Judaisms) of the Jewish People is to analyze it (or them) as instances of this larger set of human individual and group creativity and imagination.[2]

As a consequence of the foregoing, one important element of the pursuit of the humanities and social sciences is to identify, understand and, when possible, to explain similarities and differences in human behaviour and thought across individual human beings and across human communities.[3] In so doing, we gain critical and well-founded perspective, both on the range and the practical limits of the range, of expressions of humanness across individuals and across groups. As scholars of the humanities and social sciences, we, thereby, implicitly or explicitly participate in a collective exercise of building a taxonomy, a classification system, of human expression and recurrent patterns of behavior. On this foundation, we are able to articulate and test theories that move us along on a continuum from observing correlations to positing reasons for, and at times causal relationships among, correlated phenomena.[4]

If we seek to understand the ranges and limits of human similarity and difference through comparison, then humanists and social scientists must supply, or be supplied with, well-documented, individual cases of what heuristically appear to be more widely observed phenomena across individuals or across human communities. This paper offers such a case: the place of a literary creation, the Mishnah, and, specifically, of dedicated Mishnah study, in the nascent rabbinic movement around the turn of the third century CE, arguably, the period of social formation (or perhaps re-formation) of the early rabbinic group.[5]

Why focus on Mishnah? Because it was the first major literary production of the early rabbis, and Mishnah's production and promulgation as an authoritative text is contemporaneous with social developments within the rabbinic movement in the last decades of the second and first decades of the third century. Why Mishnah *study*? Because a significant body of extra-mishnaic evidence from rabbinic literature, dating soon after Mishnah's promulgation, attests to the centrality of Mishnah study and the mastery of Mishnah as the *summum bonum* activity that qualifies one for membership in the rabbinic group.[6]

As intimated earlier, a particular historical instance is illuminating, because it can be related to a wider set of phenomena of which our case in point may then provide a telling example—as a result of similarities to, and differences from, *meaningful* comparators. In the case of Mishnah and Mishnah study, the more immediate, important, culturally and historically relevant comparators come from two fronts. One is the study of authoritative texts (canonical texts, if you will) within ancient Judaism and Judaism of Late Antiquity, and the role of such mastery in social formation within Jewish society. That is to say, Mishnah study as a socially formative activity within the early rabbinic group did not arise within Jewish society *ex nihilo*, as it were, but emerges from a social history within antecedent Jewish communities. The second immediate arena to turn to for meaningful comparators is the social role of textual study within the contemporary Middle Eastern and Mediterranean world(s),[7] of which ancient Israelite/Judaic polities and Jewish communities of Late Antiquity were a part. As I shall point out below by way of introduction to the case of Mishnah study, institutionalized forms of study of one sort or another in the Middle East, Egypt, and the Eastern Mediterranean regions in Hellenistic and Roman times both created and reinforced well-defined social/class boundaries and social strata. Such institutionalized forms of instruction also served the process of defining authoritative occupational groups. It is, then, to these comparators to which I now turn, in order to provide, albeit summarily, some context before proceeding to the case at hand, Mishnah study in the early rabbinic movement in Roman Palestine.

CONTEXTUAL ELEMENTS: TEXT, STUDY AND OCCUPATIONAL GROUPS IN ANCIENT JUDAIC SOCIETIES

The (temporarily successful) Deuteronomic reformation associated with King Josiah of Judah in the seventh century BCE (2 Kings 22 and 23) laid the seeds for major, more enduring changes to come several centuries later in the Jerusalem-centred, Persian-ruled territory of Judah (Yahud), associated with the careers and followers of Ezra and Nehemiah in the fifth and fourth centuries BCE. These changes placed a document, "the Torah of Moses,"[8] at the center of all systems of legitimation and authority within the community. From that period onward, only those communities that claimed to possess this "true blue" text, to command the "true blue" interpretation of it, and, faithfully, to behave in accordance with that interpretation could lay claim to legitimacy, that is, to be the People of Israel under covenant with Yahweh.

As a consequence, other competing groups with roots in ancient Israel were delegitimized—the authors of Ezra-Nehemiah dismissed competing groups as mere "country folk" (*amei ha-aretz*), cast aspersions on their bloodlines, and questioned their monotheism (see Ezra 4)[9]—not because of any intrinsic "rightness" of the

Torah-of-Moses-alone community, but because of power politics of the region, first within the Persian Imperial system (see Ezra 4:1–6:15), and, subsequently, within the periods of Ptolemaic and Seleucid hegemony in the Land of Israel and, more broadly, the Levant. As a corollary, those who, backed by the imperial powers of the day, claimed mastery of the Torah of Moses (see Ezra 3:2, 6:18, 7:6, 7:10–12, 14, 21, 25–26; and Nehemiah 8, 9:13) and who possessed and were edified by the Torah's companion literature (which eventually encompassed the books of *the* Prophets and *the* Writings[10]) commanded the People of Israel, the People of Yahud, namely "the Jews." While the historical and social processes that brought about this state of affairs in the fifth, fourth, and early third centuries BCE are sketchy, for lack of descriptive evidence beyond the production of the Books of Ezra and Nehemiah, the outcome by Hasmonean times (second and first centuries BCE) is both clear and seemingly so well entrenched as to appear irreversible.

By late Hasmonean times, something else appears well established: the existence of a cadre of "learneds" (excuse the neologism) as a distinct social or occupational "class,"[11] if that is an appropriate term, by reason of their scholarship of the Torah of Moses and of associated authoritative literature. They functioned as an identifiable occupational group within the Jewish "state" and Temple administrations. They called themselves, and were called by others, "scribes" (*soferim*, a well-documented title) and perhaps "sages" (*hakhamim*). So well-established is this class by the first century CE in the Land of Israel, that scribes appear as "stock" figures in the Gospels, a point to which I return later.[12]

Institutionalized education of *soferim* or *hakhamim* also seems attested to in, for instance, the Book of Ben Sira (51:23). (I deliberately set-aside here what rabbinic literature says or implies about the education of "sages" in Hasmonean or earlier times, as that testimony is late and perhaps an anachronistic retrojection). The by-then-mythologized "model" for such scribes was Ezra, entitled in Ezra-Nehemiah, as "the Scribe, expert in the Torah of Moses" (Ezra 7:6). As to what form such instructional institutions took, the evidence does not permit us to say. Were they institutions in which several or more instructors worked together as an organized school? Or were there individual tutors, each with a restrained number of private clients? We do not know, although both models are well attested to in Middle Eastern or Mediterranean society in the late Hellenistic or Roman Periods.[13]

That the Torah-of-Moses-alone ideology should favor the emergence or enhancement of the roles of such groups of "scribes" or "sages" as an occupational class is not surprising in many respects. Nonetheless, it is worth noting how remarkable a transformation of early Judaic society this represents in the system of social authority within Israel. The Torah of Moses itself imagines no such authoritative group of "learneds," but does acknowledge kings,[14] prophets,[15] priests and Levites, and judges.[16] What the Torah of Moses does do is to make the authority of the latter subservient to that of a document, the Torah, and Moses (long dead, of course) is now the only source of revelation that matters. According to Deuteronomy, kings are to study the Torah. Prophets whose utterances contradict the teachings of the Torah are *ipso facto* false prophets. One is to go to the priest or to the "judge" for authoritative rulings based on Torah law, which assumes the priest (an hereditary post) has studied Torah (an acquired expertise). Clearly, the rug is being pulled out from under the forms of traditional authority that were normative and well-established in ancient Israel, and sapiential authority is being given a "leg up."

For an occupational group to be given a "leg up," it is more likely that they will have already existed, and less likely for them to have emerged *ex nihilo*. The "sage" and the "scribe" are well referenced in biblical literature for the period prior to the ascendency of the Torah-of-Moses-alone ideology. They are figures in the royal court of ancient Israel,[17] as they were in the Middle

East generally in this period.[18] These figures appear to be retainers of the monarchy, acting as advisors and senior bureaucrats. The qualifications that suited them for their positions and the training regime that prepared them for their appointments can only be surmised by indirect methods. But they clearly had to have acquired "high literacy," including not only the capacity to read and write,[19] but familiarity with the literatures and knowledge of the day, some of which seems to be reflected in the "wisdom" texts of the Hebrew Bible (even if these biblical texts were produced in later periods).

For such occupational groups, the self-transformation to purveyors of "Torah-literacy," specifically, would not have been a bridge too far. The "scribes" encountered in the Gospels as Jesus's strawmen are portrayed as precisely that—recognized, retained purveyors of Torah literacy, as the "scribes of the priests" and the "scribes of the Pharisees."

CONTEXTUAL ELEMENTS: SAGE AND SCRIBAL "CLASSES" IN MIDDLE EASTERN AND EASTERN MEDITERRANEAN SOCIETIES OF THE GRECO-ROMAN PERIOD

As intimated, "scribes" and "sages" were "high-literacy," occupational retainers of the ancient Israelite monarchy, modelled on contemporary, royal-court administration in the Middle East or Eastern Mediterranean generally. Evidence for this institutionalized occupational class comes from Egyptian sources, where some form of educational system to produce court or temple-scribal magistrates and bureaucrats from among the sons of the wealthy (and perhaps, at times, the very intellectually gifted among the poor) is clearly exhibited as early as the end of the Old Kingdom, as in the wisdom text attributed to Dauf. Indeed, the scribal "wisdom literature" of Egypt and that of Israel resemble one another to an extent that cannot be by chance. The story of Ahikar, documented among the Elephantine Papyri of the fifth century BCE, has already mythologized a scribal/sage figure that the narrative sets in the Assyrian imperial period. The books of Ezra-Nehemiah (Ezra 5:8), in addition to describing Ezra as a "scribe," use the term to designate officials in the Persian Imperial government of the territories "beyond the river," of which Jerusalem was a part.[20]

Even more important are governmental administrative systems of the Ptolemaic and Roman imperial periods in Egypt (and in the Land of Israel under Ptolemaic and Roman hegemony).[21] The Ptolemies divided Egypt (and the Land of Israel, when the latter fell to their rule for about a century) into larger administrative districts, or nomes, and subdivided the latter into geographical "toparchies." Within toparchies, villages and towns constituted subordinate administrative units. Only constitutional, self-governing "cities" fell outside this administrative system; constitutional cities were accountable directly to the monarchy, from which their city charter derived. At the apex of the governmental administration of each of the nomes, toparchies and towns were two administrative figures: (a) the archon, and (b) the scribe, who served as the chief bureaucratic retainer. Obviously, the archons and scribes of the nomes were far more powerful figures than those of toparchies and the towns, and with exemplary service officers of latter two might rise to positions in the former.

It is not clear me whether or in what manner the Hasmoneans in the Land of Israel retained this organizational structure when the dust settled from, first, the Seleucids wresting control of the Land of Israel from the Ptolemies, and, second, the Hasmoneans winning (limited?) home rule for the Land of Israel under Seleucid hegemony. Nonetheless, I lean toward the conclusion that much of the Ptolemaic system of administration was retained, because of what we know about the region under Roman rule. When Rome assumed hegemony over Ptolemaic Egypt, they retained the system of nomes/toparchies and archons/scribes, even though it differed substantially from the system of Roman administration elsewhere.[22] And as I have already noted above, the prominence of scribal retainers in a Roman-ruled Land of Israel is well documented in the Gospels for the first century CE.

I cannot give an account of how specifically these scribes or archons were prepared for their occupations and careers, but it is well known that the gymnasium-system of education of Greek-Macedonian (upper-crust) boys of Ptolemaic society was very well established and that it was intended to prepare young men for military, political, and administrative leadership at the court and in the cities—and I would imagine in the imperial administration of the territories generally. In addition, throughout the Eastern Roman Empire various philosophical schools operated. Some were small tutor-student affairs; others were organized on a larger, more institutionalized scale. In the Roman Imperial Period, Athens was one center for such schools; Alexandria, too, was such a locus. Libanius, writing in Syria, in the fourth century CE, tells us much about his "school days" as a student in Athens, and he implies a great deal about his own illustrious career as a private teacher of aspiring aristocratic youth, in competition with other private teachers in his region of the Roman Levant. His students, like those of the gymnasium, were preparing for high-ranking roles in the imperial government and its administration and for assuming their rightful place as decurions in the governing councils and in the magistracies of their towns and cities.

Finally, and tellingly, if we turn to evidence from Jewish communities in the Mediterranean world outside of the Land of Israel, the titles "archon" and "scribe" appear liberally in Roman period inscriptions. The former title sometimes appears honorific or hereditary, like membership within the class of decurions in Roman cities. But the latter seems invariably occupational, referring to an administrative role in the Jewish community accountable to the political governance system of the "synagogue," vested in an (aristocratic) council headed by the archon(s). This evidence is either contemporary with Mishnah's promulgation and with the nascent period of rabbinic movement or (more frequently) from the several centuries immediately following the promulgation of Mishnah.[23]

This, then, constitutes a brief account of the general, more immediate, historically, and culturally relevant contexts for looking at Mishnah study as a socially formative activity within the early rabbinic group. The existence of administrative retainers, as an occupational group, class, or guild characterized by "high literacy" and education in sapiential traditions, is well attested within the Judahite/Judean communities for the centuries preceding the advent of the rabbinic movement. After the reforms which biblical literature associates with the careers of Ezra and Nehemiah, Torah study and mastery would likely have occupied a place of primacy in scribal preparation. But as the content of Ben Sira indicates, other sapiential traditions continued to have their rightful place in the education of scribes.

The existence of scribal occupational groups have been equally well documented for eastern Mediterranean society generally well before, at the time of, and in the era just after the production and promulgation of Mishnah near the turn of the third century CE. And, not surprisingly, a scribal administrative group was part and parcel of Jewish communal organization in the Roman-ruled Mediterranean.[24] Against this backdrop, let us examine Mishnah study in order to glimpse aspects of the socially formative, core identity of the nascent Rabbinic group.

MISHNAH STUDY AND EARLY RABBINIC SOCIAL FORMATION, A CASE STUDY

In the remainder of this paper, I seek to summarize two distinct types of evidence that bear upon our chosen task. One type of evidence attests to the importance, even the primacy, of Mishnah study and the mastery of Mishnah as a hallmark of becoming and being a "rabbi," beginning at the turn of the third century CE, when Mishnah was first produced and promulgated by and within the early rabbinic group, and continuing in the subsequent several centuries. The other type of evidence has to do with the most pervasive literary and rhetorical traits of Mishnah itself. I will broach the question, "What type of occupational or sapiential expertise is reflected in or engendered by focused and intensive study of a document with these traits?"[25] The former type of evidence helps establish the *centrality* of Mishnah study within the nascent rabbinic group. Evidence of the latter type allows us to glimpse the probable *socio-cultural impact and meaning* of Mishnah study in the formation of an early rabbinic social identity or "professional" profile.

Before summarizing these two types of evidence, I wish to state that I will *not* consider in this paper evidence concerning what *institutionalized, organized forms of rabbinic education* existed before, at the time of, or in the decades and centuries immediately following the authoring of Mishnah. This matter, in my view, was been well researched for more than 40 years, commencing with the work of David Goodblatt.[26] The evidence and subsequent scholarship on this topic has been more recently reviewed and reassessed by Jeffrey Rubenstein.[27]

Extra-Mishnaic, Early-Rabbinic Evidence for the Centrality of Mishnah Study to the Inner-Group Life of the Early Rabbinic Social Formation

Let me begin with the centrality of Mishnah study in the early rabbinic movement. For the most part, evidence supporting this claim comes, as one might expect, from sources external to Mishnah itself, *if* one is of the view that "Mishnah" Tractate Avot is a later addition to Mishnah—added, perhaps, some half-century later.

Avot (the Fathers), in form and substance, might well be characterized as a distinctively rabbinic version of Israel's wisdom literature. At one level, Avot is a collection of wisdom teachings with a characteristically rabbinic ethos.[28] The text touts the importance of Torah study and associated rabbinic discipleship, and it contextualizes other wisdom-type advice about the good life and traits of the sage within that frame. At another level, particularly in the first several chapters, Avot establishes a pedigree for rabbinic teachings and tradition, and, therefore, in effect, provides an authoritative pedigree for Mishnah, when later—perhaps as early as the mid-third century—Avot is inserted among Mishnah's tractates. That insertion in effect declared Mishnah to be Torah, and Mishnah study to be Torah study.

But, taken on its own, outside of its current placement among Mishnah's tractates, Avot is not a panegyric for Mishnah study, specifically, but it is for Torah study and rabbinic discipleship generally. However, Avot de Rabbi Nathan (AVRN), an elaboration and expansion of Avot, contains passages that explicitly designate the core curriculum of rabbinic study, as in AVRN (version a) 8:1 (my translation, AVRN's citation of Avot in boldface type):

AVRNa 8:1

A. **Joshua b. Perahiah and Nithai the Arbelite received [the transmitted Torah] from them.**
B. **Joshua b. Perahiah says,**
   1. **"Appoint for yourself a rabbinic master [as a teacher] (rav);**
   2. **and acquire for yourself an associate [with whom to study];**
   3. **and judge every person as meritorious [on balance, that is, give everyone the benefit of the doubt]."**
C. "Appoint for yourself a rabbinic master." How so?
D. This teaches that one should appoint for oneself a rabbinic master [that is, one should not flit from one rabbinic master to another] [with whom to study on a] regular basis.
E. And one should learn from him scripture, and mishnah, and legal midrash, and aggadot [that latter being edifying tales about/from the rabbis].[29]

The order of the mandated curriculum at AVRNa 8:1:E is not arbitrary. Mishnah's primacy is exceeded only by biblical Scripture itself. And Mishnah study is preeminent over other substance of rabbinic learning. Nor is it fortuitous that after Mishnah in the list comes "legal midrash" (halahkic midrash), the extant rabbinic compositions of Late Antiquity that serve to argue the necessity of a close reading of Scripture, in which no element of a biblical verse is superfluous, this in order to derive rabbinic law (halahkah). Jacob Neusner, among others, has argued that halakhic midrash functioned to temper the ascendency and primacy of a solely logical-analytical approach to the study of Mishnah's substance.[30] The perceived need for such a corrective serves to bolster our claim.

Similar to the assertion in AVRNa 8:1 about the primacy of Mishnah study is another found in a *beraita* tradition—a tradition purported to come from authorities outside of, but contemporaneous with, those of the Mishnah—cited in the Babylonian Talmud (b. B.M. 33a). But, in contrast, b. B.M. 33a seems to register the necessity to *re-assert* the primacy of Mishnah study in the face of the increased stress on the study of post-mishnaic Talmudic traditions.

b. B.M. 33a:

> Our Rabbis taught: Those that occupy themselves [just] with [the study of] scripture are of limited value; with [the study of] Mishnah [but not of subsequent rabbinic teachings] are certainly of value and will be recompensed [for their study]; with [the study of] Talmud, nothing is of greater value. But always pursue the [study of the] Mishnah more than the [study of the] Talmud.[31]

But, of course, the most compelling evidence external to Mishnah of the centrality of Mishnah study to the interior life of the group comes from the following two fronts: (a) at the turn of the third century and in the subsequent several centuries, the rabbi or would-be rabbi was expected to have memorized Mishnah, and serving groups of masters and students were a company of official memorizers of Mishnah (i.e., the *tannaim*), who were living repositories of the textual tradition;[32] and (b) entire literary-rhetorical genres of rabbinic traditions and study materials were collected or authored as companions to Mishnah study under the two generic designations of *beraitot* (or *tosafot*) and *gemarot*, with the Mishnah text providing the only overarching organizing structure[33] for the eventual compilation of these materials into the extant Tosefta, Palestinian Talmud, and Babylonian Talmud.

In summation, briefly, the claim that Mishnah study and Mishnah mastery were central to the inner group life of the early rabbinic group from the turn of the third century CE and over the subsequent several centuries is very much an over-determined claim, based on the extra-mishnaic evidence from late antiquity.

Intra-Mishnaic Evidence and the Nature of Inner-Group, Normative Traits Modeled and Re-enforced by Mishnah Study

In a preceding section, I broached the question, "What skills or traits of mind, on the one hand, and what social/professional relations, on the other, are the requisites of, or are engendered by, life-long devotion to Mishnah study?" To some degree, the answer to these questions is reflected in the major post-mishnaic compilations, the two Talmuds, organized as commentaries of sorts on Mishnah.[34] But, as stated earlier, if we are interested in the nascent rabbinic group at the turn of the third century, when Mishnah and Mishnah-study were initially promoted, and in the decades or the century immediately following, we must look principally to the Mishnah itself for answers, and, specifically, at its most pervasive literary and rhetorical features at both the *macro* and *micro* levels. It is these traits that would have confronted the student of Mishnah on a regular basis and placed specific demands upon the student's resources, intellectual and otherwise. Moreover, the acquisition of these resources bespeaks, indirectly, of a social network in which they may be accessed and in which they are valued.[35]

Macro Literary Traits: Mishnah's Topical Agenda and Scripture

Mishnah's content is legal in nature, spanning sacerdotal ritual and priestly gifts, religious-festive practice, purity maintenance, some civil and family law, and certain judicial processes, torts, and criminal law. However, while the treatment of many *subtopics* is extensive and seemingly exhaustive, for example, the signatory requirements for writs of divorce, Mishnah's coverage of a number of its grand themes (the subject matter of its "tractates" and "orders") is not; rather, coverage is episodic.

By what heuristic standard do I make such an assertion? Mishnah's treatment of many of its grand topics would require much in the way of complementary and supplementary materials even to begin to approach the comprehensiveness that one would expect of a "working" law code for a "living" Judaic society. To satisfy the latter's requirements, whole additional chapters would have to be added to many of Mishnah's thematic tractates, and entire additional tractates would be needed.[36] This contrast between apparent exhaustiveness at the level of many sub-topics and "gross lacunae" at the level of Mishnah's topical agenda is an important datum,[37] to which I will return. Moreover, while Mishnah sometimes articulates overarching legal principles from which detailed law follows, more often it does not. Rather, the reader is left to induce the law or legal principles from a series of specific rulings on minutia—that is, unless knowledge of the former type is assumed to already be part of the Mishnah student's toolbox in some fashion—also a matter to be further discussed later in the paper.

One feature of the spectrum of Mishnah's major topical themes is that while some of Mishnah's legal content is relevant to Palestinian Judaic life at the time of Mishnah's promulgation at the turn of the turn of the third century, a great deal of Mishnah's substance concerns a Judaic world and society that disappeared before Mishnah's authors undertook their work. When Mishnah was composed near the turn of the third century CE, the Jerusalem Temple, its associated institutions (its courts and tribunals), and its leadership (priests, Levites and temple scribes) had been defunct for more than a century. But one can barely surmise this from Mishnah's substantive agenda in many of its tractates. Other parts of Mishnah's agenda are, however, completely relevant to the post-destruction period and assume none of the Temple-era's institutions in their articulation (e.g., m. Megilah and m. Eruvin). On still other occasions Mishnah's substance proffers odd-ball anachronisms, such as, when Mishnah enjoins (rabbinic) sages to give instructions to Temple priests, because only the latter, by law, may act, but only the former know with accuracy what the priests must do (e.g., m. Yoma).

Social scientists and humanists (particularly historians) are used to studying evidence in historical time to provide important context. Synchrony and diachrony are important dimensions in scholarly analysis.[38] But the social world that emerges across Mishnah's agenda and topics is curiously "unstuck in time," to use the novelist Kurt Vonnegut's term.[39] As a result of being so "unstuck," the world that Mishnah's content adumbrates in law is an "imagined" one. On the one hand, that world very likely *never* existed in the manner that Mishnah law portrays, and, on the other, it is a world that did not and could not exist *as a whole*, as a religio-cultural *system*, at the time of Mishnah's production.

I use words such as "whole" and "system" for specific reasons and as important qualifiers. Three reasons are foremost, among potentially others: First, because my own work and that of my teacher, Jacob Neusner, as well as that of many of his other former students, strongly support the claim that an integrated religio-cultural system underpins Mishnah throughout.[40] To a large extent, it is the system that also underpins the Pentateuch, which I argue elsewhere in this paper is the core touchstone of Mishnah's substantive agenda, even though Mishnah more often than not tends not to cite its dependence on scripture. Second, and in a completely opposing vector, I use the terms "whole" and "system", because I do *not* wish to imply that all of Mishnah's content is irrelevant or un-implementable at the turn of the third century. In theory, any Mishnah law that does not require the Temple cult and its administration is implementable in principle. Earlier, I pointed to tractates like Megilah and Eruvin. But one may also look to passages in many other tractates, including, for example, in Gittin, Kiddushin, Berakhot, and others. And indeed, when the rabbis came to wield sufficient power and authority—a state of affairs that emerged well after Mishnah's production—the rulings of such tractates were taken as the basis for normative practice within Jewish communities. One has only to look at the bases in Mishnah for significant sections of the great medieval rabbinic codes. Third, and perhaps the most intriguing for some social historians of late Roman Palestine, while Mishnah's "whole system" was not implementable at the time of Mishnah's production, at a number of junctures in the text, those who produced Mishnah could not help but reflect *in passing* the historical or social reality of their times. Why? At these junctures, it was likely more difficult for Mishnah's authors to "imagine" things to be otherwise than they actually were in the world around them. For example, one of the foundational underpinnings of Mishnah tractates Shabbat and Eruvin is the authors' conceptual model of the typical layout of a late second-century Palestinian town or city, when translating biblical Sabbath prohibitions, which do not adequately take account of urban life,

into an urban setting. Mishnah's framers, *by the way*, tell us much about the towns and cities of their day, because it is much less likely that they are trying to imagine the structure of towns and cities of ancient Israel. Not so, by contrast, when Mishnah refers to cities of refuge enjoined in the Pentateuch itself.[41] The same may be said for tractates dealing with agricultural gifts, like tithes and the heave offering, given to the poor and the Levitical-priestly caste. Here, Mishnah's framers reflect the modes of agricultural production of their day, because at these junctures they are less likely or simply less able to "imagine" other ones.[42]

So, to summarize our observations thus far—Mishnah's treatment of its subject matter oscillates between the exhaustive, when dealing with subtopics, and the highly episodic and incomplete, when covering themes relevant to a living Judaic community. Mishnah concerns itself with social, cultural, and religious norms and institutions, which as a *cultural system* did not exist at the time of Mishnah's production and that likely never existed in the form that Mishnah gives it in law.

I remarked earlier that in terms of substance, Mishnah's content seemed "unstuck in time." Mishnah is not, however, as unstuck in topographical space. With so much of Mishnah's content referring to a Jerusalem-Temple-centered praxis, the geography of the "imagined" world of Mishnah clearly has its axis in Jerusalem and in the Land of Israel. Since the early rabbinic movement emerged in Palestine, Mishnah may simply reflect the decidedly Roman-Palestinian social location and social identity of its authors and its initial intended users.[43]

I do not think such reasoning is compelling. At best, it is an incomplete explanation. Mishnah's Land-of-Israel and Jerusalem-Temple centrism is at the same time an epiphenomenon of another abiding literary trait of Mishnah—namely its pervasive, first-order dependence upon biblical-Pentateuchal law, which is itself Jerusalem-Temple centric.[44] Permit me to elaborate. Mishnah is faithfully grounded in the laws and injunctions of the Pentateuch, when and where topically there is corresponding scriptural material. Chapter after chapter, in tractate after tractate, Pentateuchal injunctions underlie Mishnah passages. The former are authoritative axioms of the latter throughout Mishnah, even though nine times out of ten—I mean this rhetorically, not statistically—the relevant Scripture is neither cited nor alluded to. At times—some might say, not infrequently—Scripture is cited as a proof text. But episodic proof texting is very different than systematic citing or than pointing to the underlying scriptural basis of passage after passage in tractates and chapters; the latter rarely happens. Yet without a thorough knowledge of Pentateuchal injunctions, Mishnah's content is all but incomprehensible. That knowledge is assumed to be possessed by the reader, or it is assumed that the reader has immediate and continuing access to someone who does have that knowledge. We will hold that thought for later, as we have held others, but I would recall here in passing the extra-mishnaic evidence of Late Antiquity (referred to earlier) about the hierarchy of the rabbinic core curriculum in the several centuries following Mishnah's promulgation:[45] The primacy of Mishnah study was exceeded only by the study of Scripture. To *openly* assert the inverse would be ideologically unthinkable in any post-Ezra-Nehemiah Judaic community.

Mishnah's often undocumented and unstated dependency on scripture is odd in two other, diametrically opposing ways.[46] In some cases, Mishnah passages seem to deal with an uncited scriptural injunction, as if no intervening centuries of practice or interpretation existed—as if scripture were composed a mere day before the Mishnah passage in question, and the latter is a first attempt at understanding the former. For instance, m. Menahot 5:8 proffers a dispute concerning what the difference is between a *mahkreshet* ("a firepan") and a *mahvat* ("a firepan"). Both terms are biblical (see Lev. 7:9–10), and Mishnah at this juncture is engaged *in effect* in first-order exegesis (or eisegesis) of biblical terms—to sort out a fuzzy matter in the scriptural injunctions. But the scriptural passages were not composed the day before the Mishnah passage. Surely, more than five centuries of practice in the Jerusalem Temple had long settled the issue in question. So, either Mishnah's editors were unaware of five centuries of practice, or, far more likely, the established practice was beside the point, given Mishnah's purpose for its intended readership, a core topic of the latter sections of this essay.

At the other end of the spectrum, Mishnah is, at times, based on Scripture (still uncited), but one or several (also) unstated premises or postulates may logically intervene between the datum in Scripture and the starting point in Mishnah's treatment of a topic. In such instances, one may readily surmise what (uncited) Scripture is the premise, but the starting point of the relevant Mishnah is two or three logical removes from or beyond the premise in Scripture, and the intermediate logical postulates or suppositions are nowhere to be found in Mishnah (or elsewhere in Scripture, for that matter). Since without these intermediate postulates one cannot even begin to understand the Mishnah passage, then the reader, again, is assumed to already know them or to have ready access to someone who does.

What, then, might we begin to see reflected about a specific community, the community of those who first produced and studied Mishnah as a *summum bonum* of their social formation? First, that they valued the utopian, hypothetical, and theoretical over the historical. Second, their interest was directed more to the very concrete and specific, as opposed to the articulation of general legal principles or deduction from those principles. Third, in the production and study of Mishnah, the exhaustive attention to the specific was far more important than being comprehensive; exemplifying how to articulate and fully ramify some topics outweighed the value of covering all topics to produce a usable code.

Fourth, much in the way of anterior knowledge was demanded of the reader to even start understanding Mishnah, since many of the logically essential premises to reading a Mishnah passage or "chapter" are not there in the text. Fifth, and returning to the first observation, the world of/in Scripture mattered more than the world since; and the identity of the Mishnah's producers and users was grounded and legitimated in their command of scriptural law.

On these bases, one can discern, as an interim proposition, that Mishnah reflects a community of scholarly elite, whose members are expected to have, or to acquire, a considerable body of antecedent knowledge. Moreover, Mishnah students practise (in entirely hypothetical-theoretical acts of imagination focussed on the world defined by biblical law) the application of that knowledge to the exquisitely concrete and specific.[47] At first glance, based on macro-literary traits of Mishnah, we are dealing with a community of scholarship that values and inculcates quite specific capacities among its members.

Micro-rhetorical Traits: Inculcating "High Grid" Taxonomical Vision

A number of micro-rhetorical traits of Mishnah seem consistent with, and further bear out, these interim conclusions. First, most of Mishnah's language is both highly formalized and decidedly laconic—economical to the extreme.[48] This is evident to any first-time translator of Mishnah, who must continuously interpolate (often in square brackets) the language required to turn a *mishnaic* declarative sentence into a declarative sentence in English, French, German, etc.

A prime illustration can be found in m. Bekhorot 1:1a. I chose this passage not only because it is, in my view, typical of so much of Mishnah but, specifically, because it is the *opening* pericope of the *opening* chapter of a tractate of Mishnah. In other words, there is absolutely nothing that precedes this passage that provides any additional intelligible context for the reader. What the first-time reader of m. Bekhorot 1:1a sees (or more precisely, "does not get") is all that the reader must be provided from somewhere or someone outside Mishnah itself to interpret/understand the pericope for him/herself. Below, then, I present two translations of m. Bekhorot 1:1a. The first represents Mishnah's language as closely as I am able, in its fully laconic style; the second provides interpolations (in square brackets) to make the passage (more) intelligible.[49]

m. Bekhorot 1:1a (as is, without interpolations)

1. He who purchases the fetus of an ass of a Gentile,
2. And he who sell to him,
3. Even though it is not permitted.
4. And he who forms a partnership with him,
5. And he who receives from him,
6. And he who gives to him in trust—
7. is exempt from the law of the firstling,
8. as it is said, "Of an Israelite" (Num. 3:13),
9. but not of others.

m. Bek. 1:1a (with my interpolations)

1. He [an Israelite] who purchases the fetus of an ass of a Gentile[, and the fetus, when born, if it turns out to be male, will be a firstborn of the ass owned by the Gentile],
2. And he [an Israelite] who sells to him[, the Gentile, the fetus of an ass of the Israelite, and the fetus, when born, if it turns out to be male, will be the firstborn of the ass owned by the Israelite],
3. Even though it is not permitted [for an Israelite to contract such a sale to a Gentile].
4. And he [an Israelite] who forms a partnership with him [the Gentile, so that they co-own the fetus of an ass owned by either the Gentile or the Israelite, and, subsequently, when the fetus is born, it is both male and a firstborn of the ass],

5. And he [an Israelite] who receives [a pregnant ass] from him [a Gentile, and, subsequently, when the fetus is born, it is both male and a firstborn of the ass],
6. And he [an Israelite] who gives [a pregnant ass] to him [a Gentile,] in trust [and, subsequently, when the fetus is born, it is both male and a firstborn of the ass]—
7. [in all of the foregoing cases, the fetus, when born] is exempt from the law of the firstling [of unclean species as enjoined in the biblical scriptures].
8. as it is said, "Of an Israelite" (Num. 3:13),
9. but not of others.

The contrast between the two versions is stark and typical of so much of Mishnah. As we can see from our exemplary passage, m. Bekhorot 1:1a, the very micro-literary-rhetorical traits of Mishnah's language bespeaks of a document the study and understanding of which is impossible outside of an organized social context in which vital information is learned that renders Mishnah's content intelligible.[50] That requisite information is of several sorts. One sort is captured in the question, "What is Mishnah actually talking about in this passage?" That is, Mishnah does not provide enough information to surmise the circumstances that together comprise the often-hypothetical cases upon which Mishnah proffers a ruling. The cases (the "protases" of the sentences in m. Bekhorot 1:1a) cannot be understood without the explicatory interpolations, and these must come from somewhere or someone. The other sort is captured in the question, "What background law must one know to make sense of the ruling or rulings (the 'apodoses') that m. Bekhorot 1:1a offers?" In the latter instance, one must know the biblical injunctions about the gift of the firstborn males, of humankind and of clean and unclean animals. And one must also know that Mishnah, although not the biblical text, further *assumes* that the biblical laws concerning firstborn males of unclean species apply only to the ass. Those of us who have spent years reading Mishnah and related documents forget or are no longer cognizant of the significant knowledge gap that the un-interpolated text of Mishnah presents to the novice reader, a gap that had to have been bridged by some organized social context and institutions, of which the novice reader would have had to have become a part, studying, then, together with resident experts.

Primarily post-mishnaic rabbinic documents talk specifically of such Palestinian-rabbinic institutions, notable among them, the House of Study (*bet ha-midrash*), and perhaps it is anachronistic to project these back into the period in which Mishnah was first authored, promulgated, and studied. We can suspend judgment on that issue for the purpose of this paper and its argument.[51] My point rather is this: we do not need these post-mishnaic sources to reasonably conclude that a social institution or institutions of some facilitating type existed at the core of the organization of the rabbinic movement at the time of Mishnah's initial promulgation in order to provide what the novice reader of Mishnah needed to gain sufficient mastery. At this juncture, we may say, first, that the very micro-literary-rhetorical traits of Mishnah itself beg the existence of such institutions by indirection (*derekh ha-gav*). It is warranted, preliminarily, to conclude from such evidence that (1) entry into the early rabbinic movement and (2) passage from a more or less novice status to full membership were via study in some such organized setting. Moreover, we may further hypothesize that the passage from the status of novice to the status of full membership involved becoming an "autonomous," "self-sufficient" reader and analyst of Mishnah, in so far as the mastery of Mishnah was the *summum-bonum* activity of the group.

Second, not only do Mishnah's micro-literary-rhetorical traits reflect and, indeed, beg a specific type of knowledge acquisition in the passage from novice to member, but they also foster the inculcation of particular types of analytic skills, once that antecedent knowledge is mastered.

Again, let me demonstrate this point using m. Bekhorot 1:1 (although very many Mishnah passages would do equally well). For the purposes of this illustration, we must play a mental game. We must strip sections 8 and 9 from m. Bekhorot 1:1a. Sections 8 and 9 adduce a scriptural proof text for the ruling at section 7. My excuse for this request is this: more often than not such an appeal to a scriptural proof text would *not* be included in a typical Mishnah passage. But my reason for asking that you bracket out the appeal to Scripture is that it helps make the point I have in mind when one looks at the "raw" un-interpolated text of m. Bekhorot 1:1a.

One will note that there is not one case, but five cases that are the subject of the ruling at section 7. The five cases are created, or more appropriately, "spun out," by simply varying one word in each of sections 1, 2, 4, 5, and 6. That word in each case is the use of the *heh*-emphaticus together with a verb in the third-person, singular, masculine, present-participial form in order to create a substantive in Hebrew:

1. he who purchases;
2. he who sells;
4. he who partners;
5. he who receives; and
6. he who gives.

All other circumstances that comprise the cases are held constant: an Israelite contracting with a Gentile; an unborn fetus, the gender of which is unknown; a pregnant ass that has never before given birth to offspring. What the reader is asked to surmise is whether the stated *systematic variation* in the contracted activity between the Israelite and the Gentile, with all other variables held constant, changes the outcome. Mishnah's answer is no, it does not. The ruling (given at section 7) for all five cases is the same. The question that is now begged, but not stated is, "Why should the outcome be the same in all five instances?" Because as long as the Israelite does not have *total, unrestricted* title and control of the unborn fetus and its dame, the offspring is not subject to the law of the firstling, should the fetus end up being a male firstborn of the ass. But that general answer is not given, although it could have been proffered as a general rule at the outside. It has to be "doped out" by the reader from contemplating the five "spun-out" cases and analyzing their salient differences and similarities. If the general rule had been given at the outset by Mishnah, then the rest of m. Bekhorot 1:1a would have been, strictly speaking, unnecessary, indeed, superfluous. But it is also true, and this is my point, that the student of m. Bekhorot 1:1a would have been intellectually engaged in a very different manner. The student would have (simply) learned a rule, rather than having had to figure out the rule, or when it applied to similar but still slightly varied circumstances, or both.

I could repeat this demonstration over and over again with dozens or hundreds of Mishnah passages. All examples would give similar indirect evidence of privileging of this type of intellectual engagement by reason of the micro-literary-rhetorical traits that pervade Mishnah: vary the circumstances and tell me when or whether this (biblically grounded) rule or that applies, or still applies.

In m. Bekhorot 1:1a, only one variable was changed each time. Many passages in Mishnah will systematically vary, in turn, first one then other variables to spin out more cases of increasing complexity, requiring increasingly complex intellectual engagement. In fact, we do not have to stray far in Mishnah to find such a text. M. Bekhorot 1:3 to 1:4a is an apt example. Permit me to provide a translation without any explanatory interpolations.[52]

m. Bekhorot. 1:3

1. An ass which had not given birth,
2. and bore two males—
3. one gives a single lamb to the priest.
4. Male and female—
5. he separates a single lamb for himself.
6. Two asses which had not given birth
7. bore two males—

8. one gives two lambs to the priest.
9. a male and a female,
10. or two males and a female—
11. one gives a single lamb to the priest.
12. They bore two females and one male,
13. or two males and two females—
14. there is nothing here for the priest.

m. Bekhorot. 1:4a

15. One which had given birth, and one which had not given birth,
16. and which bore two males—
17. one gives a single lamb to the priest.
18. A male and a female—
19. one separates a single lamb for himself.

Again, we may begin by asking, "What must one know of the law of the firstling as an antecedent to engaging with the 'whys and wherefores' of this passage?" First, biblical law declares that the firstborn males of humankind and animals, both of clean and unclean species, are holy. That holiness must be dissipated by being redeemed and transferred back to its originator, the deity, in some fashion. The firstborn male of an ass—we now know that, for Mishnah, the only unclean species to which the law of the firstborn applies is the ass—is redeemed with a lamb (a clean species), which, in turn, is given to a member of the priestly clan as his due, effectively returning it to the deity. The firstborn ass is now de-sanctified and may be used by the owner. The passage also assumes that in cases of doubt—when we do not know whether the male offspring is a firstborn—one de-sanctifies it by redeeming it with a lamb, but one need not give the lamb to the priest. When all this is understood by or conveyed to the novice reader, one may *begin* to contemplate the series of cases spun out before us by varying first one hypothetical factor and then another, by simple concatenation and permutation of the highly laconic terms of the extended passage. My point is, again, the literary-rhetorical features that are the atomic building blocks of extended passages demand of the student, particularly of the novice, considerable intellectual engagement. One must dope out the legal principles from a series of slightly differentiated, hypothetical cases, when one could have been given the general rules and principles first, rather than having to induce them. But to do this one must first inform oneself, or be informed, of the relevant biblical law and its subsequent developments, and one must mentally fill in the lacunae in Mishnah's highly laconic language, in order to begin to comprehend the hypothetical factors that are being permuted to create cases.

I cannot here provide a complete catalog of Mishnah's micro-literary-rhetorical traits. However, one other is so prominent and pervasive that it warrants a fulsome discussion. It is the dispute form.[53] In the dispute, the reader encounters two rulings (apodases) for a single case (protasis). The literary-rhetorical features of disputes' protases (cases) and apodases (rulings) are typical of other passages of Mishnah, but one or more of the apodases is attributed to a named rabbinic sage, from whose authority the ruling is portrayed to stem. Generally speaking, one can identify three sub-species (with several variations of each) of the dispute form in Mishnah. They are the following:

1.
   -circumstances,
   -ruling,
   -Rabbi x says,
   -ruling;

2.
   -circumstances,
   -Rabbi x says,
   -ruling,
   -the sages say,
   -alternative ruling;

2'.
   -circumstances,
   -ruling,
   -the words of Rabbi x,
   -the sages say,
   -alternative ruling;

3.
    -circumstances,
    -Rabbi x says,
    -ruling,
    -Rabbi y says,
    -alternative ruling.

3'.
    -circumstances,
    -ruling,
    -the words of Rabbi x
    -Rabbi y says,
    -alternative ruling.

The circumstances (protases) and rulings (apodases) in mishnaic disputes display the same highly laconic, concatenative and permutative literary-rhetorical characteristics as other passages in Mishnah. Disputes are constructed by the simple interpolation of: "Says/say," or "the words of"; and "Rabbi" plus name, or "the sages." That is it. Nothing more.

Given the specific purposes of this paper, what are we to conclude from the presence and literary-rhetorical character of disputes in Mishnah? First and most obviously, thanks in large part to the literary-formal characteristics of the dispute form, Mishnah has told us unequivocally that "full" members of the group that produced and studied Mishnah referred to themselves collectively as "the sages," and addressed individual authorities within the group by the honorific "My Lord/Master" so-and-so, for that is the most reasonable translation of the term "rabbi." Both would be highly loaded terms in late-Roman, Palestinian-Jewish society. We may additionally read here a respect and reliance upon some specific lineage of tradition and opinion, the lineage of those named: Yohanan ben Zakkai, Eliezer ben Hyrcanus, Joshua ben Hananiah, Aqiva, Yose ben Halafta, Judah ben Ilai, and the list goes on.

The adducing of named authorities is significant to this essay's issues, because it could have easily been otherwise from a literary-rhetorical perspective. We could have had attributions to named authorities without disputes. And while sometimes we have just this, it is overwhelmingly the case that attributions to named authorities appear in one or another of the variations of the dispute form. Moreover, we must also consider that it was entirely within the realm of literary-rhetorical possibility that Mishnah could have had disputes without named attributions. For example, we could have had something that displays this literary-rhetorical patterning:

-protasis;
-apodasis;
-[and] there are those who say:
-alternative apodasis.

What, then, are we to make of the fact that (a) we have names and (b) they largely appear in highly formalized, laconically worded, disputes?

Unless we wish to conclude that the number of members of the early rabbinic movement was very small in the decades leading up to the production of Mishnah (which is certainly a possibility), and that, consequently, Mishnah names virtually all early rabbis, we would be wise to consider that the named authorities in Mishnah are a subset, a particularly important and noteworthy subset of early members. These important early-rabbinic VIPs, if you will, are *portrayed* by Mishnah as often having diametrically opposed positions. I say "portrayed," because the laconic, formulaic, and permutative nature of Mishnah's particular micro-literary-rhetorical traits makes it highly unlikely that any real, historical, early rabbinic VIP's language is portrayed, or that "his" legal position was articulated on precisely the case as articulated by Mishnah.[54] What is portrayed is that the divergent legal traditions that may have come from various early rabbinic VIPs all find their place in Mishnah's disputes, more often without any indication of which person's view is the correct one.

A number of years ago, Shaye Cohen made essentially the same argument in proffering his "big tent" theory of the rabbinic movement's origins.[55] I accept Shaye Cohen's view, and offer an additional claim about the social significance and meaning of the Mishnaic dispute for the community that produced, revered, and studied Mishnah.

Earlier, I wrote about the intellectual engagement required by Mishnah's laconic language in the construction of its cases. We spoke as well of the use of concatenation and permutation of terms to generate a series of related cases, in order to test in each whether similarities outweighed differences such that one or another ruling should apply or not. Imagine now a passage in which *not only* the laconically stated elements comprising the case (the protasis) are varied to examine differentiation, *but also* the ruling is varied by the presentation of diametrically opposed outcomes in the apodases for a single protasis. The Mishnah student is, thereby, additionally invited to ask, "Why might someone legitimately rule one way in these circumstances, while someone else would legitimately rule otherwise in the same circumstances?" In other words, adding alternative rulings expands the matrix for active, engaged analysis.

That the dispute begs such additionally active analytic engagement, perhaps intentionally so by Mishnah's authors, is indicated by the use in Mishnah of the debate form, in which a dispute is followed by very laconic justifications for the disputing parties' different rulings. Debates (unlike disputes) are less common in Mishnah. But debates are more common in post/extra-mishnaic rabbinic sources, such as Tosefta, composed as companions to Mishnah study. This last observation, in my view, serves to bolster my claim about one important (intended?) effect of the dispute for the Mishnah student's engagement.

CONCLUSIONS

Let me now summarize and characterize the sort of Mishnah-student engagement seemingly engendered by Mishnah's pervasive micro-rhetorical traits. One may describe what is demanded of the engaged student as "matrix analytics." Across the top of the matrix are various related cases, often spun out by varying the several circumstances that combine to define the case. Down the side of the matrix is the ruling or rulings that apply in each case. Where there is a dispute, down the side of the matrix there are more items than there would be otherwise. In every "box" formed by the matrix, there is a "Yes" or a "No." "Yes," rule x applies; "No," rule x does not apply. In the case of a dispute, there are more boxes with "Yes" or "No," providing opposing positions for the same case. To understand Mishnah, the engaged student is invited to figure out *why* Mishnah has placed a "Yes" or "No" in each box of the matrix. Why, upon reflection and analysis, are discrete cases more or less similar to one another in ways that are compelling and relevant in Torah law?. As one increases and permutes those elements that together define a case—take for example, m. Bekhorot. 1:3-4a—one increases the number of boxes with "Yes" or "No" in them; the matrix gets larger, and, visually, the boxes smaller to fit the page. In other words, the greater the number of variables that define a hypothetical situation for which a ruling is given, the finer the gradations that differentiate one situation from another in a manner that is potentially significant in the application and ramification of Torah law.

The study of Mishnah, then, prepares one to expect, recognize, and deal with—in the sense of making judgments about—such potentially highly or finely differentiated circumstances.[56] Mishnah models, invites, demands, and inculcates high-grid thinking and analysis on the part of its life-long students as a professional or occupational set of skills, founded, as we have seen, on thorough knowledge of Scripture's law and, at times, on legal traditions that intervene between the "raw" dicta of Scripture and the starting point of a mishnaic treatment of a related matter. And we know that the study, mastery, and life-long analysis of Mishnah constituted principal activities of the inner-group life of the nascent rabbinic social formation, and defined, in (large) part, "who" became qualified as a full member in the early rabbinic group.

We need to know more about the positions in Roman Palestine at the turn of the third century CE to which members of this group were appointed by reason of being rabbis. That is an historical inquiry in its own right; Mishnah itself tells us little or nothing of value in this regard. But Mishnah does hint at the aspirations of the early rabbinic group—to serve as *the* authoritative administrators and arbiters in the organized religious, civil, and judicial institutionalized structures of Jewish society in the Land of Israel, by reason of their unique professional competencies. They aspired, moreover, to a monopoly over these positions. Have I not just described the goals of a professional guild?

No evidence that I know of confirms that their broader aspirations were fulfilled in the third century, particularly their monopolistic ones. But some rabbis did fill some relevant positions, sometimes by appointment to them by the Palestinian patriarchate.[57] Several centuries later in Palestine and Babylonia and, certainly, in the early Muslim period, they largely achieved the positions and levels of authority to which they seemed to aspire from the beginning.

In conclusion, what we glimpse is the core nature of a specific social formation in the late second- or early third centuries in Roman Palestine, that of the nascent rabbinic group. We have an indication of what turns the group's novices into full-fledged members. We understand what knowledge and capacities are to be nurtured in that transformation. We surmise something of the expert resources the novice must access. We can see that, however particular the early rabbinic group is in these regards, it stands synchronically and diachronically within historical and social contexts in which such groups and the social institutions that support their continued existence were quite normal, even normative. These other groups (some antecedent to the rabbis in the Land of Israel itself) provided sapiential, high-literacy retainer classes—professional guilds, if you will—for their respective communities, governments or temple administrations in the Middle East well into the Roman imperial period. And it stands to reason that the members of the early rabbinic group aspired to much the same.[58] That and how they acted on these aspirations, first in Roman Palestine, and soon after in Persian-ruled Babylonia, is another topic altogether with its own challenges of evidence and methodology.

REFERENCES

1. Of course, our biology and physiology are key conditioners of our human and social expressions. Psychology, for example, has been transformed by neuroscience. My point is simply that this relationship between biology, on the one hand, and human expression, thought, social systems, and culture, on the other, has tended not to be central to most of the issues that the humanities and social sciences have sought to address.

2. This is a point that my recently deceased doctoral supervisor, Dr. Jacob Neusner, made frequently and emphatically, when I and my fellow graduate students studied with him in the early 1970s. This may be an obvious statement now, but it was not then, as the scholarly study of Judaism was still largely undertaken in Jewish institutions of higher learning and most faculty in secular universities who dedicated their careers to the research of Judaism's classical and medieval literatures had themselves acquired their expertise in these texts while studying in Jewish institutions such as seminaries and *yeshivot*—Jacob Neusner himself being among

that generation. Also among the most cogent and articulate writers on the study of religion, from the perspectives of the humanities and social sciences, in general, and the academic study of Judaism, is, to my mind, Jonathan Z. Smith. He has been consistent in continuing to reflect on these matters in light of his career experiences. In this regard, see Jonathan Z. Smith, "When the Chips are Down," in *Relating Religion: Essays in the Study of Religion* (Chicago: University of Chicago, 2004), 1–43.

3. The writings of Jonathan Z. Smith, in the 1970s and early 1980s, were the first to drive these points home for me in the study of religion. See, for example, his essay, "In Comparison a Magic Dwells," in *Imagining Religion: From Babylon to Jonestown* (Chicago: University of Chicago Press, 1982), 19–35. For an informative and quite comprehensive discussion of the comparative methodologies, particularly in the modern and post-modern study of religion, see David M. Freidenreich, "Comparisons Compared: A Methodological Survey of Comparisons of Religion from 'A Magic Dwells' to 'A Magic Still Dwells,' " *Method and Theory in the Study of Religion* 16 (2004): 80–101. For a study of the early modern efforts to compare religions from the perspective of the history of philosophy and the history of ideas, see Laura Ammon, *Work Useful to Religion and the Humanities: A History of the Comparative Method in the Study of Religion from Las Casas to Tylor* (Eugene, OR: Pickwick Publications, 2012).

4. The theoretical perspectives, methodological approaches, and sought-for-ends of the humanities and social sciences are diverse and increasingly so. Moreover, the boundaries between the two disciplinary families have become more difficult to draw. For an exemplary attempt to sort these out, see Abhijit Kundu, "Understanding the Humanities," chap. 1 in *The Humanities: Methodology and Perspectives,* ed. Abhijit Kundu, Pramod K. Nayar, and Shweta (Delhi: Pearson, 2009). See also Jerome Kagan, *The Three Cultures: Natural Sciences, Social Sciences and the Humanities in the 21st Century* (New York: Cambridge University Press, 2009); on the ramification of theoretical perspectives in the humanities (and social sciences) in contemporary scholarship, see Vincent B. Leitch, *Theory Matters* (London and New York: Routledge, 2003). An example of the adoption of scientific-like methods in the contemporary humanities may be seen in the handbook by Willie von Peer, Frank Hakemulder and Sonia Zyngier, *Scientific Methods for the Humanities* (Amsterdam and Philadelphia: John Benjamins Publishing, 2012).

5. There is no doubt that early rabbinic texts themselves implicitly or explicitly place the development of the emergence of "the Rabbis" earlier than the dawn of the third century. The Mishnah itself attributes traditions to named "rabbis" who flourished just before and just after the destruction of the Jerusalem Temple in 70 CE. These texts also attribute rulings to proto-rabbinic figures like Hillel and Shammai and to their "Houses." See Jacob Neusner, *Rabbinic Traditions about the Pharisees, before 70, 1–3* (Leiden, NL: Brill, 1971). But "the Rabbis" did not produce and promulgate a *common* major text, even if traditions or collections of traditions may have circulated among them before, or other than, Mishnah. Post-mishnaic rabbinic texts consistently portray Rabbi Judah the Patriarch (last decades of the second century and first decades of the third century) as a pivotal figure in Mishnah's production or promulgation, or both; see Lee Levine, "The Status of the Patriarch in the Third and Fourth Centuries," *Journal of Jewish Studies* 47 (1996): 1–32, and David Goodblatt, *The Monarchic Principle* (Tuebingen, DE: Mohr Siebeck, 1994). Whether the attribution of Mishnah's production to Rabbi Judah the Patriarch is historically accurate or, as is more likely, an honorific attribution only does not matter for our purposes. It serves only in combination with other evidence stemming from attributions to date "our" Mishnah's production and promulgation to sometime near the turn of the third century CE. "Our" Mishnah is the only one extant, although Judith Hauptman has argued for the existence of a proto-Mishnah in *Rereading the Mishnah* (Tuebingen, DE: Mohr Siebeck, 2005). Concerning the above, see Jacob Neusner, *Judaism, the Evidence of the Mishnah* (Chicago: University of Chicago Press, 1981) and Martin S. Jaffee, *Torah in the Mouth: Writing and Oral Tradition in Palestinian Judaism: 200 BCE to 400 CE* (Oxford: Oxford University Press, 2001); see also Martin S. Jaffee, "Oral Tradition in the Writings of Rabbinic Oral Torah: On Theorizing Rabbinic Orality," *Oral Tradition* 14, no. 1 (1999): 3–32; Elizabeth Shanks Alexander, "The Fixing of Oral Mishnah and the Displacement of Meaning," *Oral Tradition* 14, no. 1 (1999): 100–139; Elizabeth Shanks Alexander, *Transmitting Mishnah: The Shaping Influence of Oral Tradition* (Cambridge: Cambridge University Press, 2006). See also David

Kraemer, "The Mishnah," in *The Cambridge History of Judaism: The Late Roman Rabbinic Period*, ed. Steven S. Katz, vol. 4 (New York: Cambridge University Press, 1984), 299–315, cf. 313, 314. n.13, which references David Weiss Halivni's "The Reception Accorded to R. Judah's Mishnah," in *Jewish and Christian Self-Definition: Aspects of Judaism in the Greco-Roman Period*, vol. 2, ed. E. P. Sanders, A. I. Baumgarten and A. Mendelson (Philadelphia: Fortress, 1981), 204–12. See also Steven J. Fraade, "Introduction to the Symposium: What is (the) Mishnah?" *AJS Review* 32, no. 2 (2008): 221–23.

6. See, for example, Avot de Rabbi Nathan, version a (AVRNa), 8:1, cited in part and discussed later in this paper. See also Jaffee, *Torah in the Mouth*, 4; Alexander, "The Fixing of the Oral Mishnah;" 100–139; and Alexander, *Transmitting Mishnah*, 1–3.

7. I would recall at this juncture what Émile Durkheim wrote more than a century ago about "social facts." He defined "social facts" as any shared norms or institutions that constrained human behaviour in one fashion or another. However, he also maintained that the explanation of a social fact was to be sought in its diachronic and synchronic contexts. Diachronic—in the history of other, related social facts that constituted an influential historical context; synchronic—in the contemporaneous systems of social facts within which the social fact under examination fit. See Émile Durkheim, *The Rules of Sociological Method*, (New York: Free Press, 1982), first published (in French) in 1895.

8. See Deut. 4:8, 45; 2 Kings 22:3, alternatively designated "the Book of the Covenant" in the next chapter, 2 Kings 23:2; and in Ezra 3:2, called "the Torah of Moses, the man of God."

9. The tendentiousness of these criticisms is proven by Ezra-Nehemiah's authors' own admission that the very leadership of the fifth-to-fourth century BCE Jerusalem-centred community, including members of the priestly class, had to be forced on several occasions to divorce their foreign wives and to cleanse the Jerusalem cult of cult objects of foreign deities (see Ezra, chaps. 9 and 10; Nehemiah 13:23–31). Moreover, it seems that some Judean "nobles" (possibly landowners) were among those that resisted the Ezra-Nehemiah group's reforms and (re-)establishment of Jerusalem's centrality and power in Judah (Yahud) (see Nehemiah 7:15–19, see also Nehemiah 3:5; 5:7). Apparently, only with time did these reforms "stick."

10. Clearly attested in the prologue to the Greek translation of Ben Sirah (a.k.a., Sirach or Ecclesiasticus). The prologue was added by the translator, who identifies himself as the grandson of the author, Simeon or Yeshu, of the original Hebrew. The translator describes his grandfather as someone who had dedicated himself to the study of "the law, and the prophets, and the other books of the ancestors," and a person who promoted "the love of learning," that is, the study of these texts and of associated "wisdom."

11. Ben Sirah (10:1–5ff), who probably wrote just prior to the Hasmonean war and subsequent Hasmonean rule over Jerusalem/Judah, seems explicitly to link formal study in "wisdom" to high-ranking administrative bureaucratic roles in Hellenistic Jerusalem/Judah; the author also links such functions to the designation of "scribe."

12. See M. D. Goodman, "Texts, Scribes and Power in Roman Judea," in *Literacy and Power in the Ancient World*, ed. Alan K. Bowman and Greg Woolf (Cambridge: Cambridge University Press, 1994), 99–108. See also Philip R. Davies, *Scribes and Schools: The Canonization of the Hebrew Scriptures* (Louisville, KY: Westminster John Knox, 1998), 15–36. In addition, see Jaffee, *Torah in the Mouth*, 15–26, and Meir Bar-Ilan, "Scribes and Books in the Late Second Commonwealth and Rabbinic Period," in *Compendia Rerum Iudaicarum ad Novum Testamentum*, Section 2, vol. 1, *Mikra*, ed. M. J. Mulder (Assen-Maastricht: van Gorcum, and Philadelphia, PA: Fortress Press, 1988), 21–38.

13. Davies, *Scribes and Schools*, 15–36; Emanuel Tov, *Scribal Practices and Approaches Reflected in the Texts Found in the Judean Desert* (Leiden, NL: Brill, 2004), 7–30; and Karel Van Der Toorn, *Scribal Culture and the Making of the Hebrew Bible* (Cambridge, MA, Harvard University Press, 2007). See also Michael Wilkins' treatment of the "learner/disciple" in the ancient and Greco-Roman periods in *Discipleship in the Ancient World and Matthew's Gospel* (Eugene, OR: Wipf and Stock, 1995), 1–125.

14. See Deut. 17:14–20.

15. See Deut. 13:2–6; 18:18–22.

16. See Deut. 17:8–13; 19:17.

17. See esp. Jeremiah 18:18; see, for example, the role "Shaphan the Scribe" in Josiah's administration in 2 Kings 22 and 23.

18. See, again, Davies, *Scribes and Schools*, 15–36; and Van Der Toorn, *Scribal Culture and the Making of the Hebrew Bible*, chaps. 3 and 4.

19. Their skills probably included numeracy as well. Shaphan the Scribe is clearly portrayed as handling both administrative and financial matters in Josiah's court (2 Kings 22).
20. Ezra 5:8 refers to two senior governmental posts in the Persian Imperial district, the "commander" and the "scribe," implying that some clear division of labor existed between these two positions. This provided a striking parallel to the twinned positions of *archon* (ruler) and *grammateus* (scribe) in the subsequent Ptolemaic system of imperial rule, as discussed in the next paragraph of this paper.
21. These early administrative systems have been well documented by scholars for more than a century. See, for example, Abdallah Simaika, *Essai sur la Province Romaine d'Egypte Depuis la Conquete Jusqu'a Diocletien: Etude d'Organisation Politique et Administrative* (Paris: Imprimerie generale de Chatillon-sur-Seine, 1892).
22. Again, this system of administration is well documented in modern scholarship as early as the late nineteenth century; see discussion and evidence throughout Simaika's *Essai sur la Province Romaine d'Egypte*.
23. See Jack N. Lightstone, "Roman Diaspora Judaism," in *A Companion to Roman Religion. Blackwell Companions to the Ancient World*, vol. 9, ed. Jörg Rüpke (Oxford: Blackwell, 2007), 345–77.
24. Instances of scribal administrative presence in diaspora Jewish communities are well documented in the inscriptional evidence for the late Roman period. A tally of that documentation may be found in Lightstone, "Roman Diaspora Judaism," 345–77.
25. This paper's summary of the two designated types of evidence draws heavily on my analyses in Jack N. Lightstone, *Mishnah and the Social Formation of the Early Rabbinic Guild: A Socio-Rhetorical Approach* (Waterloo, Ontario: Wilfrid Laurier University Press, 2002) and further extrapolates, the observations made in that book. In a sense and to some extent, this question and the analyses and arguments of this paper constitute a type of "mirror-image" of the questions, analyses, and issues that drive the work of Elizabeth Shanks Alexander's work. See both Alexander, "The Fixing of the Oral Mishnah," 100–139 and Alexander, *Transmitting Mishnah*, 1–30. One could recast her research focus accordingly: What effects did the "oral" study of Mishnah have on the evolution of the text of Mishnah and its ultimate "fixity"? Understandably, then, some of the same rhetorical-literary conventions exhibited in Mishnah play heavily in her work and in mine as evidence, but, on the surface, the search for effect and cause or just influence are in opposing directions. While it is beyond the scope of this paper to provide a more complete assessment of Alexander's theses, conceptual framework, and methods, I am inclined toward two highly general assessments. One, both she and I have articulated complementary, not opposing, phenomena. Two, after a close reading of her work, it seems to me she must start with the premise that Mishnah was composed by a process of oral transmission in order to show the effects of oral performance on the very composition of the Mishnah text, not just argue that Mishnah after its production was promulgated and studied via an oral performative process, which kept the text somewhat fluid for a period. From the point of view of method and evidence, the former (creation via oral transmission, with embedded rhetorical impact) is a much more difficult hill to climb; the latter (oral retelling/rehearsal) is not, even if both are possibilities. I suspect that one of the side effects of asserting the former position as well as the latter, versus asserting only the latter, has to do with how one views Tosefta, its purpose and its composition. At the risk of putting words into Alexander's mouth, at times I have the impression she sees Tosefta (or its materials) as the first "Mishnah" that in the end was supplanted by the extant Mishnah, rather than viewing Tosefta as the earliest post-mishnaic composition that reflects something of how the Mishnah was received and studied, and which served the study of Mishnah. Again, both views are not necessarily logically incompatible, but the former is the steeper hill to climb as regards method and evidence.
26. David Goodblatt, *Rabbinic Institutions in Sassanian Babylonia* (Leiden, NL: Brill, 1975).
27. Jeffrey L. Rubenstein, "Social and Institutional Settings of Rabbinic Literature," in *The Cambridge Companion to the Talmud and Rabbinic Literature*, ed. Charlotte Elisheva Fonrobert and Martin S. Jaffee (New York: Cambridge University Press, 2007), 58–74.
28. See Daniel Bernard, "Listing and Enlisting: The Rhetoric and Social Meaning of Tractate Avot" (PhD diss., Concordia University, Montreal, 2008).
29. The dating of Avot de Rabbi Nathan (AVRN) has been much disputed by modern scholarship. A century ago, the scholarly consensus was that the AVRN was compiled sometime in the seventh to ninth centuries CE. In the early 1970s, A. J. Saldarini undertook

a careful comparison of the two recensions of AVRN and Avot. He concluded that in all probability early versions of AVRN, likely circulating in oral form, were almost contemporaneous with early versions of Avot, dating from near (or perhaps just prior to) the time of Mishnah's authoritative composition at the turn of the third century CE. Saldarini also points out that all recensions of AVRN take pains to attribute traditions to rabbinic authorities contemporaneous with mishnaic sages (tannaim), save for three exceptions that prove the rule. One must be cautious in drawing conclusions from the latter observation, because of a penchant for anachronistic attribution to earlier authorities in rabbinic literature. My own view is that in its earliest version(s) AVRN likely predates the authoring of the Palestinian Talmud sometime from the mid-fifth century to mid-sixth, and so sits in the period bounded by Avot in the mid-third century and the Palestinian Talmud. See A. J. Saldarini, *The Fathers According to Rabbi Nathan (Avot de Rabbi Nathan) Version B: Translation and Commentary* (Leiden, NL: Brill, 1975), 1–16.
30. Jacob Neusner, *Uniting the Dual Torah: Sifra and the Problem of the Mishnah* (New York: Cambridge University Press, 1990). See also, Jack N. Lightstone, *The Rhetoric of the Babylonian Talmud: Its Social Meaning in Context* (Waterloo: Wilfrid Laurier University Press, 1994), chap. 4. See also Jack N. Lightstone, "Form as Meaning in the Halakic Midrash: A Programmatic Statement," *Semeia* 27 (1983): 23–36.
31. This is my own translation, which is influenced by that of Joel Zaiman. For his, see "The Traditional Study of the Mishnah," in *The Modern Study of the Mishnah*, ed. Jacob Neusner (Leiden, NL: Brill, 1973), 3. Similar views of the place of Mishnah in the early rabbinic core curriculum are expressed in Avot 5:21; but Avot 5:21 together with Avot 6 are generally agreed to be later additions to Avot. In this last regard, see H. Albeck's commentary in *Shishah Sidre Mishnah: Seder Neziqim*, no. 20. ed. H. Albeck (Jerusalem and Tel Aviv: Mosad Bialik and Dvir, 1953), 380.
32. See Jaffee, *Torah in the Mouth*; see also Jaffee, "Oral Tradition in the Writings of Rabbinic Oral Torah: On Theorizing Rabbinic Orality," *Oral Tradition* 14, no. 1 (1999): 3–32. See Alexander, "The Fixing of the Oral Mishnah," 100–139; Alexander, *Transmitting Mishnah*, 1–29, 174–75. See also David Kraemer, "The Mishnah," in *The Cambridge History of Judaism: Volume 4, The Late Roman Rabbinic Period*, ed. Steven S. Katz (New York: Cambridge University Press, 1984), 299–315, cf. 313, 314. n.13, which references David Weiss Halivni, "The Reception Accorded to R. Judah's Mishnah," in *Jewish and Christian Self-Definition: Aspects of Judaism in the Greco-Roman Period*, vol. 2, ed. E. P. Sanders, A. I. Baumgarten, and A. Mendelson (Philadelphia: Fortress Press, 1981), 204–12. See also Steven J. Fraade, "Introduction to the Symposium," 221–23. On the oral rehearsal of rabbinic traditions as a superior act of piety for the rabbi to participation in the synagogue liturgy and listening to public readings of Scripture during the liturgy, Jacob Neusner is apt to cite the tale about Rav Sheshet conveyed in b. Berahkot 8a; see Jacob Neusner, "Rabbis and Community in Third Century Babylonia," in *Religions in Antiquity: Essays in Memory of Erwin Ramsdell Goodenough*, ed. J. Neusner (Leiden, NL: Brill, 1968), 438.
33. A point also made by Jaffee in Jaffee, "Oral Tradition," 3–32, and by Alexander in Alexander, "The Fixing of the Oral Mishnah, 100–139"; Alexander, *Transmitting Mishnah*, 174–75.
34. And to some extent they are reflected, although less explicitly, in materials in the Tosefta, which serve to ramify correlative sections of Mishnah in the guise of supplementing Mishnah. I realize that in making this claim I am implicitly taking a stand on the literary relationship between Tosefta and Mishnah, or, at a minimum, between Mishnah and materials that came to be included in Tosefta. See Jacob Neusner, *Judaism, the Evidence of the Mishnah* (Chicago: University of Chicago Press, 1981), and Jacob Neusner, *The Mishnah: An Introduction* (New York: Aronson, 1994). Compare the position argued by Judith Hauptman over the course of her book, *Rereading Mishnah*. See also the position defended in Alberdina Houtman's volume, *Mishnah and Tosefta: A Synoptic Comparison of the Tractates Berakhot and Shebiit* (Tübingen, DE: Mohr Siebeck, 1996); Houtman's introduction provides a good summary of the scholarly debate in the modern period about the nature of Tosefta and about Tosefta's relationship to Mishnah. The recent scholarly literature positing some version of the thesis that some or much of Tosefta's materials predate Mishnah includes: Joshua Kulp, "Organizational Patterns in the Mishnah in Light of their Toseftan Parallels," *Journal of Jewish Studies* 58, no. 1 (2007): 52–78; Judith Hauptman, "Does the Tosefta Precede

the Mishnah? Halakhah, Aggada, and Narrative Coherence," *Judaism* 50 (2001): 224–40; "The Tosefta as a Commentary on an Early Mishnah," *Jewish Studies, Internet Journal* 4 (2005): 109–32; Shamma Friedman, *Tosefta Atiqta, Pesah Rishon: Synoptic Parallels of Mishna and Tosefta Analysed with a Methodological Introduction* (Ramat Gan: Bar Ilan University Press, 2002); "The Primacy of Tosefta to Mishnah in Synoptic Parallels," in *Introducing Tosefta*, ed. Harry Fox and Tirzah Meacham (New York: KTAV, 1999), 99–121. A similar position on Tosefta may be found in Alexander, *Transmitting Mishnah*, 49–54.

35. What follows in this section largely reproduces the lion's share of section IV of a paper I presented in July 2016 to the Research Group on "Sociological and Anthropological Approaches to the Evidence of the Mishnah" at meetings in Leuven, during the European Association of Biblical Studies (EABS); the paper is entitled "The Bases for Social Cohesion and Group Identity of the Early Rabbinic Guild: What does the evidence of the Mishnah show?" I rely throughout the sections that follow on my own research published in Lightstone, *Mishnah and the Social Formation*, cf. chaps. 2 and 5. See also Jack N. Lightstone, "Whence the Rabbis? From Coherent Description to Fragmented Reconstructions," *Studies in Religion* 26, no. 3 (1997): 275–95. The influence on my own thought processes of Jacob Neusner's studies of Mishnah are evident in my *Mishnah and the Social Formation*, chap. 5; see Jacob Neusner, *Judaism, the Evidence of the Mishnah*, and Jacob Neusner, *The Mishnah: An Introduction*. In the intervening period, Jaffee's work (*Torah in the Mouth* and "Oral Tradition") on the topic of Mishnah's orality has increasingly impacted my thinking about Mishnah's traits, as has Alexander in "The Fixing of the Oral Mishnah," 100–139" and *Transmitting Mishnah*, 1–40.

36. Within the history of Rabbinic legal texts, one need only compare Mishnah to the breadth of Maimonides' Mishneh Torah (12th c.), or to Jacob b. Asher's Arba'ah Turim (13th c.) and Yosef Karo's Shulkhan Aruk (16th c.). For indication of the validity of this observation consider that Tosefta, beraitot in the Talmuds, and the later "minor tractates" exhibit a tendency to complement and complete Mishnah's topical agenda.

37. This is an observation made in passing by Jaffee in "Oral Tradition," 3–12, for quite other purposes and interpreted in relation to a quite different set of questions than those addressed in this paper.

38. A point made very early on about social facts in the writings of Émile Durkheim; see above n. 7: Émile Durkheim, *The Rules of Sociological Method*.

39. Kurt Vonnegut Jr., *Slaughterhouse Five, or The Children's Crusade: A Duty-Dance with Death* (New York: Delacorte, 1969).

40. See Lightstone, *Mishnah and the Social Formation*, chaps. 1 and 5; see Neusner, *Judaism, the Evidence of the Mishnah*, 167–229; and Neusner, *The Mishnah: An Introduction*, 40–199. However, to say that a vision of a "system" underlies Mishnah is not to say that Mishnah is a systematic articulation of that vision. It clearly is not, as I have already intimated. Moreover, it is easy to overstate the systemic qualities of Mishnah as a unified literary work, a point emphasized by Jaffee in "Oral Tradition," 12–26. Jaffee proposes that the compositional processes that produced Mishnah and other early rabbinic texts might better be understood as a type of anthologization.

41. With respect to urbanization in late second-century Palestine and its reflection in both Mishnah and Tosefta, see my presentation and analysis of the evidence in Jack N. Lightstone, "Urban (Re-) Organization in Late Roman Palestine and the Early Rabbinic Guild: What Toseftan Evidence Indicates about the City and its Institutions as an Emerging Salient Category in the Early Rabbinic Legal (Re-) Classification of Space," *Studies in Religion/Sciences Religieuses* 36, no. 3–4 (2007): 421–25.

42. On Mishnah-Tosefta and agricultural realia in late Roman Palestine, one need only refer to the classic work by J. Feliks, *HaHaqla'ut BeErez Yisrael BiTqufat HaMishhah VeHaTalmud* [Agriculture in Palestine in the Period of the Mishna and Talmud] (Jerusalem: Magnes Press, 1963).

43. A good example of this is the first chapter of Mishnah, Tractate Gittin, which concerns writs of divorce issued *outside* of the Land of Israel for use by parties *inside* the Land of Israel. The entire composition assumes this uni-directionality.

44. For example, see Deut. 12 and 14:22ff.

45. As in AVRNa 8:1 and Avot 5:21.

46. At first glance, so compellingly odd ideologically is Mishnah's explicit literary penchant not to systematically document its dependence on scripture that David Weiss Halivni, in his magisterial work covering the range of early rabbinic legal literary genres, concluded that substance antecedent to Mishnah was a now lost literary genre, some form of earlier

halakhic midrashic literature, that did explicitly derive Mishnaic teachings from scripture. The producers of Mishnah, in his view, stripped away those scriptural exegetical parts to produce the Mishnah genre we now possess, and post-mishnaic rabbinic writers recreated, subsequently, a halakhic midrashic literature. See David Weiss Halivni, *Midrash, Mishnah, and Gemara: the Jewish Predilection for Justified Law* (Cambridge MA: Harvard University Press, 1986). I agree with Jaffee's elegant comment on Halivni's claims: Halivni has the genres right, but the historical order wrong (see Jaffee, "Oral Tradition," 3–12).

47. Again, this is a trait of Mishnah captured by Jacob Neusner when he called the religion of Mishnah, "a religion of pots and pans." While I remember him using the phrase in the early 1970s, in the late 1980s, it became the title of one of his books: Jacob Neusner, *A Religion of Pots and Pans?: Modes of Philosophical and Theological Discourse in Ancient Judaism: Essays and a Program* (Atlanta: Scholars Press, 1988).

48. See Jacob Neusner, *A History of the Mishnaic Law of Purities, Part 21* (Leiden, NL: Brill, 1977), 164–246.

49. Both translations are my own and draw on my translations in Jack N. Lightstone, *The Rhetoric of the Babylonian Talmud*, 79, 175.

50. Some may wish to argue at this point that Mishnah's laconic style is merely a by-product of its composition for oral transmission, as with other literary traits of Mishnah. But such an argument does not undermine the point I am making in the least. It matters not at all why Mishnah is this way or how it came to be this way. Rather Mishnah *is* this way, with attendant consequences for the ancient Mishnah-student, which I will continue to detail below.

51. I refer the reader once more to Jeffery Rubenstein's survey of the evidence on early rabbinic institutions in Rubenstein, "Social and Institutional Settings," 58–74.

52. Again, the translation is my own and is based on the one I prepared for Lightstone, *The Rhetoric of the Babylonia Talmud*, 177–78.

53. The identification of the dispute form and its variations in Mishnah was a product of Jacob Neusner's analyses of the rabbinic traditions of proto-rabbinic figures who flourished before the destruction of the Jerusalem Temple in 70 CE. It is from that point that he began to undertake what he called "form analysis." See Neusner, *Rabbinic Traditions, 3, Conclusions*, 5–179.

54. See William Scott Green, "What's in a Name? The Problematic of Rabbinic Biography," in *Approaches to Ancient Judaism: Theory and Practice*, vol. 1, ed. William Scott Green (Scholars Press: Missoula, 1978), 77–96.

55. Shaye J.D. Cohen, "The Significance of Yavneh: Pharisees, Rabbis and the End of Sectarianism," *Hebrew Union College Annual* 55 (1984): 27–53.

56. I have just defined in other terms what the late anthropologist, Mary Douglas, described as "high-grid" thinking and competence. See Mary Douglas, *Natural Symbols: Explorations in Cosmology*, 2nd ed. (London: Routledge, 1996). See also Mary Douglas, *Purity and Danger* (London: Routledge and Kegan Paul, 1966).

57. See Lee I. Levine, *Ma'amad HaHakhamin*, translated as *The Rabbinic Class of Roman Palestine in Late Antiquity* (Jerusalem: Yad Yitzhak ben Zvi, 1989).

58. A matter treated throughout both Lee I. Levine, *Ma'amad HaHakhamim*, and Catherine Hezser, *The Social Structure of the Rabbinic Movement in Roman Palestine* (Tubingen, DE: Mohr Siebeck, 1997); see also Lightstone, *Mishnah and the Social Formation of the Early Rabbinic Guild*, chap. 5.

Genealogies of the Future*

Jonathan Boyarin

Abstract

A very brief story titled, "At That Time: or, The History of a Joke," by the twentieth-century American Jewish writer Grace Paley, appears enigmatic at first, but upon examination alludes to key moments in the relation between Jewishness, Christianity, and the rhetoric of futurity and "pastness" in kinship and genealogy. While initially taking off from and then returning to the Paley story, a number of additional texts are identified and discussed that, together, demonstrate an emerging notion that genealogy is a means for not only fixing the past but also for projecting our present selves and family structures into the future. Examples presented range from the powerful ancestral self-portrait photography of Rafael Goldchain to the fiction of A. B. Yehoshua and the ethnography of Joshua Friedman.

The study of kinship is a mainstay of what is called in Britain social anthropology. In the United States, the study of kinship is virtually central to what we have been calling cultural anthropology since the days of Franz Boas. However, studies of what were once called "kinship structures" may be seen as somewhat out of fashion now, as they are linked to the period of high imperialism and colonialism, when anthropology on both sides of the Atlantic was understood to be primarily the study of peoples then called "primitive," usually with more or less derogatory intent. By the time anthropologists began turning their attention toward their own societies and, often, to their own peoples, the notion of attempting to establish a group's kinship structure as a central concern of ethnography had become somewhat passé. Nevertheless, as anthropologists know, kinship in its protean forms remains a dynamic and shaping aspect of the realms of power, authority, prejudice, and solidarity that shape all of our lives.

My colleague Lucinda Ramberg at Cornell University sees kinship at work in an unlikely place, among the Jogati, who are Indian devotees of the goddess Yellama, and provide sex as part of their temple service. Ramberg, along with other anthropologists, reminds us that what we properly call "kinship" is not simply a matter of biological generation but a complex symbolic system. She, therefore, argues for a very inclusive notion of what she calls "kin-making"—pointing to these Jogatis' assertions that they truly are, in the words of her book's title *"given to the goddess."*[1] Ramberg offers an expanded concept of kinship:

> As a technology, kin-making is innovative. . . . To think of kin-making as a technology of human generation and transformation is to get beyond the distinction between 'real' and 'fictive' kin and out of a field conscripted by blood and alliance. It might seem that we long ago left this field, but to the extent that the genealogical grid continues to delimit our categories of gendered personhood and relatedness, we have not.[2]

The things I talk about this evening, unlike Ramberg's fascinating ethnography, will hardly escape the realm of what she calls here, "blood." Blood, in our common culture, is a common enough metaphor for biological descent, albeit not a particularly Jewish one. And Jewish kinship remains very much about alliance, that is,

---

*First presented at the Jewish Museum London, December 9, 2015.

the strategies of matchmaking that parents and extended families engage in for the purpose of their larger projects, their individual and shared projections of the future, and their innovative making of time using the tools of kinship.

Though I confess to being an anthropologist myself, my examples tonight will largely be drawn from literature and art, with ethnography making the odd guest appearance. My primary text—the text with which we will begin and to which we will return—is a very short story by our late friend and colleague Grace Paley. Grace was a longtime chronicler of everyday life, especially in New York City, and especially its Jews, women, and poor people. She was a tireless activist for peace and for women's rights, and a beloved teacher at Sarah Lawrence College.

Her tale is enigmatically titled "At That Time, or the History of a Joke," published in Paley's 1985 volume of short stories *Later the Same* Day as well as previously in a literary journal (fig. 1).[3] Upon recently rereading this text, I was astonished at how well the story seems to capture the potentially distinctive ways that Jews shape time through their practice of kinship and gender. And so, I sent the story to my very clever son, Jonah, but he was puzzled, asking me: What was he to make of it? I hope to provide some clues to answer his question in this talk. I can't guarantee that at the end of it this talk you will find the story as insightful as I do. But I hope it will help frame a set of references and questions, all of which circle somehow around these distinctive modes of Jewish time and kinship.

To begin, the story surely alludes to the continuing controversy surrounding the birth of Jesus of Nazareth over two thousand years ago, but it is still primarily about an *imaginary* baby, born in the future. At least since the ministry of Jesus' contemporary Paul of Tarsus, what we now call, in retrospect, Judaism, has been linked in the dominant discourse of the West to an outmoded past, while what we have come to call Christianity is now understood to be oriented toward the future. As argued among some authors, to include my brother, Daniel, in his book *A Radical Jew: Paul and the Politics of Identity*,[4] Paul's rejection of marriage and procreation was part and parcel of his expectation that the *end-times* were imminent. Paul, that is, rejected genealogical identification in favor of individual freedom and future-orientation. This rejection of the past and concomitant stress on novelty as liberating is dramatized in his writings, as where he declares that for the sake of the Redeemer:

> I have accepted the loss of all things and I consider them so much rubbish, that I may gain Christ and be found in him. . . . Just one thing: forgetting what lies behind but straining forward to what lies ahead, I continue my pursuit toward the goal, the prize of God's upward calling, in Christ Jesus. (Philippians 3:8–14)

As Paul makes clear in this text, he now considers ancestral Jewish Law and the Jewish Law of ancestry to be rubbish. Paul, thus, signals a set of concerns focused around problems of genealogical and legal identity formation, which found expression over the course of centuries in the dialectic of Jewishness and Christianity. It is important to insist at the outset that these tensions remain with us. Indeed, abstract and lofty notions as seemingly distant from family life or even family trees as a philosophy of history are inseparable from the problems of personal identity through time, hence of connections to ancestors and to some expected future outcome, whether for oneself or one's dependents. Thus, when, for example, the German Jewish philosopher Karl Loewith writes that "[h]istory has time and again to be recovered and rediscovered by the living generations,"[5] the word "generation" needs to be understood not only collectively as a body of "contemporaries" but also in a more literal sense than he seems to have intended. That is, children have to rediscover history, and their children's children will have to do the same.

At that time most people were willing to donate organs. Abuses were expected. In fact there was a young woman whose uterus was hysterically ripped from her by a passing gynecologist. He was distracted, he said, by the suffering of a childless couple in Fresh Meadows. The young woman said, "It wasn't the pain or the embarrassment, but I think any court would certainly award me the earliest uterine transplant that Dr. Heiliger can obtain."

We are not a heartless people and this was done at the lowest judicial level, no need to appeal to state or federal power.

According to the *Times*, one of the young woman's ovaries rejected the new uterus. The other was perfectly satisfied and did not.

"I feel fine," she said, but almost immediately began to swell, for in the soft red warm interior of her womb, there was already a darling rolled-up fetus. It was unfurled in due time, and lo! it was as black as the night which rests our day-worn eyes.

Then: "Sing!" said Heiliger, the scientist, "for see how the myth of man advances on the back of technological achievement, and behold, without conceiving, a virgin has borne a son." This astonishing and holy news was carried to the eye of field, forest, and industrial park, wherever the media had thrust its wireless thumb. The people celebrated and were relatively joyful and the birth was reenacted on giant screens in theaters and on small screens at home.

Only, on the underside of several cities, certain Jews who had observed and suffered the consequence of other virgin births cried out (weeping) (as usual): "It is not He! It is not He!"

No one knew how to deal with them; they were stubborn and maintained a humorless determination. The authorities took away their shortwave and antennas, their stereo screen TV and their temple videotapes. (People were not incarcerated at that time for such social intransigence. Therefore, neither were they rehabilitated.)

Soon this foolish remnant had nothing left. They had to visit one another or wander from town to town in order to say the most ordinary thing to a friend or relative. They had only their shawls and phylacteries, which were used by women too, for women (by that time) had made their great natural advances and were ministers, seers, rabbis, yogis, priests, etc., in well-known as well as esoteric religions.

In their gossipy communications, they whispered the hidden or omitted fact (which some folks had already noticed): The Child WAS A Girl, and since word of mouth is sound made in the echo of God (in the beginning there was the Word and it was without form but wide), ear to mouth and mouth to ear it soon became the people's knowledge, outwitting the computerized devices to which most sensible people had not said a private word for decades anyway.

Then: "O.K.!" said Dr. Heiliger. "It's perfectly true, but I didn't want to make waves in any water as viscous as the seas of mythology. Yes, it is a girl. A virgin born of a virgin."

Throughout the world, people smiled. By that time, sexism and racism had no public life, though they were still sometimes practiced by adults at home. They were as gladdened by one birth as another. And plans were made to symbolically sew the generations of the daughters one to another by using the holy infant's umbilicus. This was luckily flesh *and* symbol. Therefore beside the cross to which people were accustomed there hung the circle of the navel and the wiggly line of the umbilical cord.

But those particular discontented Jews said again, "Wonderful! So? Another tendency heard from! So it's a girl! Praise to the most Highess! But the fact is, we need another virgin birth like our blessed dead want cupping by ancient holistic practitioners."

And so they continued as female and male, de**scending and** undescending, workers in the muddy **basement of** history, to which, this very day, the **poor return** when requiring a cheap but stunning **garment for** a wedding, birth, or funeral.

FIGURE 1. Text of Grace Paley's short story "At That Time, or the History of a Joke," 93-96. Reproduced by permission from Farrar, Strauss and Giroux © 1985.

Moreover, this tension between "past orientation" and "future orientation," which I have suggested has been understood to help structure the tense dialogue between Jewishness and Christianity in the West, found expression in twentieth-century debates about the best way to organize revolutionary forces.

In the twelfth "illumination" of Walter Benjamin's now canonical essay "Theses on the Philosophy of History," written on the eve of World War II and near the end of his too short life, he writes that revolutionary passions are really fueled more by "the image of enslaved ancestors rather than that of liberated grandchildren."[6] To me, when I was a young graduate student trying to recuperate a sense of East European Jewish life while also willing himself a political radical, the "enslaved ancestors" part, the call of memory, resonated as "Jewish," while the future-oriented promise of liberated descendants sounded vaguely Christian.

Of course, Jewish families and broader kinship networks are not only oriented toward the past. Nor, for that matter, have the lives of most lay Christians been characterized by actual freedom from kinship ties or by even the desire for such freedom. Still, given the common association of Jewishness with the past, one might have expected more work by anthropologists on Jewish kinship patterns. Rhonda Berger-Sofer's analysis of the kinship patterns of the Schneersohn family (the leaders of Lubavitch Hasidism), for example, dramatically shows the rich potential for social anthropology in studying marriage patterns among Hasidic elites.[7] Yet her analysis itself is not distinctively Jewish. Rather, it is a product of the culture of social anthropology, in this case, using Jews as its material. Kinship *studies* until now, indeed, have been past-oriented, largely because they depend on patterns derived from data already established, more than on imaginations or projections of the future.

There is now some research into the workings of what I'm trying to name this evening as *Jewish genealogies of the future*. And in the culture of liberal United States Jewry, we perhaps find something most like Ramberg's idea of kinship divorced from biological genealogy or marriage alliances per se. In a fascinating recent dissertation on institutions in the contemporary United States that work to further the transmission of the Yiddish language and the resources of secular Yiddish culture, Joshua Friedman articulates a related useful notion of "abstract kinship." "Abstract kinship" involves a diffuse sense of intergenerational relations, in which notions, especially of grandparenthood and, if you'll permit me, "grandchildhood," implicitly underlie the connections made between elderly financial donors and youthful students of Yiddish language and culture. The Yiddish Book Center in Massachusetts, where Friedman did his fieldwork, has become both a prime repository for printed Yiddish books and a leading center for education, dissemination, and translation related to Yiddish heritage. The Center's publicity calls Yiddish language and culture *yerushe*, a term whose base meaning conveys material inheritance, as of money or property, but which has long been rhetorically stretched to include symbolic resources. Unlike money or property, these symbolic resources dissipate if there is no descendant to act as an heir.

The college-aged and young adult interns Friedman interviewed at the book center were smart and reflective. They were well aware that, in return for a summer in New England and a guided entrée into the world of Yiddish, they were being recruited into the role of "abstract heirs." However, their participation was not always abstract, since the program includes carefully staged opportunities for major donors to meet with the interns. Sometimes, specific cross-generational relationships combined with the prospect of wealth transfer and the creation of new family bonds. Friedman recalls in his dissertation a conversation as students prepared for one such meeting:

"Do you think if I become my donor's best friend she'll fund my trip to Vilnius?" asked Mary, who had coincidentally met her donor earlier that summer on the latter's visit to the book center. "Seriously, though," she only half seriously insisted, "that woman loved me."

"I'm gonna get set up with someone's granddaughter!" Brian said to the laughter and a few eye rolls of those around him.[8]

One of the interns, whom Friedman calls Evan, even compared himself to one of the Yiddish books that was on display for visitors to the center, suggesting that the center collects young Jews like it collects old Jewish books. The interns, even more than the Yiddish books at the center, thus, serve as abstract heirs to donors who love this language and culture but, except in rare cases, have not managed to pass it on to their own children and grandchildren. Of course, as Friedman also explains, this attempt to secure the future through kin-making does not always work, as he explains further:

> In the case of students like Evan, a college freshman still in the process of determining the objects of his devotion, he may very well refuse such interpellations; he might, in other words, turn out much less "Yiddish" than the book to which he compares himself. But where Evan may opt out, another student potentially opts in and enacts the desirable future of possible Yiddish (and indeed Jewish) returns.[9]

Citing Pierre Bourdieu's critique of Levi-Strauss, Friedman notes that even when intergenerational relationships may lend themselves to structural analysis, they remain contingent in practice: they don't always work out. Of course, the chances that an individual who is designated as an heir or marriage partner will reject her assigned role in the kinship structure may be and seem greater when that individual is a free-thinking student at an American university than when she is the daughter of a Hasidic rebbe. And, thus, the prospect of slippage—the uncertainty about reciprocation that means the supposed structure may at any moment potentially be violated—may seem both slimmer and potentially more dramatic in the traditional case than in the "modern" one. But the principle remains the same: kinship as a *project*, an attempt to throw ourselves and our identities forward, is always plagued by the uncertainty of that which only the future will tell.

While kinship is a strategy to mold the future, the future cannot guarantee success. Perhaps this very uncertainty—the notion that we might be betrayed by the future—propels research in genealogy back into the past. Here we are certainly on unstable ground, where it is not clear whether our projections are based on our values or whether what we claim and articulate as our "values" is based precisely on our future anxieties. As Susan Buck-Morss has similarly asked, in the context of debates about the multiple effects of Muslim presence in contemporary Europe, "Does such a thing as Europe exist that is threatened by the future or is the future [a] threat to the concept, Europe, itself?"[10]

I suggest that we must acknowledge if we are honest with ourselves that our values and our anxieties reciprocally shape each other. And one of the most promising forms of response to this knowledge is a consciously artistic invocation of kinship, explicitly understood as a message to the future. That is the kind of work the Chilean-Canadian Rafael Goldchain, a grandchild of emigres from Poland, performed in his series of ancestral self-portraits as various relatives: maternal and paternal, male and female, known and unknown, and sometimes purely imagined altogether.

In the series' web presence, prior to its eventual publication as an album, titled *I Am My Family*, Goldchain writes of the interconnected symbolism across the portraits:

> On Familial Ground is an autobiographical installation work that includes digitally altered self-portrait photographs, reproductions of pages from an artist's book, videotapes, and aural works. It is about grounding identity within a familial and cultural history subject to erasures. . . . The self-portraits in On Familial Ground are detailed reenactments of

ancestral figures, and can be understood as acts of 'naming' linked to mourning and remembrance. . . . They propose a form of inter-subjective connection between us and those we mourn. . . . [They] suggest that we look at family photographs in order to know ourselves through the photographic trace left by the lost ancestral other . . . [and they] remind us of the unavoidable and necessary work of inheritance.

Familial Ground [he continues] is the product of a process that started several years ago when my son was born. I gradually realized that my new role as parent included the responsibility to pass on to my son a familial and cultural inheritance and that such inheritance would need to be gathered and delivered gradually in a manner appropriate to his age. My attempts at articulating histories, cultural and familial, public and private, made me acutely aware of how much I knew of the former, and how little of the latter. . . These images are the result of a reconstructive process that acknowledges its own limitations, in that the construction of an image of the past unavoidably involves a mixture of fragmented memory, artifice, and invention, and that this mixture necessarily evolves as it is transmitted from generation to generation.[11]

This work offers something like hope, a word that I usually regard with suspicion. I regard hope as a name for a drug that offers illusion at least as often as genuine inspiration, especially when we are most insistent that "we must not lose hope." What warms me in Goldchain's statement is the forthright acknowledgment that *artifice*—and not merely dogged research—is necessary if he is to shape a record of ancestry that he can transmit to his son. To use Lucinda Ramberg's words again, Goldchain's art is a work of "kin-making" as an "innovative technology," oriented both to the past and toward the future. In truth, not only the future but also the past, to a great extent, is not known but must be imagined.

This artistic work of recuperation is not easy. In fact, it is not only difficult, it is precisely *uneasy*. In one notable moment of slippage in Goldchain's very lucid text, he asserts that his images suggest "*we look at family photographs in order to know ourselves through the photographic trace left by the lost ancestral other.*" But his are not family photographs; they are self-portraits sometimes and not always inspired by the documentary photographs that he has gathered. His portrait work is inescapably a work of self-knowledge. Here, however, he skirts the risk of authorizing his audience to simply and uncritically look at their own collections of ancestral images and think that, thereby, they know themselves. Does this perhaps, in turn, betray some anxiety about the balance Goldchain had to constantly maintain between recuperation and illusion? We may, I think, fairly call this anxiety one that is distinctively if not uniquely Jewish, and one that centers on the relationship between kinship and time.

The temptation to overcome anxiety about lost ancestry is betrayed in the current fascination with the supposed ability of DNA analysis to tell you, as anthropologist Naida Abu El-Haj's interviewees put it, "who you really are." Through new technologies of kinship such as the study of the genome, the past can be not only recuperated but become even more fixed than it was before. The rhetoric used in this search is sometimes most flamboyant, as is apparent in one author's words in 2008:

DNA is at once an atlas and a time machine that can transport us to biblical times and beyond, awakening us to the shared roots of civilization and the promise of designer therapies to target disease. . . . [W]e carry pinpoints of DNA that suggest that maybe human population groups aren't really quite so alike. However slight our genetic differences may be, they are defining. . . . And they mark me indelibly as a Jew.[12]

So wrote a man named Jon Entine, a male carrier of the BRCA gene that is tied to a greatly increased risk of breast cancer and father of a daughter whose mother is identified as Christian. The anthropologist Kaja Finkler eloquently summed up the temptations of the idea that DNA testing tells us, once and for all who we really are as she writes, "Knowledge of shared DNA may substitute for our fragile memories and may transcend memories of ancestors recorded in faded photographs and other artifacts, or embedded in the consciousness of sounds, smells, affect, and tales, and leaves little to mystery in the absence of experience and feelings."[13]

American Jews, largely of Ashkenazi descent, are among the most avid consumers of the new technologies promising to tell you where you come from and who you're related to through DNA testing. They are not the only ones, and the similar popularity of such tests among African-Americans might suggest something about the relation between traumatic breaks in generational continuity and the desire for a technology to restore a semblance of the past.

I suggest, however, that there are several good reasons, none having to do with any putative neurotic tendencies, why Jews may have been and may remain particularly anxious about the future of kinship.

First, for millennia, and almost certainly for most of the time they have been called and have thought of themselves as Jews, they have lived not in a land they and others called "their own," but in diaspora. Diaspora, as a technology of identity, depends, in turn, more on the maintenance of kin boundaries than do collective identities grounded in shared territory.

The second reason why Jews may be especially anxious about is the still recent experience of genocide. The last poem in Yiddish writer Chaim Grade's volume of poetry *Doyres* (Generations), published immediately at the end of World War II, begins with the demand, "*O mames yidishe, hot kinder!*"[14] that is, "Jewish mothers, have children!" And while it is possible, I suppose, to bear children without kinship, surely the plea here was not only a demographic one, but expressed a fervent desire to have the skein of genealogy stretching forward and backward renewed.

Third, whether or not antisemitism is somehow endemic to the West, there have certainly been threats to the autonomous responsibility of Jewish parents for the fate of their progeny on many occasions, long predating the disaster of the twentieth century. Just one remarkable example is Canon 60 of the Fourth Council of Toledo, in the year 633, which mandated the removal of children of forcibly baptized Jews from their parents, in order that they may be raised by devout Christians. As Lindsay Kaplan explains, during the thirteenth century, "The French Dominican William of Rennes argued that Jews were legally 'slaves' of the princes, 'And just as these Princes are able, against the parents' wishes, to give to others or to sell into servitude the same little children, like his own slaves, so they can offer them to baptism.' "[15] However common this actual forced removal combined with baptism may have been, William of Rennes's rhetoric here links the detachment of the child from Jewish kinship networks to a notion of baptism as the alternative to slavery. The analogy to twentieth-century coming-of-age narratives of Jewish children breaking away from the confines of their supposedly stifling family background is chilling in this light.

Fourth, in premodern Christian doctrine, the Jews were mostly supposed to wither away anyway. True, Augustine argued for the persistence of a degraded remnant, arguing against the idea that there is no place in Christendom for Jews after the revelation of the Messiahship of Jesus and their stubborn refusal to acknowledge that Messiahship. This is, of course, what is known as the doctrine of supersession: the idea that "Judaism" (whatever the status of that term) is now obsolete. Hence, also, the trope of the "old Jew" that persists through European Christian folklore, as richly documented, for example, in Claudine Fabre-Vassas's remarkable book on Jews, whose subtitle is, "Jews, Christians, and the Pig."[16]

Fifth, and last in this list for now, the perceived prospects of future Jewish generations are oddly skewed toward the negative for the following reason: Those sectors of the contemporary Jewish population that have the strongest and most strictly regulated kinship bonds—the Hasidim and other Haredi groups—are frequently perceived as belonging to the past. One contributor to a 1994 volume on *The Jewish Family and Jewish Continuity* wrote of the Hasidim as a "dynamic" group, but he dismisses them as "remain[ing] in the nineteenth century."[17] As I pointed out recently in my book on *Jewish Families*, "That doesn't make sense: everyone you or I might talk to today, which fortunately includes Hasidim, is living at the same time as you or I."[18] Actually, the notion that communities persisting in strictly regulated and gendered kinship patterns are inherently stuck in the past is only one horn of the dilemma of "Jewish continuity." The other horn is its mirror: the sense, prevalent in some Jewish communities for centuries now, that Jews can only "get ahead"; that is, they can only join the march toward some presumptive better future for all by escaping the bonds of in-group marriage and identity. Such a sense, it needs to be said gently, harmonizes well with the millennial Christian view that Jewish particularism needs to be overcome if all, and not only the Jews, are to be redeemed.

It's worth pointing out here that, while I've been emphasizing the pulls of both the past and the future on kinship, the desires that technologies of kin-making are designed to express may also be desires for stasis, or more prosaically, maintenance of the status quo. When representatives of Jewish community organizations speak about the imperative of "continuity," might this not sometimes betray a covert wish that things remain as they are rather than continue to be transformed? To be sure and to be fair, the rhetoric of Jewish continuity in organized Jewish organizations recognizes that change is necessary. But, perhaps far too often that change is understood as learning how to make "Jewishness" fit what a new generation, already understood as having escaped the constraints of Jewish kinship, might respond to. In that respect, "Jewish continuity" is not so much about past, present, or future, as about a perpetual attempt to catch up—often with nothing more substantial in justification than by a passing fashion as dictated by the marketplace.

Early in this talk, I invoked my intellectual hero Walter Benjamin and his dictum pointing to enslaved ancestors rather than liberated grandchildren as a major source of revolutionary zeal. It should be mentioned that in his own writings he had little to say about the specifics of his own ancestry. In his memoir, *A Berlin Childhood Around 1900*, he recalls one elderly aunt living in an already obsolete quarter of that very new city. He passes on few details of what she told him about his ancestors, beyond the very suggestive observation that their recently acquired last names were often toponyms, the names of small towns and hamlets in the countryside and, hence, smacked more of the memory of place than the memory of family. But he also gives us enough to suggest a narrative trajectory from the past, intended to guide the neophyte toward a future anticipated by his ancestors. The bits of information about his family learned from relatives offered him some insight into how his ancestry was meant to determine his own trajectory:

> Such stories brought to light what little I knew of my forebears. The career of an ancestor, a grandfather's rules of conduct, were conjured up before me as though to make me understand that it was premature for me to give away, by an early death, the splendid trump cards which I held in my hand, thanks to my origins.[19]

Nothing is said in Benjamin's memoir about the Jewishness of these forebears, and, in fact, one gets the impression that what was distinctive about them was their origin in the countryside as opposed to the city. After all, Benjamin's emphasis in that memoir is his Berlin childhood, not his Jewish childhood. When he recalls a childhood ritual of springtime, that ritual is an Easter egg hunt, rather than the search for *khomets*.

Our patience is short—shorter, perhaps, than that of our ancestors, if a bit longer than that of our children. We will read Grace Paley's story again, in just a moment, but this time trying to shed more light on some of its possible deeper meanings than we were able to perceive on the first hearing. Before we do that, let me linger a bit with one more text, hundreds of times longer than Paley's sketch. I refer to Aleph Bet Yehoshua's novel *Mr. Mani*, published in English in 1992.[20] The novel comprises five parts. Each part is told as one side of a dialogue between a younger person and a parent or other "parent" figure. Each part features a different "Mr. Mani," another in a direct line of Sephardi males. Each part as well focuses on the upbringing of the one who is to become the next Mr. Mani. The parts are told in reverse chronological order; that is, each successive part is set in a time and describes a generation earlier than the one that precedes it. Rather than "back to the future," this narrative moves forward to the past.

The first section, set in Jerusalem at the time of the novel's writing, describes an encounter between a young woman with the provocative name Hagar, who believes herself pregnant, and the father of her boyfriend. The father seems in suicidal despair over the recent death of his wife. The young woman's intervention, at least as she perceives it, prevents his suicide. Thus, in a sense, Hagar takes the place of her boyfriend's father's deceased wife.

If we skip *forward* in pages, and *back* in time, to the fifth and final section of Yehoshua's novel, set in Athens, in 1848, another Mr. Mani visits, consoles, and confronts his revered rabbi from childhood. That revered rabbi, by now quite aged and utterly incapacitated following a stroke, had belatedly married the Dona Flora, whom Mr. Mani had desired in his own youth. The rabbi's marriage to Dona Flora has borne no fruit. Meanwhile, Dona Flora's niece has married Mr. Mani's son, and the couple are now living in Jerusalem. In the course of this, Mr. Mani's one-sided conversation with Dona Flora and then only with his stricken rabbi, he reveals the secret that his supposed grandson, recently born in Jerusalem and presumed to be the child of his recently deceased son, is actually his own son, conceived during the year of mourning for the Mr. Mani, who was his son. The question he desperately and, it seems, tauntingly, and vengefully seeks an answer for from his mute rabbi is this: Will he, by his own suicide, be able to expiate the grave sin of incest that he has committed in getting his son's widow with child? Later, we are told in a passage that Yehoshua calls a "biographical supplement" that, having received no answer from his rabbi, Avraham Mani did not commit suicide.

Are we, the readers, then to understand that suicide as being deferred from generation to generation in the Mani family, down to the near suicide that our Hagar of the narrative's first but most recent part thinks she has interrupted? Perhaps even she, in the course of her relation to her own widowed kibbutznik mother, has confessed that she felt like she was part of some much larger tale. It would, of course, not be the first time in the history of Jewish literature that the arc of the collective's future is foretold in terms of a number of generations. Indeed, the Mishnah in Tractate Eduyot (4a) asserts that a son benefits his own father by helping to fulfill the number of generations that God has already declared will come before the end of the Exile, as it is stated in Isaiah (41:4), *kore hadoros marosh*: He announced the generations beforehand. Thus, each new generation brings us one step closer to redemption.

Though the allusion to Isaiah might tempt us to read *Mr. Mani* as a tale of redemption with the fulfillment of the male line, the book itself does not end on anything like a triumphant note. In any case, the multigenerational narrative's first but culminating episode seems to have brought us to some degree of healing. Possibly that healing has something to do with the fact that the generation whose stories are told in the book's first sections are all citizens of a Jewish state, unlike their ancestors whose distracted longings and fantasies had much to do with the lack of homeland and territorially grounded peoplehood. Hagar, the current-day narrator, becomes "pregnant" again, this time for real, and while her lover is abroad in graduate school, his widowed father comes from time to time to visit the kibbutz and to get to know his own grandson. Perhaps the widowed father and Hagar's widowed mother will marry each other, perhaps not. It is not even clear that this tale of generations has been about an inherited curse or about what its fiercely Zionist author believes are the inherent pathologies of families in diaspora. What is clear is that a family story can be told not only going forward, but also going backward, and perhaps more powerfully so.

If Grace Paley's "At That Time, or the History of a Joke" can be called a family story as well, it is only be in the very broad sense that the Jews are a big family or that all members of *Homo sapiens* constitute an even greater family of humankind. As I mentioned, Jonah didn't immediately share my enthusiasm for the story. I suppose I thought he might since, even more than I, he is sensitive to the continuing workings of white Christian privilege in our own United States. Thus, these ruminations are sparked, in part, by my own disappointment at a failed attempt to connect with my own descendant and also constitute, in part, the work of trying to recuperate that failure. Still, I'm not sure I can fully answer my son's puzzlement, because like all great fiction, "At That Time" surpasses any one individual's interpretation; or perhaps because Grace Paley herself was not quite sure what to make of this story. But here are a few signposts toward understanding this "history of a joke" that I hope will make it easier to understand.

The story was published in 1981 and again in 1985, yet, it includes reference to a "stolen uterus" and then to a uterus transplant, which we, in our own world and in our own time, hear of happening for the first time just a few years ago in Sweden. So the "at that time" of the story's title refers to what might just be in "our own time," more than thirty years in the future from when the story was conceived. The doctor who commits this theft is referred to as "hysterical," suggesting that not only those who actually possess a womb are subject to the diagnosis of hysteria. The "passing gynecologist" might not just have been hurrying by but pretending to pass as a Christian rather than a Jew; certainly, his name, "Dr. Heiliger" or "Holy Man," is ambiguous enough for him to pass as either. The reference to Fresh Meadows is harder to read, but I should tell this London audience that it names a neighborhood in the borough of Queens, New York, outside the city proper.

There are a series of transformations in the story or, perhaps, said better, a set of conveyances that strike us as magical, whimsical, or both: a stolen uterus replaced by transplant; a virgin birth assumed to be a boy child and announced as such but who is actually a girl; a child unexpectedly born black (though why did we readers assume that the young mother herself had white skin); a repetition of the birth of a savior rather than the annunciation of his return as the Messiah, mature and ready to redeem; and then—not a transformation but a mythic repetition, not "the Jews" *tout court* but only "certain" of them, evidently two thousand years old, because they had "observed and suffered the consequences of other virgin births," crying yet again, "It is not He! It is not He!"

As a result of their denial of this new advent, these "certain Jews," this "foolish remnant," as Paley also calls them, are cut off from electronic media—thus, in the world of the tale, from all contact with anyone except themselves—and must actually come face to face in order to maintain everyday contact. They are materially reduced to the most basic religious symbols but not thrown into the past, for these symbols—"shawls and phylacteries"—are by now routinely worn by woman as well. Moreover, this "foolish remnant," like the naïve child who declares that the emperor has no clothes, is the first to announce that the product of the virgin birth is a girl. Not a problem for most people in the world of this story, since everyone else except the "particular discontented Jews" is ready to modify the old myth by adding the symbol of a circular navel and wiggly umbilical cord.

The Jews—let's just call them that after all, since particularity is characteristic of Jewishness in any case—are by now quite ready for a female Divinity, offering their "Praise to the most Highess!" Yet they continue stubbornly, nostalgically if you will, to refer to twentieth-century left-wing politics ("Another tendency heard from!") and to premodern medical practices, doubtless quoting their grandmother's Yiddish to insist that another virgin birth *vet helfn vi a toytn bankes*—it will do about as much good as the old folk remedy called cupping.

I grant that the identity of "they" in the final paragraph (see fig. 1) is a bit ambiguous: Did only the Jews here "continue as female and male" as the God of Genesis had created them, stubbornly denying the triumphal supersession of gender difference Paul announces in his letter to the Galatians? The "if so" suggests that their persistence as gendered humans is a consequence of their rejection of the newborn's saving power. Certainly, they continue in their generations, "descending" by continuing to conceive and bear in the old-fashioned way and in the old-fashioned way as well to stick it out in the "shmatte" business. The "muddy basement of history" they continue to occupy suggests the "bargain basements" of New York City department stores in the mid to late twentieth century. And the poor Gentiles as well, it seems, also continue to "descend;" else why would they need to be dressed for such life-cycle rituals as "weddings, births, or funerals?"

If one didn't know Grace Paley better—at least through her many writings—one might be forgiven for wondering what the author of this curious brief fantasy thinks about "those particular discontented Jews." Are they stubbornly remaining behind, refusing universal redemption? After all, the world of this story is one where "sexism and racism had no public life": real progress no doubt. But shining through Grace Paley's stories is a fierce, tremendous, and unsentimental love for the skepticism, the stubborn difference of "those particular Jews" and also of those poor people—many but by no means all of them also Jews—about whom she so often wrote. The Jews descend, every day but Saturday perhaps, to the "muddy basement of history," finding the right clothes for those moments that make it possible, somehow, always tentatively, in ways that are transformed whether we celebrate the transformations or attempt to deny them, to locate ourselves forward and backward in time through our practices of genealogy.

References

1. Lucinda Ramberg, *Given to the Goddess: South Indian Devadasis and the Sexuality of Religion* (Durham, NC: Duke University Press, 2014).
2. Lucinda Ramberg, "Troubling Kinship: Sacred Marriage and Gender Configuration in South India," *American Ethnologist* 40 (2013): 671–72.
3. Grace Paley, "At That Time, or the History of a Joke," in *Later the Same Day* (New York: Farrar, Strauss and Giroux, 1985), 93–96. The story was also published in *The Iowa Review* 12.2 (1981): 266–67, accessed June 24, 2017, http://ir.uiowa.edu/iowareview/vol12/iss2/91/.
4. Daniel Boyarin, *A Radical Jew: Paul and the Politics of Identity* (Berkeley, Los Angeles: University of California Press, 1994).
5. Karl Loewith, *Meaning in History* (Chicago: University of Chicago Press, 1957), 2.
6. Walter Benjamin, "Theses on the Philosophy of History," in *Illuminations: Essays and Reflections*, ed. Hanna Arendt, trans. Harry Zohn (New York: Schocken Books, 1969), 260.

7. Rhonda Berger-Sofer, "Political Kinship Alliances of a Hasidic Dynasty," *Ethnology* 23 (1984): 49–62.
8. Joshua Friedman, "Yiddish Returns: Language, Intergenerational Gifts, and Jewish Devotion." PhD diss., University of Michigan, 2015, 51.
9. Friedman, "Yiddish Returns," 165.
10. Susan Buck-Morss, "Globalization, Hegemony, and Sovereignty," in *Anti-Semitism and Islamophobia*, ed. Matti Bunzl (Chicago: Prickly Paradigm Press, 2007), 59.
11. Rafael Goldchain, "Familial Ground," accessed May 9, 2017, http://v1.zonezero.com/exposiciones/fotografos/goldchain/.
12. Jon Entine, "Is DNA Embracing Difference?" *Ancestry* (March-April 2008), 45.
13. Kaja Finkler, "Family, Kinship, Memory and Temporality in the Age of the New Genetics." *Social Science & Medicine* 61 (2005), 1069–70.
14. Chaim Grade, *Doyres* (New York: IKUF Publishers, 1945), 217.
15. Quoted in Lindsay Kaplan's soon to be published book, *Servitus Judaeorum: Biblical Figures, Canon Law and the Construction of Hereditary Inferiority* (manuscript in progress), 37. The translation is hers, and I thank her for allowing me to consult her manuscript. For the Toledo canon, she cites Amnon Linder, ed., *The Jews in the Legal Sources of the Early Middle Ages*, (Detroit: Wayne State University Press; Jerusalem: Israel Academy of Sciences and Humanities, 1997), 487–89 and Pakter, *Medieval Canon Law and the Jews*, 315. For the William of Rennes quote, Kaplan cites Pakter, *Medieval Canon Law*, 322, n. 295.
16. Claudine Fabre-Vassas, *The Singular Beast: Jews, Christians, and the Pig* (New York: Columbia University Press, 1994).
17. Gerald Bubis, "Policy Considerations for American Jewish Life," in *The Jewish Family and Jewish Continuity*, ed. Steven Bayme and Gladys Rosen (Hoboken, NJ: KTAV Publishing, 1994), 298.
18. Jonathan Boyarin, *Jewish Families* (New Brunswick, NJ: Rutgers University Press, 2013), 153.
19. Walter Benjamin, *Berlin Childhood Around 1900* (Cambridge: Harvard University Press, 2006), 74.
20. A. B. Yehoshua, *Mr. Mani*, trans. Hillel Halkin (New York: Doubleday, 1992).

The Role of Life Motifs in Commitment Journeys of Ba'alei Teshuvah

Roberta Rosenberg Farber

Abstract

In this article, findings from my interviews with *ba'alei teshuvah*, the Hebrew term for Jews who "return" and adopt a religiously observant lifestyle, are examined. I identify the presence of a non-rational, holistically known theme, which I call a *life motif* that inspires and guides the journey towards religious commitment. The *life motif* is symbolic of a person's life purpose and goal. It is encapsulated in a specific *mitzvah* (commanded deed) and or ideal which strongly attracts and symbolizes what it is in Judaism that leads a person to make a religious commitment.

The growth of the American *ba'alei teshuvah* movement began in the 1960s, a tumultuous time in American history. The Civil Rights Movement began in the 1950s; the Counterculture Movement dominated the 1960s and 1970s, along with the Berkeley Free Speech Movement and the Women's Movement. It was a time when young Americans were moving towards a life of fewer restrictions and greater freedom of expression. Thus, it was particularly puzzling that some young Jews were attracted to religiously observant Judaism, a system generally regarded as restrictive and patriarchal. At a time when women's freedoms and opportunities were being publically debated, examined in the media, and clearly increasing the attraction of young women was especially puzzling.

Several sociological studies examined these paradoxical trends and concluded that, in general, the young men and women attracted to Orthodox Judaism wanted or needed fewer choices and so chose to adopt a life structure that was imposed from the outside. Other studies found that women tended to reconfigure the restrictions of Orthodox Jewry to be consistent with feminist values.[1]

Recently, emphasis has been given to the study of persons who leave an Orthodox Jewish lifestyle and become more secular.[2] Absent family struggles, the primary reason for leaving seems to be a desire for greater intellectual and emotional freedom. These studies offer insight into the same radical life change processes as those experienced by *ba'alei teshuvah*, the critical difference, of course, being the direction of the change.[3]

In 1985–1986, I developed an approach to exploring the epistemological dimensions of the change process experienced by Jewish returnees (*ba'alei teshuvah*).[4] What puzzled me was how a person who had no intention of becoming religious or even spiritual came to make a commitment to a form of Judaism that required a radical life change. How did it happen? Was there a road map and, if so, what constituted the road signs? How did the returnee make her decisions and how did this new way of life become integrated with an earlier sense of self? In other words, how did it all come and stay together? Methodologically, it was unclear how the topography of this journey could be known.

To find answers to my questions, I conducted interviews with returnees, during which they were asked to tell me their story. It was important to know not only events that occurred on their journey but "to hear" what Max Weber called "*verstehen*," the subjective dimension of the person's experience. Therefore, the returnee was asked to tell me in his or her own words why and how he or she became religiously observant of Jewish law. This approach allows the significance of events and relationships to emerge naturally, their meanings embedded within the order and flow of the narrative. Objectively, the outcome of the process was clear—the person became a religiously observant Jew. Understanding how this happened from a subjective perspective was my goal.[5]

METHODOLOGY

Earlier studies of *ba'alei teshuvah* focused primarily on persons who were still in the process of deciding whether religiously observant Judaism was a lifestyle they wanted to live.[6] They were still in the process of learning about religiously observant Judaism, often in a seminary type setting. Because I wanted to understand the completed decision process, I only interviewed persons who had made a commitment to live as a religiously observant Jew. Because of the potential for backsliding, only persons who had been living an Orthodox Jewish lifestyle for five or more years were chosen.[7] This seemed a sufficient amount of time to assume lifestyle stability.

To achieve a random sample, the snowball method of recruitment was used. This means I needed to find one returnee who would then recommend another and so on. In all, I conducted in-depth interviews with sixteen *ba'alei teshuvah*, ten women and six men in Jerusalem and New York City in 1985–1986. Interviews were conducted in the respondent's or interviewer's home, office, or a public setting, such as a hotel lobby or café. They lasted approximately 2 to 4 hours, and were conducted in two sessions when necessary.

Of the ten females and six male interviewees, all but two were born in the United States; one woman was from England and one man was born in and living in Israel. The American respondents were generally second- or third-generation or some combination thereof. A few were fourth-generation American. The age of the respondents at the time of their interview ranged from 24 to 54 years old, with an average of 36 years. Five respondents had master's degrees; one had a PhD, and all but one had completed college. Twelve respondents were married, three were divorced, and one expected to marry soon. All the women had children except two, one of whom was expecting her first child. Of the six men, five were married and had children.

During the interview, one woman mentioned that she was a convert to Judaism. I retained this interview to determine whether her experience differed significantly from *ba'alei teshuvah*, who are born into the Jewish faith. No significant difference was found in the decision process per se, such as how she knew when and where to turn in her travels and how she knew when she found what she was searching for. Excluding this one convert, the background denominations of the respondents were as follows: one woman was raised in an Orthodox family, seven respondents (4 men, 3 women) were raised in Traditional or Conservative Jewish families; two women had a reform background, and five respondents (2 men, 3 women) came from secular Jewish households. Eight respondents came from families with fairly strong connections to the Jewish world and seven from families without any or only a tenuous connection. After collecting specific personal data, an open-ended interview format was employed using probes as necessary. Taped in-depth interviews lasted between two and four hours. They were transcribed.

In this paper, I re-examine the study described above. Although the societal context has clearly changed, I find that discussions about the role that life goals play in forming and shaping a person's identity and life path remain relevant and important. The identification of a non-discursively known *life motif* as the inspiration and guide to an individual's life journey is especially relevant today, in that it addresses the incompatibility between religious faith/knowledge and scientific knowledge. This conflict hinges on the distinction (and incompatibility) between discursive and non-discursive perceptual forms and ways of knowing.[8] The rational perceptual form builds sequentially, one unit at a time, each of which can be abstracted from the whole and still retain its meaning. In comparison, a non-discursive perceptual form is known intuitively and holistically. It is an all-at-once apprehension of the whole. It cannot be taken apart without losing its meaning which is dependent upon context.

The conflict between the non-rational (non-discursive) and rational (discursive) ways of knowing and being in the world are noted by Rav Soloveitchik[9] in his well-known essay, "The Lonely Man of Faith." He observed that faith knowledge, being non-discursive, cannot be translated into the discursiveness of modern thought:

> There are simply no cognitive categories in which the total commitment of the man of faith could be spelled out. This commitment is rooted not in one dimension, such as the rational one, but in the whole personality of the man of faith. The whole of the human being, the rational as well the non-rational aspects, are committed to God. Hence, the magnitude of the commitment is beyond the comprehension of the *logos* and the *ethos*.[10]

This distinction in ways of knowing has methodological implications for the examination of the religious commitment of *ba'alei teshuvah*. It is the reason I asked my interviewees for "their story" rather than asking specific questions drawn from sociological and psychological theories of change. In doing the latter, I would have had to fit personal experiences into existing theoretical conceptual categories. Instead, I wanted my analysis to be based on and emerge organically from the interviewees's experiences.

Life Motifs

After carefully listening to and analyzing the transcribed accounts of the interviews, I found the presence of a non-discursively known theme that inspires and guides a person's life journey. I call this a *life motif*. It may be an idea, ideal, or quest to resolve a conflict. The *life motif* may signify the personal meaning that becoming religiously observant of Jewish law has for the individual. However, at the start of a person's journey, his *life motif* need not be connected to or expressive of religion in general, or of Judaism in particular. However, because it functions as a conceptual link between the old identity and the new Jewish one, the *life motif* is re-conceptualized within a Judaic framework at some point in the commitment process. This reconceptualization connects and gives coherence to the shift in identity, thus, providing the consistency necessary for personal stability and integration. So too, it facilitates the shift from an individually-oriented identity to a more communal Jewish one.[11]

Typically, a *life motif* emerges when a person is young and sometimes is barely noticed or given much attention. Because a person's deepest life goals are often hidden to them, shaded by the light of other pursuits, one's *life motif* may not be a strong activating force in a person's life until some event or understanding triggers it. Over the years, however, its strength grows with its recognition as something important, something symbolic of a person's life purpose.

In his groundbreaking study of adult male development, Daniel J. Levinson[12] identified a comparable, non-discursive knowledge that propels and guides a person's life development. Levinson called this the "Dream":

> In its primordial form, the Dream is a vague sense of self-in-adult-world. It has the quality of a vision, an imagined possibility that generates excitement and vitality. At the start it is poorly articulated and only tenuously connected to reality, although it may contain concrete images such as winning the Nobel Prize or making the all-star team.
>
> Whatever the nature of his Dream, a young man has the developmental task of giving it greater definition and finding ways to live it

out. It makes a great difference in his growth whether his initial life structure is consonant with and infused by the Dream, or opposed to it. If the Dream remains unconnected to his life it may simply die, and with it his sense of aliveness and purpose." (pp. 91–92)

Like the Dream, the *life motif* must be concretely expressed to be realized. Of the sixteen persons interviewed, all were found to have *life motifs* that motivated and guided their process of change. Examples of the most interesting *life motifs* follow. In all cases, pseudonyms are used to refer to the interviewees.

Leah's Life Motif: "Service to God"

Brought up in a traditional Jewish household, Leah's journey may be said to have begun when she was thirteen years old. While at summer camp, she had "a very strong sense of God's presence." A few hours after this experience, she wrote a poem: "I wrote about knowing. . . . Knowing, not in terms of thinking specifically about God, but like knowing there was a certain purpose in life. The strong feeling of contentment and being at peace with myself came from knowing there was a purpose to the world—that I was being taken care of and had a specific destiny in life. . . . The experience made a really big impression on me, and when I was home, I wanted to be back in camp just so I could have those feelings again. It was like the experience had become a real place for me, one I wanted to return to."

Over time, the memory of this experience and the desire to return to it remain, but only faintly. As she matures, Leah seems to intuitively comprehend the idea that Orthodox Judaism is the correct way to live; but she fights this knowledge, resisting the radical life change it would require. Instead, she takes on Jewish obligations half-heartedly. For example, while in college, Leah decides to keep kosher but does so only when at home and not outside her house. She recognizes that the Jewish dimension of her identity is of central importance to her, and she knows she should only be dating Jewish boys. And yet, Leah falls in love with a non-Jewish boy, rationalizing her behavior by proclaiming that since he is vegetarian, the relationship does not interfere with her standard of keeping kosher.

In another situation, Leah decides to keep the Sabbath but does not want to give up her Friday and Saturday activities and so tries to do both, keep and not keep the Sabbath by invoking technicalities. Upon completing college, she feels that she must go to Israel. But once there, she goes to a non-religious kibbutz even though she is trying to keep kosher. Leaving the kibbutz, she travels around the country and finally ends up in an Orthodox yeshiva for *ba'alot teshuvah*. Here, Leah is forced to confront the conflicts between her primarily secular value system and Jewish religious laws and understandings. One example of this conflict is the issue of abortion, which has particular resonance for Leah since she had worked for an American abortion clinic.

The *life motif* intuited while at summer camp, that she has a life purpose, is referenced in her discussion of marriage. "Before becoming religious," she says, "it was, like, to be married would be a nice thing. I needed it emotionally. But now, it was different. I figured I couldn't go any farther in my *avodas Hashem* (service to God) without being married." This perspective on marriage does not mean that love and romance are missing, only that the relationship, like her other life actions, occurs within the context of the greater purpose her life has assumed, namely, "service to God." This *life motif*, first intuited in the spiritual experience she had at summer camp, motivates her search and guides her decision to become a *ba'alot teshuvah*. Importantly, it continues to provide the background meaning and context for her life. At the time she was interviewed, she understood her *life motif* to be most clearly expressed in her role as a wife and mother.

Sara's Life Motif: "Confronting the Holocaust"

Sara's journey is one of only two of the sixteen in which the Holocaust plays a central role. Her parents, both born in Poland, were survivors of the Holocaust. They were also Bundists, a secular Jewish socialist movement popular in the early to middle 1900s, which emphasized Yiddish culture but not the Jewish religion. Sara was five years old when her mother began to teach her Yiddish by reading Bible stories to her. It was, however, the stories and not the Yiddish language that inspired Sara and sparked her imagination. Sara's mother did not believe in God. But because of the stories she read to Sara when she was only five years, Sara decided that unlike her mother she believed in God. It was a defining moment for her and can be understood to prefigure her commitment to a life of religious observance. In addition to reading her Bible stories and teaching her Yiddish, Sara's mother also told her Holocaust stories. Sara responded with a need to hear even more despite their horrible and frightening character.

Raised on these stories and inspired by the religious dimension of the Jewish people, Sara understands her relationship to religious observance to be like the historical birth of the State of Israel, which she understands as an outgrowth of the Holocaust. Her commitment is like the phoenix that rises from the ashes of destruction. Sarah understands her confrontation with the Holocaust as the *life motif* that motivates and guides her determination to become a *ba'alat teshuvah*.

Linda's Life Motif: "As Above, So Below: A Search for Congruency"

When she was fifteen years old, Linda remembers saying, "I wanted to be the kind of person who if everybody did what I did the world would be a better place. I didn't want to litter, because if nobody littered, the world would be perfectly clean. . . . Then I started to feel this way about all of my actions. Like, I wouldn't be able to live with myself if somebody, by imitating me, if the whole world imitated me, the whole world would [become] worse. Littering is a minor thing, but it was symbolic of how an individual's actions have the potential to transform an entire society, an entire world."

This ideal is stated when Linda is fifteen years old and her thoughts could easily be dismissed as youthful idealism. Nevertheless, she neither forgets nor abandons this ideal. It continues to inform her actions and relationships as she becomes an adult.

As a political activist during and after her college years, she is consistently disillusioned by the gap she perceives between stated ideals and behavior. Discouraged, Linda takes time off to travel through Europe and Greece, deciding only at the last minute to go to Israel. Quite unintentionally, Linda ends up at a yeshiva in Jerusalem where she begins to explore Judaism. In the learning environment of this yeshiva, Linda begins to see Judaism as a religious-social-political system and realizes that this was what she'd been searching for all her life:

I was always searching for the right structure within which to become a good person. The key to the structure working was that it had to account for and acknowledge the importance of personal action. It had to recognize that as a result of personal action society could be transformed. . . . Intuitively, I knew this structure existed. I was looking for it when I worked for those organizations after college, but I didn't know where to find it. So, from that perspective, I can say that all my life I've been searching for Orthodox Judaism. I just didn't know it.

At the end of the interview, Linda explains her feelings and thoughts in greater detail:

I knew that just as there's a physical order in the world, there must be a moral order as well. It's possible to establish a logical basis for this idea, but my feeling was purely intuitive. In other words, I didn't formulate it in terms of a physical order because I'm not a scientist. I didn't believe that because everything else in the physical realm interacts so perfectly, the human being should do the same. Rather, I felt that our purpose is to create a moral harmony to parallel the harmony of the physical realm, taking into account the profound difference between the two realms: in the physical world there are rules, whereas in the moral realm we have choices. In the physical world, gravity is gravity and you can't choose in or out of it, but you do choose whether or not to conform to an existing moral law. It's by choice that people decide whether or not to create a perfectly ordered society that parallels the perfection and order of the physical realm."

This "search for congruency" is the central goal that informs Linda's narrative and so, constitutes the *life motif* of her journey.

Naomi's Life Motif: "A Longing of the Soul"

A "longing of the soul" is Naomi's *life motif*. The feeling motivates and guides her decision to learn about Judaism in a yeshiva and become a *ba'alat teshuvah*. Brought up as "a completed absorbed, assimilated British Jew," Naomi says she was closer to Christianity and

> so absorbed that I knew Christmas [well] and I knew Easter. And I only knew about Judaism that I was Jewish, that I was different. I knew I was different because in school they told me I was different. For instance, 'Would Jewish girls please leave the hall until the prayers are over.' And if they hadn't told me I was different I probably wouldn't even have known it.

Nevertheless, she notes that as a child she had a strong emotional attraction to "anything Jewish." Later she understood this as a desire to come closer to Judaism:

> Whenever I went past a synagogue," she says, "my soul was tugging. I could feel it. It was yearning. . . . And whenever I came across anything Jewish, a challah in a shop window for instance, this soul would activate itself, and I would feel hungry. Not physically hungry but spiritually hungry, like I've got to go in because that belongs to me: Not as if I'm starving hungry, no. Rather, this is mine; this is me." But I could couldn't have it because we didn't observe Shabbat.

It takes Naomi more than twenty years and a great deal of traveling before she becomes a *ba'alat teshuvah*. Towards the end of her narrative, she observes that when she lived in Canada and began to study Judaism for the second time her epilepsy disappeared. She says, "I think this was all part of the distress of my soul. I believe I had the epilepsy because my soul was in distress, mainly because it was out of its element—it was in a strange and hostile environment struggling to find its identity. I've never had an attack since [becoming religiously observant]."

David's Life Motif: Tefillin

David was thirty-two years old at the time of the interview. He begins his narrative by discussing his *tefillin*, the phylacteries worn by religiously observant men every day except the Sabbath and Holy Days:

> I mean the fact that I had now graduated Hebrew school [and] I had my pair of *tefillin* to, you know, to show off. That was my diploma. I reached the end of the line and just like everyone else in my circle of friends, Conservative, Reform, assimilated, and unaffiliated—once you graduate Hebrew School means . . . you never have to go to shul again. This is the end. This is the end of your Jewishness. This is the end of your education. It's the last time you have to open up a siddur [prayer book]. It's the last time you'll ever go to shul, except for a wedding or bar mitzvah. . . . And I figured the same. So, I took my *tefillin*, stashed them away in the drawer, and that was the end of it.

When David speaks about his decision to observe the Sabbath and became an observant Jew, he returns again to the topic of his *tefillin*:

I just made a decision that one of these days I'm going to become Orthodox. I'm going to become *shomer Shabbos*, put on a yarmulke, everything—*tzitzits, tefillin,* go to shul. . . . And then I said to myself, I'll have to move out of my parent's house because they aren't *shomer Shabbos,* and there'd be no way I could be observant and still live with them. . . . Then I got my big break. My friend Larry called me up and said there's an apartment available near him. . . . And I said to myself, "This is it. This is from heaven." But I didn't say it in those words. Instead, I said, "This is meant to be." I promised myself, as soon as I pack my bags and move out that's the day that I'm going to become observant. . . . And I, you know, I bought a couple of yarmulkes, bought a siddur, packed, and left that day. It was on a Sunday. That was it. I went over to my friend Larry's house, and he refreshed my memory about putting on *tefillin.* It was fifteen years since I'd put on the *tefillin.* The *tefillin* lay in my drawer, but I fetched them. I got them out of the drawer. He [David's friend] showed me how to put them on. But the very strange thing is that in those fifteen years when I didn't put on *tefillin,* I'd say, once every year or once every couple of years, I'd go open the drawer and take them out. I'd look in the bag, and I'd see the *tefillin* there. Somehow, some way I knew that I'd be, maybe one day wearing them. I just had this feeling. I'd just open the drawer to look at them. . . . It was basically something I wanted to do.

At the end of the interview David says:

I said to myself, I've got one life, so I might as well live it as a Jew. You know, it's like sort of a buried treasure in my backyard. All I have to do is dig it up. I figured out that there's such a small percentage of Jews in the world, it's such a miracle, and it's such a waste to go through your life living like a non-Jew when you have these riches. That's the way I feel. You're just wasting your life if you don't live it the way you're supposed to.

A boy puts on *tefillin* when he turns thirteen. This is the age when he becomes responsible for his actions. Religiously, the act means that the boy is now responsible for observing all the *mitzvoth* (girls reach the age of responsibility at twelve). It is also the age at which he can be counted as a man for a *minyan,* a quorum of ten men. For David, the act of leaving his parent's home signifies that he is taking responsibility for his life, something he was obligated to do at the age of thirteen, when a boy becomes obligated in the ritual of *tefillin* and all the *mitzvoth* for which he is responsible. He waited and, thus, it was symbolically significant that his commitment to don *tefillin* converges with his decision to leave his parent's home and begin a new life.

Life motifs, in other words, constitute the symbolic meaning towards which a person strives. It constitutes the meaning that provides both motivation and direction in one's life. In the above illustrations, the *life motif* is the meaning, or the symbol that functions as a beacon illuminating a life path in the process of change. Without these directional signals, how else would a person know in which direction to go, when to stop, when to keep moving, or when to change directions in the often chaotic experience of radical life change?

In the following sections, I examine my interview data from the perspectives other scholars have used when analyzing *ba'alei teshuvah.* Importantly, these studies are of persons in the process of deciding whether or not to make a commitment. All of my interviewees, on the other hand, did make a commitment to live a religiously Orthodox lifestyle and had been living this way for five years or more.

Search Paths

In their study of *ba'alei teshuvah* Davidman and Greil[13] identified three paths taken by individuals they interviewed—accidental contact, casual search, and committed search. I apply these categories to the interview data from my study.

Since extensive change is required when becoming a *ba'al (at) teshuvah,* the most logically relevant category would seem to be the committed search path, characterized by persons "who eventually made a decision systematically to 'search in their own backyards,' that is, in Jewish religious directions."[14] And indeed, this is the category with the greatest fit. Thirteen respondents (including Andrea, a convert) were on a committed search before examining Orthodox Judaism. The casual search category fits the early part of the change process for one of the respondents. The accidental contact category applies to two male respondents, who, without prior intention, encountered Judaism, and this encounter provided the catalyst that led them to become *ba'alei teshuvah.*

Unlike Davidman and Greil, I interviewed only persons who completed the process of radical life change to become *ba'alei teshuvah.* As previously stated, because of the radical nature of this change, all *ba'alei teshuvah* can be expected to exhibit the characteristics of a committed search path before making the decision to become religious, even when their search begins differently. In all the journey narratives of my interviewees, a *life motif,* the subjective meaning structure that enables a person to interpret an experience in such a way that it leads him or her to begin the process of radical life change, is identified.

Accidental Contact

Accidental contact "refers to the experiences of those newcomers who were not deliberately and self-consciously seeking a spiritual path or greater knowledge about Judaism."[15] The key phrase is "deliberately and self-consciously seeking." Two respondents, Daniel and Ari, can be said to have encountered Judaism as a consequence of accidental contact. Daniel's friend asked him to come with him to hear Rebetzin Jungreis, a noted and dynamic speaker. Though not particularly interested, he went to keep his friend company. Daniel expressed an interest in being religious when he was younger but did not pursue this interest as he was growing up. Thus, he was not "deliberately and self-consciously" seeking a spiritual path when he went to hear Rebetzin Jungreis. Nevertheless, he was so impressed by her words that he decided to lead (as he phrased it) "a real Jewish life and become religious." But where did Daniel's notion of a "real Jewish life" come from? His narrative reveals his *life motif* to be the image of his Orthodox grandmother, who he identifies as "an authentic Jew." The life of Daniel's grandmother sharply contrasted with the Jewish life led by his parents, which he termed "hypocritical." This earlier understanding enabled Daniel to recognize the authenticity of the Jewish life expressed by Rebetzin Jungreis. Her speech illustrated a path to pursue the goal of Jewish authenticity that he desired.

Ari went to a party at which he happened to meet a rabbi with whom he got into a discussion about "Truth." The discussion so interested him that he continued to pursue various ideas and beliefs with this rabbi. After several years, these discussions led Ari to become a *ba'al teshuvah.* His focus on the pursuit of Truth is the *life motif* that motivates and guides his journey. Nevertheless, he was not consciously seeking a spiritual path or even greater knowledge about Judaism when he attended the party and met the Rabbi. He was just going to a party. Importantly, however, he was committed to a search for Truth.

Casual Search

Casual search is the path taken by "individuals who became interested in learning more about Judaism and who sought a place in which to do so, although not always in a systematic way."[16] Only Naomi, whose journey was discussed above, exhibited this pattern. Since the process of becoming a *ba'alat teshuvah* requires intensive study and a radical change in behavior, the latter part of all *ba'alei teshuvah* journeys is expected to exhibit the characteristics of a committed search, as was, indeed, the case for Naomi. However, because it took such a long time to reach the committed search stage of her journey (approximately 20 years), Naomi's path is here characterized as a casual search.

Committed Search

The committed search path is characteristic of the journeys experienced by the majority of respondents in my study. As characterized by Davidman and Greil, "Committed searchers are those *ba'alei* and *ba'alot teshuvah* who had been on a spiritual quest for many years and who eventually made a decision systematically to "search in their own backyards," that is, in Jewish religious directions."[17] Among the interviewees for this study, Tamar's journey is perhaps the best example of a committed search path, which she defined as a spiritual search.

Tamar's search began when she started taking drugs in college. As she says, "the drugs really started me on a spiritual search at that point ... Plus, like, there were a lot of spiritual people." She notes that her drug use was mostly in the presence of like-minded friends who were also into spiritual growth. Comparing herself with another close friend at the time, she separates her drug experiences from his, saying, "Well, he liked getting high, and it made him feel good and, you know, taking drugs was a very communal experience and everything like that. For me, it was a very spiritual thing. It transformed a lot of things about myself, and he didn't really do that. You know, I got into meditation and this and that and foods and yoga and all these alternative things, and he didn't really do that."

Tamar decided that two years "on drugs" was long enough, and she returned to New York City and began to work at the New York Public Library. Then she went back to school to finish her undergraduate degree. She taught in a private school for a while, traveled cross-country, and was into communes, macrobiotics, yoga, gurus, ashrams, Erhard Seminar Training, therapy, food co-ops, jogging, camping, backpacking, and color therapy. Her initial introduction to Judaism came about through a friend who learned about it in San Francisco. At that time, Judaism did not appeal to her; it sounded too dry and not spiritual enough. But then Tamar and the person she was living with went to a friend's house for Shabbos, and they really liked it. Her friend's husband found funding for her to attend a *ba'alei teshuvah* yeshiva in Israel, where she studied for two and a half months. Her response to this experience was, "I just felt that this was it. It was really a revelation for me." She became a *ba'alat teshuvah*.

Themes

In this section, the *life motifs* that emerged from the journey narratives are organized into seven themes and subsequently discussed. The themes are: spirituality, service to God, the Holocaust, Jewish continuity, social justice, authenticity, and personal responsibility. Each *life motif* is then examined in accordance with Kanter's three dimensions of commitment.[18] The relevance of gender is integrated into discussions of the *life motifs*. I have also included a brief analysis of gender roles in the discussion of commitment. In cases of overlap, where a *life motif* may reflect more than one theme, the respondents may be referred to several times.

Spirituality

In Danzger's 1989 study of *ba'alei teshuvah*, more men than women reported spiritual experiences.[19] In my study, only Leah noted a spiritual experience that functioned as the inspiration and guide to and throughout her journey. However, the search for a spiritual connection, generally described in personal terms, is a central theme in the majority of the women's narratives. Interestingly, the men for whom a *spiritual dimension* is of central importance express its significance in terms of belonging and commitment to a community. This is particularly interesting in that it is men who are obligated to be part of a *minyan*, a quorum of ten men needed for reciting certain prayers. It is men, in other words, who are obligated to be part of prayer community.

Naomi speaks of her search for a spiritual peace, which she finds when she begins to keep the Sabbath. Leah speaks of a return to the peace experienced in the spiritual experience she had as a youth in summer camp. Ruthie refers to a desire to connect with the "spiritual background" of the universe. In her narrative, she intertwines the themes of spirituality and purity that are symbolized in the feelings she had as a child when she sees her grandfather pray, wearing *tefillin* and draped in his *tallit*, prayer shawl. Participation in the *mitzvah* of *mikvah*, the ritual bath to which married women go on a monthly basis symbolizes a process of purification. It is a pivotal event in Ruthie's process of becoming a *ba'alat teshuvah*. Tamar always considered herself to be a spiritual person. The desire to connect with a higher spirituality was the reason she sought an alternative lifestyle. She experimented with communes, drugs, health foods, yoga, and Eastern religious practices but none of these lifestyles satisfied her. Only when she encountered Orthodox Judaism did she recognize the life for which she'd been searching. Today, as a *ba'alat teshuvah*, Tamar still struggles with some of the requirements to which she must adhere as an Orthodox Jewish woman. This struggle is eased by her awareness that when doing the commanded rituals, she fulfills her destiny as a Jewish woman and connects to the spiritual dimensions of the universe.

Pinchos frequently referred to the fact that he was on a spiritual path before deciding to become a *ba'al teshuvah*. But as with most of the men, it was the idea of being part of a spiritual community that was the central focus in his *life motif*. When Kenny has his first child, a boy, he realizes that he has nothing to pass on to his child and so begins to learn about Judaism in a deeper and more spiritual way. He senses the mystical connection with generations of Jews past and those yet to come in the ritual of *brit milah*. In this act, symbolic of the covenant between God and the Jewish Nation, Kenny fulfills his role as a link in the unbroken chain of Jewish Tradition.

Service

"Service to God" is a theme related to but not identical with spirituality. Typically, this theme is expressed within the context of a particular action or set of actions understood by religiously observant Jewish communities as obligations commanded by God. Examples can be found in the activities of daily life, such as saying blessings before and after eating as well as reciting the daily prayer service and studying holy texts. For Leah, her role as wife and mother are central to her *life motif* of "service to God." From a behavioral perspective, the emphasis on the roles of wife and mother fit the gender expectation of woman in particular and, generally, of women living in traditional communities.

If one looks deeper, however, another image and meaning emerges. As Leah understands these roles, it is the activities of prayer and Torah study that constitute the context and background of her actions and provide the spiritual meaning of and direction to these roles. The specific purpose of the Jewish People (i.e., that for which they were chosen) is often symbolized in the transference of the Jewish Heritage from one generation to the next. It is through the family and the efforts of the wife and mother, in particular, that this goal is realized. Thus, within the context of the religious meanings assigned to these roles, that of the mother and the home are central. It is not the synagogue that is the central institution but rather the home where the mother has the primary role.

Leah understands her actions as "service to God." Of course, this purpose is also fulfilled in a general way by being an observant Jew; from that perspective, the idea of service to God is central to the actions of all persons who become *ba'alei teshuvah*.

Of the six men respondents, only Ari is "*learning*" Torah full-time at the time of the interview. For men, this type of learning is regarded as the highest form of service to God. It is considered to have consequence in both this world and the world to come. Learning Torah merges the concrete and spiritual realms and is efficacious in both. For Ari, learning Torah is consistent with the *life motif* that inspired and motivated his journey, the search for Truth. It is also consistent with the communal expectation for men in Orthodox communities and especially the ultra-Orthodox Jewish communities of which Ari is a member.

The concepts of obligation and personal responsibility clearly fall under the rubric of "service to God," especially when applied to a religious community. This theme is central to David's journey narrative, the *life motif* in which personal responsibility is symbolized by the ritual of *tefillin*. Because he is limited in his ability to excel in Torah learning, David fulfills his sense of community responsibility through another *mitzvah*, *zedekah*, most often translated as charity but, in fact, means "justice." Lacking other resources, David uses his physical strength to help prepare and deliver meals to those who are poor.

Holocaust

The theme of the Holocaust is central to only two respondents. Sara, whose journey was discussed earlier, is a child of survivors. She understood her turning to Orthodox observance and her giving birth to and raising Jewish children as a correction for the horrors of the Holocaust. Andrea, the only convert to Judaism among the respondents, desires not to belong to a people who could perpetuate something as evil as the Holocaust. This intertwines with a desire to transcend nature and not be confined by or be a slave to natural forces. Sociologically, her decision to convert can be understood as a transformation of an ascribed status into an achieved one.[20] In this sense, she understands her act of conversion as transcending nature in that she is no longer bound by the social and religious definitions of her birth heritage.

Jewish Continuity

For Sara, having children and being concerned with family is a direct expression of the continuing struggle of the Jewish people to be victorious over the effects of the Holocaust. This meaning is discussed earlier as her *life motif*, "confronting the Holocaust." Concern with children and family has a related though different meaning for Kenny. His *life motif* of *dor v'dor*, from "generation to generation" is poignantly symbolized by the *b'rit milah*, the ritual circumcision of a male child. The *b'rit milah* is a sign of the covenant between the Jewish Nation and God. Kenny's concern with family and children enables him to continue the chain of Jewish Tradition. Jewish continuity, in other words is the theme of his *life motif* symbolically expressed in the ritual circumcision, the *b'rit milah* of his son.

Social Justice

The theme of social justice is central to Linda's narrative, discussed earlier. Desiring to build a better world, she was involved in various social action organizations only to be disappointed by the incongruities between political position and personal behavior. In one example, she found that the desire to build a better world did not prevent the person from cheating on a spouse. In another example, she found that being the leader of an anti-poverty effort did not stop the person from stealing from her own organization. In Orthodox Judaism, Linda found not only what she perceived as a revolutionary vision of the world but also a blueprint of how to achieve it. For Linda, a more perfect and more moral world was only possible when the

Authenticity

Honesty and authenticity are central themes in many of the *ba'alei teshuvah* narratives.[21] Specifically, the respondents expressed concern that they not adopt religiously mandated behaviors that did not truly reflect their inner selves. There was the desire, in other words, that outwardly expressive behavior should match their inner feelings and understandings. This approach reflects a concern with the authenticity of their actions and, ultimately, their life. It is a concern expressed in specific issues like *sniut*, or modesty, the requirements of appropriate dress and body covering. The concern is expressed in a more general way as well. For example, Linda says that "As I went through the process of becoming religiously observant, I always tried to internalize the ideas behind the *mitzvoth* before starting to practice them. You know, I did not want to just do things because I was supposed to. I wanted to understand their meaning, to feel inside of me that it was the right thing to do." This idea is expressed in several of the journey narratives.

Daniel uses the concept of authenticity in a broader and slightly different sense when he speaks of a desire to live as an *authentic* Jew. His grandmother epitomized his image of an "authentic Jew," and his familiarity with her life enabled him to respond immediately when he found a path through which he could achieve this authenticity in his life.

Personal Responsibility

The theme of personal responsibility is present in all of the journeys. Without a sense of personal responsibility for one's life, the requisite characteristics required to bring about radical life change would be lacking. In David's story, however, this theme is his *life motif*. His decision to observe the commandments coincided with his decision to leave his parents' home and move into his own apartment. The pivotal ritual in his story is his *tefillin*, worn by men in the daily prayer service once they become thirteen years old. It is at this age, that of *bar mitzvah*, when a boy becomes responsible for the observance of the commandments and, therefore, a full member of the community. Consequently, the theme of personal responsibility is central to David's journey narrative.

Commitment Dimensions

Since commitment is the essential and central action required of a person who becomes a *ba'al(at) teshuvah*, it is appropriate to examine the interview data with reference to Rosabeth Moss Kanter's three dimensions of commitment.[22] Instrumental commitment refers to a commitment to the organization; affective commitment refers to persons in the group; and moral commitment refers to a commitment to the rules, regulations, ideas, and mores of the group. These dimensions can be analytically separated but they are deeply intertwined in life.

For the purpose of discussion, these commitment dimensions are separated with reference to the *life motifs* of the respondents. Instrumental commitment is understood, therefore, as a reference to or concern with belonging both to the Jewish Nation and with its continuity; affective commitment refers to persons who become *ba'alei teshuvah* because of a personal relationship or are primarily attracted to the relationships embedded in Jewish communal life, or both. The third dimension, moral commitment, refers to persons for whom the ideals, ideas, and way of life found in the learning, study, and observance of Torah are paramount.

Orthodox observance requires a great amount of Jewish education, and because of this, the latter dimension constitutes an essential component in the decision of all persons who become *ba'alei teshuvah*. Both men and women must know how to observe the commandments.[23] It is important to point out that the categorization of commitment based on *life motifs* does not imply less than full commitment in all three dimensions by the *ba'alei teshuvah* interviewed for this study. In some *life motifs*, the commitment dimensions overlap and so they may be counted and discussed more than once.

Instrumental Commitment

Three persons, one man and two women, may be said to have entered on the basis of instrumental commitment—that is, commitment to the continuity of the Jewish People. Kenny focused on the *b'rit milah* of his son, an unambiguous symbol of Jewish continuity. Concern with the issue of Jewish continuity is also central to the *life motif* of Sarah who understood her choice to live an Orthodox Jewish life as symbolic of the rebirth and victory of the Jewish People after the devastation of the Holocaust. In her travels through Europe, Andrea decides to convert because she did not want to belong to a people who could commit a Holocaust. Rather, she chose to belong to the Jewish People.

Affective Commitment

Respondents for whom attraction to the community and individual relationships were primary determinants in their decision to become *ba'alei teshuvah* include three men and one woman. Daniel accompanied his friend to hear Rebetzin Jungreis, a person known to give passionate, emotional speeches that open a person to becoming religiously observant. In his narrative, Daniel notes that a relationship with his religiously observant grandmother provided a critical and sustaining influence in his life and was a source of personal knowledge for the ideas and themes expressed by Rebetzin Jungreis. Pinchas followed the example of his wife who became a *ba'alat teshuvah*. Additionally, he describes his attraction to Jewish Orthodoxy as "it's the community." The *life motif* of David's journey is the ritual *tefillin*, which signifies the communal and individual responsibilities incumbent upon Jewish men. In addition, however, David notes his initial attraction to the people he used to watch from the living room window in his parent's home as they went to and from the Orthodox synagogue down the block. He wanted to be like them. Likewise, he is concerned that he fulfills his obligation to the community, which leads him to take on specific work with charitable community organizations. Leslie, the only woman for whom the affective dimension is primary, was persuaded to return to religion because of the better quality of family life that she saw because of her son's enrollment in a yeshiva.

Moral Commitment

The dimension of moral commitment refers to those persons for whom the ideals and ideas of Judaism are a central element in their decision to become *ba'alei teshuvah* as reflected in the *life motifs* of their journey narratives. Nine persons, six women, and three men, fit this category. Leah responded emotionally to her experience of God during summer camp when she was a youth. Once she began to learn in an Orthodox yeshiva, she understood the meaning of her experience as the obligation to live as an Orthodox Jew. This symbolized the essence of her life purpose and *life motif* of service to God. Naomi and Selma responded to the meanings of Jewish life as symbolized in the Sabbath celebration. Ruthie found a life of spiritual purity and authenticity in a lifestyle guided by Torah. For Tamar, being part of a transcendent spiritual reality was central; she found this in her commitment to a religiously Orthodox Jewish life. Linda sought a harmony between the physical and moral realms, expressed in the tenets of Orthodox Jewish observance. Similarly, Ya'acov also found the congruency for which he was searching in the teachings and ritual observance commanded by the Torah. Daniel's understanding of Jewish authenticity is likewise expressed in religious observance. In his search for truth, Ari found satisfaction only when he began the intellectually challenging process of learning Torah and living within the life structure of Orthodox observance.

Gender Analysis

Davidman and Greil[24] found that women were more likely to enter through personal contacts and men were more likely to be active seekers. This finding is consistent with the gender roles of traditional societies such as found in religious communities. In the study described herein, however, these roles seem reversed. Women were more likely to be the active seekers and the men were more likely to enter through personal contacts. The moral dimension, which includes ideals, ideas, and norms attracted more women than men. Men were more likely to enter because of affective ties. This analysis suggests that the substratum of meaning that underlies traditional role behaviors needs to be explored if they are to be understood and appreciated for the personal differences and complexity of meanings they represent. It is, after all, men who have the requirement to be a part of a prayer *minyan*, which makes them "count" as members of the community.

Discussion

In this study, the *life motif* that emerges from a journey narrative is understood to express the meanings that bridge and, thereby, connect an individual's meaning system to the traditional paradigm of Jewish identity. Methodologically, the identification of a *life motif* in a person's journey offers a window into an individual's personal meaning structure or cosmology and its consequences for life development. It is what enables the transformation of behavior required to belong to a religious community. Understanding this personal cosmology is necessary to achieve a deeper comprehension of the reasons a person becomes a *ba'al teshuvah*,

becomes a part of the Jewish community, and, thereby, assumes a Jewish identity.

The diversity of *life motifs* points to the idiosyncratic nature of the connection that pulls or draws a person to become a *ba'al(at) teshuvah*. Because there are so many points at which a person can be pulled in and enter Judaism, *kiruv* programs present as full a picture of Orthodox Jewish life as possible. Especially effective in this approach is the Lubavitch sect that sends out emissaries to communities where they settle and then open their homes for prayer services, learning Torah, have guests on the Sabbath, and establish a place, a *makom* to which and within which a person may find and develop his Jewish identity or as Steinsalz (1980)[25] would define it, his Jewish *neshama* or soul.[26] Importantly, the emissaries become a model of the Jewish family to which *ba'alei teshuvah* aspire.[27]

Because a greater scope of activity falls within the purview of religious action within Orthodox Judaism, there are a greater number of religious activities or rituals to which people may become attracted and attached. Once having made a commitment, there are also a greater number of spiritual and ritual pathways along which people may express themselves and still remain fully within the religious structure. In effect, this reverses the logic for leaving fundamentalist sects earlier in the last century when the appeal of "Progress," the idea that humankind was "progressing" especially due to developments in science and technology, constituted a far greater pull in society than anything today. At that time, the very inclusiveness of Orthodox observance was perceived as a restrictive barrier to participation in the modern world.

For the *ba'al(at) teshuvah*, expression of one's *life motif* within an Orthodox framework constitutes the personally integrative force in her life. Religiously based ideology, theology, and ritual practice are conceptually integrated into a personal meaning framework and held together by this *life motif*. As such, it provides the focal point for merging the psychological and sociological dimensions of the change process. It provides a vehicle by which to transcend personal understandings and, thus, enables a person to make and retain his or her commitment to the multiple facets present in a religious community.

References

1. Lynn Davidman, "Accommodation and Resistance to Modernity: A Comparison of Two Contemporary Orthodox Jewish Groups," *Sociological Analysis* 51 (1990): 35–51; Lynn Davidman, *Tradition in A Rootless World: Women Turn to Orthodox Judaism* (Berkeley, CA: University of California Press (1991); Herbert M, Danzger, *Returning To Tradition: The Contemporary Revival of Orthodox Judaism* (New Haven, CT: Yale University Press, 1989); and Debra Renee Kaufman, *Rachel's Daughters: Newly Orthodox Women* (New Brunswick, NJ: Rutgers University Press, 1993).
2. Lynn Davidman, *Becoming Un-Orthodox: Stories of Ex-Hasidic Jews* (New York: Oxford University Press, 2015); Shulem Deen, *All Who Go Do Not Return: A Memoir* (Minneapolis: Greywolf Press, 2015); Reva Mann, *The Rabbi's Daughter: A Memoir* (New York: Dial Press: A Division of Random House, 2007); and Hella Winston, *Unchosen: The Hidden Lives of Hasidic Rebels* (Boston: Beacon Press, 2005).
3. An excellent study of this process is by Helen Rose Fuchs Ebaugh in her book, *Becoming an Ex: The Process of Role Exit* (Chicago: University of Chicago Press, 1988).
4. Farber, Roberta Rosenberg, "Creative Decision-Making and the Construction of A Modern Jewish Identity," in *Jews in America: A Contemporary Reader*, ed. Roberta Rosenberg Farber and Chaim I. Waxman (Hanover: University Press of New England. 1999).
5. Debra Renee Kaufman discusses the use of narrative as a way to understand the individual experience in "Demographic Storytelling: The Importance of Being Narrative," *Contemporary Jewry* 34 (2014): 61–73.
6. Lynn Davidman, "Accommodation and Resistance to Modernity: A Comparison of Two Contemporary Orthodox Jewish Groups," *Sociological Analysis* 51 (1990): 35–51; Lynn Davidman, *Tradition in A Rootless World: Women Turn to Orthodox Judaism* (Berkeley, CA: University of California Press, 1991); Davidman and Greil, "Gender and the Experience of Conversion," 83–100; and M. Herbert Danzger, *Returning To Tradition: The Contemporary Revival of Orthodox Judaism* (New Haven, CT: Yale University Press, 1989). A significant exception is the work of Debra Renee Kaufman, who interviewed women who were living as Orthodox Jews. Her work includes "Patriarchal Women: A Case Study of Newly Orthodox Jewish Women," *Symbolic Interaction* 12, no. 2 (Fall 1989): 299–314 and *Rachel's Daughters: Newly Orthodox Women* (New Brunswick, NJ: Rutgers University Press, 1993).
7. See Lynn Davidman and Arthur L. Greil, "Gender and the Experience of Conversion: The Case of 'Returnees' to Modern Orthodox Judaism," *Sociology of Religion* 54, no. 1 (1993): 83–100; note on p. 87 that "becoming a *ba'al* and *ba'alat teshuvah* can be classified as a conversion process insofar as it involves a radical change in belief system and way of life." This paper concurs with the understanding that *ba'alei teshuvah* experience a radical life change.
8. My discussion of these perceptual forms is primarily based on the works of Susanne K. Langer, *Philosophy In a New Key: A Study in the Symbolism of Reason, Rite, and Art* (New York: A Mentor Book: The New American Library, 1942); and Susanne K. Langer, *Feeling and Form: A Theory of Art Developed From Philosophy in A New Key* (New York: Charles Scribner's Sons, 1953).
9. Joseph B. Soloveitchik, "The Lonely Man of Faith," *Tradition* 7, no. 2 (Summer 1965): 6–67.
10. Ibid., 60.
11. Roberta Rosenberg Farber, "Creative Decision-Making and the Construction of A Modern Jewish Identity," in *Jews in America: A Contemporary Reader*, ed. Roberta Rosenberg Farber and Chaim I. Waxman (Hanover, MA: University Press of New England, 1999) and Iddo Tavory, *Summoned: Identification and Religious Life in a Jewish Neighborhood* (Chicago: University of Chicago Press, 2016).
12. Daniel J. Levinson, *The Seasons of a Man's Life* (New York: Ballantine Books, 1978).
13. Davidman and Greil, "Gender and the Experience of Conversion," 83–100.
14. Ibid., 89.
15. Ibid.
16. Ibid.
17. Ibid.
18. Rosabeth Moss Kanter, *Commitment and Community: Communes and Utopias in Sociological Perspective* (Cambridge: Harvard University Press, 1972).
19. Herbert M. Danzger, *Returning To Tradition*, 1989.
20. See Phillip E. Hammond and Kee Warner, "Religion and ethnicity in Late-Twentieth-Century America," *The Annals of the American Academy of Political and*

Social Science, 527 (1993): 55–66 for a discussion of religion as achieved status.
21. See Charles Taylor for an analysis of the importance and use of this concept in contemporary society, in *The Ethics of Authenticity* (Cambridge, MA: Harvard University Press, 1991).
22. Kanter, *Commitment and Community*, 1972.
23. For different perspectives on women in Orthodox Judaism, see Susan Starr Sered, *Women as Ritual Experts: The Religious Lives of Elderly Jewish Women in Jerusalem* (Oxford: Oxford University Press,1992); Tamar El-Or, *Educated and Ignorant: Ultraorthodox Jewish Women and Their World*, trans. Haim Watzman (Boulder: CO: Lynne Rienner Pub., 1994); Sylvia Barack Fishman, *A Breath of Life: Feminism in the American Jewish Community* (New York: The Free Press, 1993); and Sylvia Barack Fishman, "Negotiating Egalitarianism and Judaism: American Jewish Feminisms and Their Implications for Jewish Life," in *Jews in America: A Contemporary Reader*, eds. Roberta Rosenberg Farber and Chaim I. Waxman (Hanover, NH: University Press of New England, 1999).
24. Davidman and Greil, "Gender and the Experience of Conversion," 1993:83–100.
25. Adin Steinsaltz, *The Thirteen Petalled Rose*, trans. Yehuda Hanegbi (New York: Basic Books, 1980).
26. Adam S. Ferziger, "From Lubavitch to Lakewood: The *Chabadization* of American Orthodoxy," *Modern Judaism* 33, no. 2 (2013): 101–24); Adam S. Ferziger, *Beyond Sectarianism: The Realignment of American Orthodox Judaism* (Detroit, MI: Wayne State University Press, 2015); Sue Fishkoff, *The Rebbe's Army: Inside the World of Chabad-Lubavitch* (New York: Schocken, 2003); and Chaim I. Waxman, "The Haredization of American Orthodox Jewry," *Jerusalem Letter/Viewpoints*, February 15 (1998) (Jerusalem: JPCA).
27. In his comprehension study of the *ba'alei teshuvah* movement, Danzger notes that "In Orthodox Judaism, family is the central plausibility structure. Within the family the individual acts out the central roles and rituals of religion" (see Danzger, *Returning To Tradition*, 43).

Mipnei Darkei Shalom: The Promotion of Harmonious Relationships in the Mishnah's Social Order

Simcha Fishbane

Abstract

This paper will examine the principal of *mipnei darkei shalom* (in the interest of peace) as it manifests itself in the social order of Mishnah. This principle was used by the rabbis to modify putative laws sometimes explicitly stated in Mishnaic texts and at other times only implied. The Mishnah presents its reader with ten cases of *mipnei darkei shalom*. Before examining the cases, I first present eight assumptions on which Mishnah is based. These assumptions are used to analyze the ten cases and search out the components that motivate and justify the rabbis' changing of an accepted law. Based upon my conclusions from the analysis of *mipnei darkei shalom*, I apply the Durkheim school of social theory to our evidence to better understand the social and cultural ideal world of Mishnah and its structure as presented by an early Palestinian rabbinic group.

My intention is that this essay is to offer a better understanding of the sociology and culture of the 'world' as defined by and in Mishnah's substance, even if that world does not mirror any contemporary or historical Palestinian Jewish world.

The Constitution of the United States has a preamble that states the goal of democracy is to create an environment of tranquility. Judaism is not a democratic religion *per se*, but includes many aspects that advocate democratic traditions. This paper will examine the principal of *mipnei darkei shalom* (in the interest of peace) as it manifests itself in the social order of Mishnah. The application of this concept creates an environment of peaceful and mutual respect between all persons irrelevant of their race or religion. This principle was used by the rabbis to modify putative laws sometimes explicitly stated in Mishnaic texts and at other times only implied. In total, the Mishnah presents its reader with ten cases of *mipnei darkei shalom*. I will first present eight assumptions on which Mishnah, in general, is based. These assumptions will be employed to analyze each case and search out the components that motivate and justify the rabbis' changing of an accepted law. Based upon my conclusions of the analysis of *mipnei darkei shalom*, I will then apply the Emile Durkheim school of social theory to our evidence—to better understand the social and cultural ideal world of Mishnah and its structure as presented by an early Palestinian rabbinic group.

Methodological Considerations

Scholars such as Neusner and Lightstone as well as my own work have written on the nature and problems of defining an approach to Mishnah in detail;[1] therefore, I will simply note them here in brief.

Mishnah is a highly redacted document. Lightstone describes Mishnah as a "distinct literary *oeuvre*, authored, not simply compiled, by some person or persons with their own agenda, outlook, style, purpose, and social provenance."[2] This work, the entire corpus, can be viewed as a self-consistent whole. Thus, Mishnah contains not only authoritative modes of behavior but also its author's message.

Mishnah represents the rabbis' view of an ideal Temple-centered society. In this ideal society, the Jerusalem Temple (destroyed in 70 CE)[3] and its related institutions stand and occupy the center 130 or so years after the Temple—everything related to it was destroyed.[4] Although there are sections or statements in Mishnah that would be relevant and can be applied to the functioning of a rabbinic post-Temple culture, these appear within the Mishnaic document that represents the Temple society. Therefore, it can only be suggested that these statements, even though they are culturally relevant, are focused on the synchronic message of the Mishnah.

In a temple-structured culture, the religious authority is the priest. In the post-Temple era, the rabbis saw themselves as the inheritors of this role, including the authority that it could embrace. The Mishnah often implicitly (and at times explicitly) manifests the importance of the rabbis within an idealized Temple society.[5]

The Mishnah, amongst the earliest authoritative rabbinic documents in our possession, offers a synchronic message. It also puts forward a diachronic view of society, and both these views serve to view the Mishnah's present order as an ideal Temple-focused society. The purpose of this essay is to seek out the message of the redactor concerning *mipnei darchei shalom* within its constructed Temple society and not to understand or shine light on the actual Palestinian culture and society of the rabbis during the third century.

As a rabbinic document, with its resolve to create a social structure for the rabbinic Jew, boundaries were created that excluded any outsider, such as the Gentile.[6] Thus, the focus of Mishnah is on the Jew. The only concern for the outsider is that which affects the life of the Jew but not of the outsider himself. The Mishnah's concern is to protect the rabbinic Jew from various types of threats or dangers, be they economic, religious, or security related.

Post-Mishnaic, Tannaic documents, Tosefta and midreshei ha-halakhah are often considered as statements not utilized by the Mishnah redactor but still having parallel authority. This essay takes an alternate view.[7] If we follow the suggestion that Mishnah is a tightly redacted document, any additional monograph would suggest the redactors had an alternate agenda. An examination of Tosefta compiled in the aftermath of Mishnah would suggest a document whose development was "dependent" upon Mishnah but was not Mishnah. Neusner[8] describes Tosefta in metaphorical terms, as a "vine on a trellis. It has no structure of its own but most commonly cites and glosses a passage in Mishnah, not differentiating its forms and wording of sentences from those of the cited passage.... The Tosefta covers nearly the whole of Mishnah's program but has none of its own." Tosefta is not Mishnah and does not necessarily seek to convey the same message as that of the Mishnah's redactor(s). Neusner,[9] in two approaches, offers a greater in-depth understanding of the relationship between Mishnah and Tosefta. First, he states: "Pericopae, which clearly present a more refined, more subtle, or more complicated picture of the same law as found in Mishnah, must be regarded as developments of Mishnah's pericopae and, therefore, as a commentary generated by Mishnah itself, not by considerations absent in Mishnah" (p. 3). Second, he refers to "autonomous" or "independent" items proffering the following: "Tosefta gives essentially the same principle as Mishnah, but in its own formulation or with its own examples." They are a (secondary) supplement to Mishnah . . . i.e., a collection of additional materials relevant to but not found in Mishnah will then apply to the autonomous and independent materials." (p. 3). The current essay is concerned with Mishnah. Therefore, following Neusner's lead, I will only refer to Tosefta when it serves as a commentary or as an exegesis to Mishnah, or are a commentary on individual pericope and not Mishnah as a complete document (p.4).

The redactor of Mishnah was not always forthcoming regarding clarification of the laws. Laws dependent on Torah passages are conspicuously absent. Statements based on basic principles are ignored and then, subsequently, laws that require elucidation are presented. The rabbi-teacher had the following answers and had to be petitioned for the explanations, as is demonstrated in our discussion below.

Mipnei Darchei Shalom

The term *shalom* is most commonly translated as *peace*. This, however, is only one way it is used, for the term often appears as a way to greet and part from people. It is also explained as meaning completeness, wholeness, health, welfare, safety, soundness, tranquility, prosperity, perfection, fullness, rest, harmony, or congeniality,[10] the absence of agitation or discord. An additional name for God is Shalom. In Mishnah, it is used as peace or something that can be referred to as a harmonious or congenial relationship.

Mipnei darkhei shalom appears in Mishnah twelve times within five separate mishnayot: Tractate M. Shabiit 4:3 (once); M. Shebit 5:9 (twice); Tractate M. Gittin 5:8 (eight times); M. Gittin 5:9 (twice); and Tractate M. Sheqalim 1:3 (once). The mishanayot in Tractate Gittin presents an overall summary and presentation of the Mishnah's entire occurrences of *mipnei darchei shalom*, except for the individual case in M. Sheqalim. Therefore, we will focus on Tractates Gittin (Table 1) and Shekalim (Table 2), but not Shabiit.

TABLE 1. M. Gittin 5:8[11]

	A.	And these rules did they state in the interest of peace:
I	B.	A priest reads first, and afterward a Levite, and afterward an Israelite, in the interest of peace.
II	C.	They prepare an *erub* in the house where it was first placed, in the interest of peace.
III	D.	A well nearest to the stream is filled first, in the interest of peace.
IV	E.	Traps for wild beasts, fowl, and fish are subject to the rules against stealing in the interest of peace.
	F.	Yose says, "It is stealing beyond any doubt."
V-G.		Something found by a deaf-mute, an idiot, and a minor is subject to the rule against stealing, in the interest of peace.
	H.	Yose says, "It is stealing beyond any doubt."
VI	I.	A poor man beating the top of an olive tree-
	J.	what is under it [the tree] is subject to the rule against stealing, in the interest of peace.
	K.	Yose says, "It is stealing beyond any doubt."
VII	L.	They do not prevent poor gentiles from collecting produce under the laws of Gleaning [*leket*], the Forgotten Sheaf [*shichikhah*], and the Corner of the Field [*peah*], in the interest of peace.

TABLE 2. M. Gittin 5.9

VIII	A.	A woman lends a sifter, sieve, handmill, or oven to her neighbor who is suspected of transgressing the law of the Seventh Year,
	B.	but she should not winnow or grind wheat with her,
IX	C.	The wife of a *haber* lends the wife of an *am haaretz* a sifter and a sieve.
	D.	She sifts, winnows, grinds, and sifts wheat with her.
	E.	But once she has poured water into the flour, she may not come near her,
	F.	for they do not give assistance to transgressors.
	G.	And all these rules they stated only in the interest of peace.
X-H.		They give assistance to gentiles in the Seventh year but not Israelite.
XI-I.		And they inquire after their welfare,
	J.	in the interest of peace.

TABLE 3. Sheqalim 1:3

A. On the fifteenth of that same month [Adar] they set up money changers' tables in the provinces.
B. On the twenty-fifth [of Adar] they set them up in the Temple.
C. Once they were set up in the Temple, they begin to exact pledges [from those who had not paid the tax in specie].
D. From whom do they exact a pledge?
E. Levites, Israelites, proselytes, and freed slaves,
F. But not from women, slaves, and minors.
G. Any minor in whose behalf the father began to pay the sheqel does not again cease [to pay].
H. And they do not exact a pledge from priests,
I. For the sake of peace.

As Basser and Basser correctly point out,[12] *mipnei darkhei shalom* refers to the need to establish standards of behavior to avoid conflict *in potential*: "This rubric offers protocols to avoid undue strife. These protocols override or amend either the intention or the explicit rulings of the Mishnaic rabbis." The issue to be considered is whether the concept of *mipnei darkhei shalom* amends or enhances an existing law. Why, in some cases, does the law transform a thing that is permitted into a prohibition, while in others it overrides a rabbinic ruling prohibiting something—to then allow it? In my analysis of such cases involving *mipnei dakchei shalom*, I will explore this query in the following set of aforementioned cases:

Case 1: "A priest reads first, and afterward a Levite, and afterward an Israelite, in the interest of peace."

This ruling is based upon a discussion of reading the Sefer Torah discussed in Mishnah Tractate Megillah 4:2, 4. These mishnayot discuss the number of individuals who are to be invited to read from the Torah (during the prayer service on days that the Torah is read in the synagogue), but no specific category of persons is identified. The Mishnah Horayot 3:8, while not specifically referring to Sefer Torah, presents the established hierarchy for the Mishnah's world, repeated below:

A. A priest takes precedence over a Levite, a Levite over an Israelite, an Israelite over a *mamzer*, a *mamzer* over a *Netin*, a *Netin* over a proselyte, a proselyte over a freed slave.
B. Under what circumstances?
C. When all of them are equivalent.
D. But if the *mamzer* was a disciple of a sage and a high priest was an *am haaretz*, the *mamzer* who is a disciple of a sage takes precedence over a high priest who is an *am haareetz*.

Although not explicitly stated, this division of status discussed in the above mishnah should also include Torah reading—the educated rabbi would supersede the priest. The rabbis, in this instance, where it is an issue of honor rather than of authority or financial implications, for the sake of harmonious relationships relinquish their prior place of honor.[13] In the Mishnah's perceived ideal Temple society, in which the priest is the religious leader, they, the priests, still enjoyed a place of symbolic honor. The rabbis chose to apply the principle "in the interest of peace" to alter and override an existing ruling. The rabbi, the inheritors of the priests, even with this awarded honor, still ruled.

Case 2: "They prepare an *erub* in the house where it was first placed, in the interest of peace."

TractateS Sabbath and Erubin both discuss the Torah prohibition against carrying any object from one domain to another on the Sabbath. One scenario regards cases when houses in an urban area were constructed within courtyards (common during late antiquity). In order to permit individuals to carry objects from their houses into the courtyard (*hatzer*) and vice-versa, an *erub hatzarot* is created. The rabbinic process requires that all the neighbors place food items in one of the courtyard houses before Shabbat. The *erub hatzarot*, thus, organizes all these domiciles into a single domain in which carrying is permitted.

There are various options for obtaining these food items. One person from the courtyard can contribute the food, or the other residents can jointly contribute towards the amount of food required to make the *erub hatzarot*. There are instances, as discussed in Mishnah Erubin 7:11, in which money is donated towards the purchase of food items.

Our paradigm, which discusses *erub hatzarot*, seems to imply that in order to reduce clashes between neighbors, maintain harmonious relationships, and not insult the householder, the *erub hatzarot* should remain in the home of the residence where it was initially placed. I believe there is an additional consideration implied in this instance—the possibility for financial gain on the part of the homeowner where the *erub hatzarot* is assigned. Although the food products belong to everyone in the courtyard, after the Sabbath, this individual would have the opportunity to acquire it before the others. As mentioned above, there are also possibilities for the transfer of monies. Although it is no more than a possibility, this consideration would offer greater clarity in understanding why *mipnei darkhei shalom* is a factor in placing the *erub* and amending the law.[14]

Case 3: "A well nearest to the stream is filled first, in the interest of peace."

This mishnah would seem[15] to portray a scenario in which a channel flows from a river alongside a series of fields. The owners of these fields use the channel's water to irrigate their fields. To avoid the possibility of water drying out before the fields are irrigated, the owners dug cisterns at the edge of their fields to collect water from the channel. To avoid conflict between the field owners as to who had first rights to the water from the channel, the Mishnah, applying the principle of *mipnei darkei shalom,* decides who has first entitlement to the water.

The Mishnah, as well, chooses to amend situations that could lead to conflict and strife. There is no halakhic ruling that the principle "*in the interest of peace*" would be required to have an override. Rather, this is a financial issue in which the strongest person would win and, thereby, cause a clash.

Case 4: "Traps for wild beasts, fowl, and fish are subject to the rules against stealing in the interest of peace."

The following three cases (4, 5, 6) are concerned with the acquisition (*kinyan*) of various objects through different methods. Our example case deals with acquisition through one's property or utensils rather than by placing or dragging it by hand.[16] Mishnah is not explicit in defining the principle of acquisition through the use of an individual's utensil with a receptacle attached to a base (*beit kibul*).[17] It is implicitly alluded to in an example of divorce in Mishnah Gittin 8:1, which says, "He who threw a writ of divorce to his wife . . . [if he threw it] into her bosom or into her basket she is divorced." The basket becomes the acquisition since it has a *beit kibul* while the trap does not; thus, preventing its owner from legally acquiring the catch. The Mishnah employs the principle *of mipnei darkei shalom* to amend the law of *kinyan* and allow the owner of the trap to keep the prey. The rabbis permit the trap owner to retain his catch, and the one who takes it is a thief.

Case 5: "Something found by a deaf-mute, an idiot,[18] and a minor is subject to the rule against stealing, in the interest of peace."

Although not stated explicitly in Mishnah, it is based on a principle that any Jews who fell within these three categories of persons (deaf-mute, idiot, minor) could not acquire property. For example, in Mishnah Baba Metzia 1:5, in discussing an object found by a minor, the

Mishnah informs us that such objects are not acquired (*kinyan*) but become the property of the father (after he makes a *kinyan*). These three categories of Jews were unable to own property and to conduct independent business transactions. The reason for the limitation on them was a lack of perceived mental capacity. This understanding was common during the Greco-Roman period by the Jews and Gentiles.[19] It is clarified in Mishnah Arakhin 1:1 in the discussion of the valuation of different type of individuals, including the use of one's monetary value of his body for determining a pledge amount to the Temple. The Mishnah rules that a *heresh, shoteh,* and *katan* may not dedicate such a valuation, since they are not mentally competent. A lack of mental capability for dealing with reality would also exclude the *heresh, shoteh,* and *katan* from making a *kinyan* on any object.

The Mishnah amends this law in prohibiting the taking of a found object for these three types of individuals. In this case, there is a clear possibility of monetary gain.

Case 6: "A poor man beating the top of an olive tree. What is under it [the tree] is subject to the rabbinic override forbidding others to take what has fallen to the ground. In the interest of peace, Yose says, 'it is stealing beyond any doubt.' "

The Mishnah commentaries explicate this scenario referring to the laws of Gleaning (*leket*), the Forgotten Sheaf (*shikhahah*), and the Corner of the Field (*peah*)—agricultural gifts awarded to a poor person.[20] The second individual claiming the right to the produce is forced to comply with this suggestion since an individual who is not poor has no right to these products, yet, if appropriated, they would be his—if not for the principle of *mipnei darkei shalom*. Again, this case is an issue of acquisition. The poor person shakes the tree, but since he does not hold the olives in his hand, he does not acquire them. Therefore, if another poor person grasped them first, if not for the case of *mipnei darkhei shalom*, they would belong to him.

The Mishnah, thus, amends a permitted circumstance and prohibits any other individual from acquiring the produce. I would like to suggest an additional consideration. The gifts offered to the deprived person can be his basic means of sustenance. If guidelines for receiving these assistances are not clearly and well defined, this could lead to brawls and possible damage to property, in our case that of the field's owner. The need for *mine dakhei shalom* would, therefore, go beyond a mere clash between two individuals and could result in financial loss to the owner of the property. The fear of violence from a poor person is implied in Mishnah Peah 4:4, which reads, "Peah, they [the poor] do not reap with sickles, and they do not uproot it [the field] with spades, lest they strike one another." This violent behavioral pattern found in a destitute individual could also result in physical and material damages.

Case 7: "They do not prevent poor gentiles from collecting produce under the laws of Gleaning [*leket*], the Forgotten Sheaf [*shichikhah*], and the Corner of the Field [*peah*] in the interest of peace."

Implied in Mishnah's statement, is that a poor Gentile is forbidden to receive gifts of produce. As stated above (work detail 5), Mishnah is not interested in the welfare of the Gentile but rather in that of the rabbinic Jew and the world of Mishnah.[21] The concern here is for the security of the destitute Jew seeking these gifts but there are also implications for financial gain/loss. As shown in the above case, the poor can tend towards violence. If the needy Gentile could not share in these gifts, that could lead to the destruction of property and, thus, to financial loss both for the Jew who is poor and for the proprietor of the field.

This amended ruling is designed to prevent gentiles from claiming that Jewish law discriminates between Jew and Gentile and is, thereby, intended to reduce conflict. Ultimately, the Jews gain, as it is in their interests to prevent enmity.

Case 8: "A woman lends a sifter, sieve, hand mill, or oven to her neighbor who is suspected of transgressing the law of the Seventh [Sabbatical] year, but she should not winnow or grind wheat with her [in the interest of peace]."

This statement first appears in Mishnah Shebiit 5:9. The Mishnah is discussing a case of a woman who is suspected of not observing the laws of the Sabbatical year and wants to lend an item that can be employed in the transgression of shebiit from one who does observe the laws of the Sabbatical year. To clarify: During the Seventh year in the land of Israel, one is prohibited from working the land or enjoying its produce in any fashion, and at a designated time must destroy food stored in the house from these fields. Our case concerns the cooking utensils, which normally would not be lent, as the receiver, who is suspected of ignoring the laws of the Seventh year, might use them with forbidden produce from the Sabbatical year.[22] Mishnah verses 6 and 7 of chapter 5 states that any utensil employed (during the Sabbatical year) for the purpose of transgression may not be sold. Selling is only permitted if the item can also be used for a permitted activity. Lending would fall under the same law. Therefore, our Mishnah would need to override the law, as it was considered prohibited to use the utensils. The assistance offered to the suspected woman would benefit her financially. For example, she would not need to buy or rent these items to use them domestically or for her business. In pre-industrial rural societies, women played an important economic role in the world of agriculture; they were core economic partners with men. Scott and Tilly correctly argue that women did work and women were necessary for the survival of the family unit (p. 41).[23] Their contribution, while being primarily in the home, it seems, could include the *family* fields. This contribution was essential for the family unit whose solidarity provides the basic framework for mutual aid, control, and socialization (p. 43).[24]

In the ideal world of Mishnah, women were also segregated and assigned specific roles. One can find in Mishnah at least a partial or limited division of labor between men and women. People resided in close proximity to one another, as demonstrated by the *hatzer*. Closeness gives rise to both great dependencies on each other as well as friction and conflict. Thus, the Mishnah rabbis choose to apply the principle of *mipnei darkei shalom* to a case that applied to women. They chose to subjugate these tensions by applying the principle of *mipnei darkhei shalom* as a way to override the law that forbade assisting a sinner.

Lending a vessel to the suspected woman would be of benefit to her financially since then she did not need to purchase a new one. The point of *mipnei darkei shalom* here is to avoid conflict caused by the usual strict application of laws,

Therefore, our mishnah would need to override the law, as the use of the utensils was considered as prohibited. The assistance offered to the suspected woman would benefit her financially. For example, she would not need to buy or rent these items to use domestically or for her business. As I stated above in the pre-industrial rural societies, women played an important economic role in the world of agriculture. They were core economic partners with men. Scott and Tilly correctly argue that women did work and that they were necessary for the survival of the family unit (p.41).[25] Their contribution was primarily in the home but also could include working the family fields. This was essential for the family unit whose solidarity provides the basic framework for mutual aid, control, and socialization (p. 43).[26]

Case 9: "The wife of a *haber* lends the wife of an *am hares* [suspected of not keeping the laws of purity] a sifter and a sieve. She may sift winnow, grind, and sift wheat with her. Nevertheless, once she has poured water into the flour [enabling the dough to contact impurity], she may not come near her, for they do not give assistance to transgressors. And all these rules they stated only in the "interest of peace."

Since both Mishnah cases discuss women, the consequences of their society's structure and assisting a potential sinner, the rabbi has grouped cases 8 and 9 together. Case 9 works on the same principle as 8 but is concerned with the violation of the laws of tithes and ritual purity (*tuma*) rather than the *haber*.[27] As in case 8, there are financial results from the cooperation of both women. In order to permit realization of Mishnah's view, it was necessary to override the law. Mishnah identifies two status levels of individuals, the *haber*, who is meticulous in the observance of Sabbatical, purity laws, and the *am haartez* (uneducated in Torah and rabbinical law), who is distrusted. There should be limited interaction between these different classes of women (as specified in Mishnah Demai 6:7 and 2:3), since the Mishnah is concerned that the wife of a *haber* would become ritually impure or eat from foods not tithed. Even so, in the interest of peace, the Mishnah overrides the law and offers restricted assistance from the wife of the *haber* to the wife of the *am haaretz* up to the point where the *tuma* becomes an actual danger and not just a concern.[28]

Case 10: "They give allow (real) assistance to [G]entiles in the Seventh year but not Israelites [in the interest of peace]."

This mishnah first appears in Shebiit 4:3, then in 5:9. It is later presented and summarized in Gittin 5:9. The opening of the Mishnah (in Shebiit 4:3) reads as follows:

> During the Sabbatical year [Jews] lease from gentiles fields newly ploughed [during that year for the purpose of cultivating them during the following year,] but (they do not [lease] from an Israelite [a field which he has plowed during the Sabbatical year, in violation of the law].

This opening is not repeated in the other two Mishnaic citations. It is clear throughout the entire Mishnah that the focus is upon the Jew and not the Gentile. The Gentile's role is to assist the Jew to better function in his world of Mishnah.

This case implies that even though the Land of Israel is holy and should not be worked by either Jew or Gentile on the Sabbatical year,[29] one cannot prohibit the Gentile from working the land. Thus, the Jew, if this were the only consideration, should not encourage the Gentile to work the land; that is, aside from the principle the rabbis applied of *mipnei darkei shalom*. By maintaining a harmonious relationship with the Gentile, the Jew will receive financial gain, by having a plowed field in the eighth year ready to plant, in addition to the security of friendship.

Case 11: "And they permit inquiring after [the Gentile's] welfare, in the interest of peace."

This statement, as in the case above, is first found in Mishnah Shabiit 4:3, then in 5:9. An examination of Mishnah will demonstrate that there is no discussion concerning a prohibition to greet pagan Gentiles even on their festivals when Mishnah prohibits various kinds of interaction with them. The Mishnah's concern is that any interface with pagan Gentiles during their religious festivals would encourage and enhance their practice of idol worship. There is no reference in Mishnah to any type of prohibition regarding asking after their welfare. To clarify the issue, one turns to Tosefta[30] in Abodah Zarah 1:2, where a discussion of pagan festivals clearly says, "Nor should one ask after their welfare. . . . But if one happened to come across [the pagan] in a routine way, he asks after his welfare with all due respect. They permit inquiring after the welfare of the gentiles on their festivals for the sake of peace."

I choose to view this Tosefta under the category of Mishnah clarification or commentary rather than as an autonomous Tosefta. Two issues are elucidated: first, that Mishnah is concerned with the different occasions when the pagan holiday was celebrated. Other than on these times (when it would be prohibited), it was permitted to greet the Gentile in a specific fashion. Second, the Tosefta clarifies that if not for the principle "for the sake of peace," it would be prohibited to ask after the well-being of the Gentile on their holiday. This is demonstrated in the language of Tosefta, identical to that of Mishnah, except that Tosefta adds the words "on their festival."

In the above case, the motivation for assisting the Gentile is economic. In our case, I suggest that it is primarily a security issue, as in case 7 concerning Peah, although financial loss is also conceivable. Religious holiday gatherings can be a time of incitement to violence and the destruction of property. The Mishnah is interested in the Jew and his welfare, not in the Gentiles. Thus, we need to look at these texts with only the rabbinic Jews' concerns in mind. If offering greetings on the pagan festival will offer greater security to the Jewish community, their physical well-being, and the protection of their property, one would seek to override the prohibitions.

Cases 10 and 11 as well as cases 8 and 9 are parallel in structure. Cases 8 and 10 override a law related to shabiit. Cases 9 and 11 are not related to shabiit but override a prohibition connected to the status of the person in the previous case. Ruling 9, which relates to women and appears in cases 8 and 11, relates to the Gentile who appears in 10.

Case 12: "And they do not exact a pledge from priests, for the sake of peace."

The Mishnah in Gittin omits the case in mishnah Sheqalim 1:4. Ancient custom saw in Exodus 30:12–16 a basis for all Israelites during the Temple period to give an annual tax of a half-shekel for community sacrifices. If a person could not pay the tax, the rabbis required the giving of a security pledge for the payment of the half-shekel tax. Priests were also required to contribute, and if they they did not, they too, strictly speaking, were subject to giving a security pledge despite their status. The authorities felt it necessary, as Safrai explains, to maintain the internal solidarity of the community by exempting them from giving security although they were expected to pay (p. 75).[31] Safrai's analysis, based upon Tosefta Menahot 13:18–19 and Zebahim 11:17, shows that the priests were aggressive when their financial gain was involved.[32] This behavior would explain why the rabbis of the Mishnah needed to employ the *mipnei darkei shalom* principle in order to avoid bickering and strife and to override the law obligating priests to give security.[33]

This ruling differs from the cases in Mishnah Gittin. In the Gittin, scenarios were all undisputed. Mishnah Sheqalim 1:4 demonstrates that not all tannaim were in agreement as to whether the priests should be exempted from paying the half shekel. The first opinion in Mishnah 1:4 exempts the priest from paying the half shekel, and, thus, they would also be exempted from giving collateral; therefore, the *mipnei darkei shalom* principle would not apply.

It is clear that there is financial gain as well as prestige for the priests in having an exemption from this tax security pledge. I would like to suggest that there is an additional advantage for the rabbis, who are the inheritors of the priests, through the inclusion of this law. Religious taxes took different forms after the destruction of the Jerusalem Temple when the half-shekel tax was no longer required. If the priests were exempt from a religious tax that could serve as a basis for the rabbis to expect exemptions from the religious taxes of their time.

SUMMARY OF *MIPNEI DARKEI* SHALOM IN MISHNAH

	Jew	Gentile	Harmony	Security	Financial gain	Amend law	Override law	Social status
Case 1	yes	no	yes	no	no	no	yes	high
Case 2	yes	no	yes	yes	yes	yes	no	middle

SUMMARY OF *MIPNEI DARKEI* SHALOM IN MISHNAH—CONTINUED

	Jew	Gentile	Harmony	Security	Financial gain	Amend law	Override law	Social status
Case 3	yes	no	yes	yes	yes	yes	no	middle-low
Case 4	yes	no	yes	yes	yes	yes	no	middle-low
Case 5	yes	no	yes	yes	yes	yes	no	low
Case 6	yes	no	yes	yes	yes	yes	no	low
Case 7	no	yes	no	yes	yes	no	implied	outsider
Case 8	yes	no	yes	no	yes	no	yes	low
Case 9	yes	no	yes	no	yes	no	yes	low
Case 10	no	yes	no	yes	yes	yes	no	outsider
Case 11	no	yes	no	yes	yes	no	yes	outsider
Case 12	yes	no	yes	yes	yes	no	yes	high

Summary and Concluding Remarks

It can be seen from the above cases that Mishnah is concerned with civil law and religious law,[34] primarily those regarding financial concerns, affecting varied strata of society, beginning with its leadership and concluding with the Gentile outsider. The Mishnah sought social stability and social order. Therefore, to avoid conflict and ensure a secure and stable society, the principle of *mipnei darkei shalom* was instituted to amend or override rabbinic stringencies that encompassed elements endangering this stability. The rabbis chose cases in which they applied the principle of "in the interest of peace" primarily in scenarios with financial implications. It was the area of economic relationships, interdependence, and cooperation that would most strongly impact the social solidarity of the collective community: what was required was the "moralization!" of economic relationships.

In order to understand how the above cases play a role in understanding the sociology and culture of the "ideal world" defined by Mishnah, I turn to the Durkheim's school of social theory. I do not believe that there is one neatly packaged world of Mishnah, but rather there is what appears as different variables, which are presented in this document. For example, we find that on the one hand Mishnah presents a Temple-based culture and on the other hand a third-century Palestinian social reality. Many pieces make up the puzzle of Mishnah. The topic of *mipnei darkei shalom* is only one piece in this puzzle, but it may reflect on, or inform, other texts or laws of Mishnah when all the pieces are examined and placed together.

Durkheim in his work *The Division of Labor in Society* presents his theory of society, moral consciousness, social order, and stability.[35] I do not believe that this theory in its entirety can be applied to the unpacking of the world of Mishnah. However, there are elements of the theory that, even taken out of context, can be used to understand the Mishnah's topic *mipnei darkei shalom* and, therefore, one segment of the Mishnah's ideal world.

Positive solidarity in society can be considered as playing an essential role in creating the social order; it is an entirely moral phenomenon. To achieve this, a legal system with a complete moral consciousness is necessary. Moral ideals and codes of conduct order the functioning of society, and when it is strong, it unites individuals in their social framework. This could then facilitate the basis of the authority necessary to retain the social order. The solidarity would result in what Mary Douglas terms a strong grid group.[36] A robust legal system in a diverse society as manifested in Mishnah brings people together. Solidarity overcomes the diversity and strengthens the collective. Furthermore, based upon our examples of *mipnei darkei shalom*, I suggest that if we apply the group grid cosmology to the ideal world of Mishnah we find that "there are visible rules about space and times related to social roles. Individuals do not, as such, transact with each other."[37] In other words, in this world, the individual is not the focus of this cosmology, as the individual's recognition would weaken the culture.

It also must be considered that, as in our case of Mishnah, religion and religious law often initiate moral consciousness. Moral bounds were provided by religion. In a religious social structure, morality is permeated with religion. Juridical life protects these moral bounds and is essential for ensuring social harmony. The rabbi's social order was religious in character and articulates moral behavior. Religion provided for all social aspects of their ideal society. The world of Mishnah had the maximum characteristics[38] for the development of a collective consciousness. Durkheim identifies these, which compose the collective consciousness of this religious social order, as the volume, intensity, rigidity, and content of the beliefs and values. For Durkheim the state was a moral agency.[39] The role of this body was to focus the collective representation on moral consciousness. For Mishnah it was the rabbi's role to take on the responsibility to implement the moral phenomenon into their ideal world, and to either develop or retain the stability required for that world and their authority. One tool they used to achieve these goals was the application of the principle *mipnei darkei shalom*.

REFERENCES

1. Jacob Neusner, *Judaism: The Evidence of the Mishnah* (Chicago: University of Chicago Press, 1981); Jacob Neusner, *Introduction to Rabbinic Literature* (New York: Doubleday, 1994); Jack N. Lightstone, *Mishnah and the Social Formation of the Early Rabbinic Guild*. Waterloo, Ont., Canada: Wilfrid University Press, 2002; and Simcha Fishbane, *Deviancy in Early Rabbinic Judaism* (Leiden, NL: Brill, 2007).
2. Lightstone, *Mishnah and the Social Formation*, 7.
3. As Cohn explains, in Naftali S. Cohn, *The Memory of the Temple and the Making of the Rabbis* (Philadelphia: University of Pennsylvania Press, 2013), 1–4, there was no one alive to testify to or even experience Temple life or ritual, and a new form of Jewish rabbinic ritual life was in the making. The Temple life, ritual, and society were chosen to serve the rabbis' agenda and enhance if not justify their authenticity and authority. As Jewish history has shown time and time again, when the new becomes the old, it acquires legitimacy.
4. See Lightstone, *Mishnah and the Social Formation*, 26.
5. Cohn's 2013 monograph focuses primarily on this hypothesis of the Mishnah placing the rabbi in the major role, even in the Temple society. I believe that Cohn's maximalist position is over-emphasized, but it is not the purpose of this essay is to take him to task. See Cohn, *Memory of the Temple*.
6. See Gary G. Porton, *Goyim: Gentiles and Israelites in Mishnah-Tosefta* (Atlanta: Brown University-Scholars Press, 1988).
7. This argument disclaiming the paralleling of Mishnah and Tosefta is developed in Jacob Neusner's *Tosefta: Its Structure and Its Sources* (Atlanta: Scholars Press, 1986).
8. Jacob S. Neusner, *Introduction to Rabbinic Literature* (New York: Doubleday, 1994), 129.
9. Neusner, *Tosefta: Its Structure and Its Sources*, 1–7.
10. Basser and Basser translate *mipnei darchei shalom* as "for the sake of congeniality," in Herbert W. Basser and Reena L. Basser, "Ideas of Human Social Concord and Discord in Judaism," *Research in Human Social Conflict*, edited by J. B. Gittler, vol. 12 (West Yorkshire, UK: Emerald Group Publishing, 2000), 147. I will demonstrate later in this essay that this translation is correct only for specific instances in Mishnah.
11. All translations of the Mishnah texts are based upon Jacob Neusner: *The Mishnah: A New Translation* (New Haven, CT: Yale University Press, 1988).
12. Basser and Basser, *Research in Human Social Conflict*, 147.
13. For a general discussion of honor and the priest to include Sefer Torah, See Shlomo Josef Zevin, ed. *Talmudic Encyclopedia*. Vol. 27. [Hebrew]

(Jerusalem: Talmudic Encyclopedia Institute, 2006), 196-214.
14. In his Mishnah commentary to our case, Maimonides suggests that this is related to a financial issue.
15. The Talmud 60b describes a scenario in which the last rather than the first cistern in the field receives the priority for the river's water.
16. See Mishnah Kidushin 1:4–5 and Baba Batra 5:7 for a discussion of *kinyan* by dragging an object.
17. Throughout, the tractate Mishnah Kelim clarifies that a utensil is an object with a proliferation. Although not relevant to Mishnah, the Babylonian Talmud Baba Batra 85a states this principle.
18. For a rabbinic discussion and definition of the deaf-mute and idiot, see Tzvi C. Marx, *Disability in Jewish Law* (London: Routledge, 2002), 96–127.
19. See Catherine Hezser, *Jewish Slavery in Antiquity*. (Oxford: Oxford University Press, 2005), 69-104.
20. Mishnah Pea 8:7–9 defines who is considered a poor person and may accept these gifts.
21. Tosefta in Gittin 5 offers an autonomous statement that the poor Gentiles are supported along with the Jew. I believe this to be a separate statement independent of the agenda of the redactor of Mishnah, with its own agenda.
22. Although the commentators intensively discuss this Mishnah, offering varying interpretations, I am looking at the direct implications of the Mishnah.
23. Joan W. Scott and Louise A. Tilly, "Women's work and the Family in the Nineteenth-Century Europe." *Comparative Studies in Society and History* 17, no. 1 (January 1975): 36–64.
24. Scott and Tilly, *Comparative Studies*, 43.
25. Ibid., 41.
26. Ibid., 43.
27. The prohibitions regarding the interactions between the *haber* and the *am haaretz* are clarified in Mishnah Demai, chapter 2.
28. For a detailed discussion of the relationship between the *am haaretz* and the *haber*, see Richard S. Sarason, *A History of the Mishnaic Law of Agriculture: A Study of Tractate Demai* (Leiden, NL: Brill, 1979), 1–21; and *Mishnah Sheviis*, rev., 1st ed., *ArtScroll Mishnah Series* (Brooklyn, NY: Mesorah Publications, 2000), 180-81.
29. This is implied in the passage in Leviticus 25:3, which states that the land should rest on the Seventh year. For a rabbinical discussion supporting this view; see *Talmud Yerushalmi Tractate Shebiit* [in Hebrew] (Jerusalem: Beth Midrash Hagavoah Bahalakhah Bahityashvut, 2006).
30. Translation of Tosefta is adapted from Neusner, 1969.
31. Shmuel Safrai, Zev Safrai, and Chana Saftai, eds., *Mishnat Eretz Israel with Historical and Sociological commentary*, vol. 109. Tractate Shakalim [Hebrew] (Jerusalem, Israel: E. M. Liphshitz Publishing House College, 2009).
32. Shmuel Safrai, Zev Safrai, and Chana Saftai, eds., *Mishnat Eretz Israel*, 73–74.
33. The Talmud chooses to explain this action by the rabbis because of the honor the priests deserve. The Mishnah implies otherwise.
34. In the case of Mishnah, it is difficult to differentiate between them.
35. Emile Durkheim, *The Division of Labor in Society* (New York: Free Press, 1997), 68-148; suggestions of reading are based on the translation of Giddens' 1973 introduction (1–50) and chapters 4, 5 and 6 (108–54).
36. Mary Douglas, *Cultural Bias* (London: Royal Anthropological Institute of Great Britain and Ireland, 1979).
37. Mary Douglas, *Cultural Bias*, 8.
38. For a discussion of each of these characteristics, see Anthony Giddens, ed., trans., *Emile Durkheim: Selected Writings* (Cambridge, New York: Cambridge University Press, 1973), 5.
39. Ibid., 18.

On the Unknown Soldier Symbol in Israeli Culture

Irit Dekel

Abstract

The "unknown soldier" symbol in Jewish Israeli commemorative discourse was referred to first by veneration in Avraham Stern's poem "Unknown Soldiers" (1932) and then by negation, such as in the popular Yehuda Amichai poem "We Do Not Have Unknown Soldiers" (1969). It is often cited and read in commemorative ceremonies. In negating this category, I argue, cultural strategies of remembrance and forgetting were used as recruiting mechanisms for missions of nation building, which demanded various forms of sacrifice that favor the collective over the individual. Reading the ways in which the "unknown soldier" symbol had been used in the Yishuv Jewish community and in Israel, I suggest that until the 1970s, losing one's life in battle was a way to regain one's name as an individual, while afterwards, the use of the symbol, whether negated or revered, points to the anonymity of an individual within a fragmented collective that does not necessarily venerate national sacrifice.

WE DO NOT HAVE UNKNOWN SOLDIERS

We do not have Unknown Soldiers.
We do not have the Unknown Soldier tomb
Whoever likes to rest his wreath
Should break apart[1] his wreath
To many flowers and divide them
To leaves and disperse them.
And all the dead return home
And they all have names.
[Yehuda Amichai][2]

"WE": THE ISRAELI COLLECTIVE AND THE FALLEN SOLDIER

The "unknown soldier" is a prominent symbol in the Jewish Israeli commemoration discourse,[3] mainly seen in commemorative texts, such as the much quoted Yehuda Amichai poem, which corresponds with an earlier poem by Avraham Stern, in 1932: "Unknown Soldiers."[4] Stern's poem cites Uri Zvi Greenberg's[5] poem that centers on unknown soldiers, both in reaction to the 1929 riots.[6] Stern set his poem to music; it was the anthem of the Irgun and subsequently became the anthem of the LEHI, a revisionist paramilitary group that violently resisted the British Mandate of Palestine. Since that time, it has been the anthem of the Israeli right wing and radical youth groups. The symbol of the unknown soldier has been central to right as well as to center and left ideas of national defense and militarism. Comparing Amichai's poem to that of Stern's, in Amichai, the speaker can be heard representing a collective voice— "We Do Not Have Unknown Soldiers" versus "We Are Unknown Soldiers" in Stern's poem.

Commemorative ceremonies for fallen soldiers often use Amichai's poem, in which the unknown soldier is negated: "we" do not have it. This negation differentiates the Israeli remembrance practices from those of Europe, described by Mosse in reaction to World War I and World War II.[7] Sivan points out the centrality of cited poetry and texts in commemorative rituals and their prevalence in other references to sacrifice.[8] Neiger, Meyers, and Zandberg describe how the use of music in memorial events creates a sonic memory, whereby certain songs—popular in commercial radio broadcasts—become identifiable with a commemorative and mourning ritual.[9] Stern's poem was part of such a canon. It was performed by self-described revisionists but also by mainstream popular singers, such as Shlomo Artzi and Yaffa Yarkoni in Israel in the 1960s and 1970s, who were often identified as supporting soldiers and the military. However, we should also remember that performances can simultaneously criticize militarism while often affirming it by separately supporting the army's missions and their consequences.

Nave considers poems as giving as well as reflecting shared meaning to historical events when a society includes them in its commemorative spaces.[10] Reciting poems and singing songs in whose center the unknown soldier was addressed, often critically, the glorification of anonymous sacrifice. Amichai's poem remains salient in commemoration discourse and high school literature instructions.[11] It is currently, in 2017, intermixed with the growing salience of Stern's poem within the current social and political climate of Israel. Thus, the symbol that developed in Europe to commemorate (and glorify) anonymous mass death, far from home fronts in World War I, became emblematic of an ongoing discourse on "war at home," in Israel. This phenomenon is in dialogue in Israeli commemoration by the Jewish imperative to remember every dead person, also salient in Holocaust remembrance ceremonies.

This article is a critical examination of the symbol of the unknown soldier in Israeli Jewish commemorative discourse. It contributes to a number of studies on militarism and its meaning in Israeli identity[12] and to understanding what is seen as a growing gap within the Israeli Jewish homogeneous "we"—whether along lines of class, ethnicity, religiosity, or age group.[13] This discussion will extend the range of these conversations, bringing the literature about the "unknown soldier" as a modernist nationalist invention [14] into the debate about Israel's case, so as to uncover a particular mechanism of collectivization (the "we do not have" of the "unknown soldiers") fraught with inner contradiction and unified by the willingness to sacrifice lives.

HISTORICAL USES OF THE UNKNOWN SOLDIER SYMBOL

As stated, an early reference to the unknown soldier as symbol in the Yishuv period was Avraham Stern's poem "Unknown Soldiers" from 1932. Stern's poem opens with the words "We are unknown soldiers, uniforms we have none / In death's shadow we march, in its terror / Volunteering to serve to the end of our days, / Only death from our duty can us sever."[15] According to Genossar,[16] the lyrical protagonist is not challenging the pioneer ideal, also based on sacrifice as one of its major pillars.[17] To the contrary, it tries to enlarge it to include the unknown soldier as a "covenant pair" to the pioneer, described in the poem in a futuristic fashion as a person who, enveloped by his own dark fate, is moved by an eternal willingness to fight and occupy. Stern's poem cites revisionist poet Uri Zvi Greenberg's own poem, with which he reacted to the 1929 Arab attacks on Jews and describes the pioneers as "kind of unknown soldiers." Indeed, Zvi Greenberg and Stern connect the European model of total sacrifice to the Jewish experience of resisting threat by using violence and tie the pioneer model to it.

The patriotic ideology was coupled with the idea that the national birth will be entangled with blood and, thereby, inevitably, the death of individuals will contribute to the existential victory of the nation. In this respect, Stern's poem "Unknown Soldiers," in which self-sacrifice is not only an unfortunate fate but a heroic aspiration of self-fulfillment, should be understood as an extreme case of Zionist martyrdom. In the past ten years, there are many new performances of Stern's song. His lyrics "With the tears of mothers bereaved of their young / Sacred infant's blood want only spilt, / We'll cement the bricks of our bodies for walls / And our homeland will surely be built" should, therefore, be interpreted as part of the revisionist Zionists' insistence of turning the dead, the scarified, into heroic icons. Thus, early Jewish nationalism transcended religious symbols. Patriotic sacrifice became the secular version of death in the name of God.[18]

However, also in the 1930s, another popular poet, Moshe Lifshitz, used the symbol to raise a possible critique of violence in "The Ballad of the Unknown Soldiers." Lifshitz was a communist-identified poet, playwright, and cultural critic. His poem was translated from Yiddish and published by acclaimed poet Nathan Alterman in 1940.[19] In this ballad, there is no collective voice; it begins with "This is the ballad of the Unknown Soldiers / in it there will be told on one big, helpless world / . . . not one, not a hundred, unknown soldiers / Come! Here millions are required, many and many / A wall of millions will be erected / worlds of human arms / Stop, guard this time, Save the World." The ballad's call to stop resonates with the communist notion of the general strike, which recruits members to *not* march or not join state-organized violence but, instead, help the world save itself. Thus, in this example of the Lifshitz Ballad translated into Hebrew by acclaimed and popular poet Nathan Alterman, who passionately supported the Zionist cause, the "unknown soldier" symbol is powerfully purposed as both nationalist and anti-nationalist when set in relation to organized violence. In Lifshitz's poem, the ballad is used as a metaphor to call to resist—by ceasing, or stopping a world that subjects millions to violence. This is the one use of the symbol that probably refers to the Jewish experience in Europe in the 1930s and was not canonized in Israeli commemorative culture.

Amichai's poem from 1969 surely corresponds with those prominent and well-known poems that were also popular songs from pre-state Jewish experiences in Palestine. Amichai challenges revisionist convictions. This correspondence, however, keeps the assembly of youth, sacrifice, and anonymity firm, which, to an extant Lifshitz, was the only one to challenge it in not using a plural collectivistic voice and in calling to cease violence while still using messianic futuristic language that Stern uses.

For sure, there are Jewish, Israeli, and European alternatives to the unknown soldier symbol as recruiting for national sacrifice, and they were explored and developed in women's writing. Siegel claims that in the case of France the unknown soldier symbol was used at the end of World War I in this way:[20] Madeleine Vernet, a pacifist educator, published criticism of such patriotic ritual under the title "To the Unknown Mother of the Unknown Soldier" in a women's journal she had started at the end of World War I, called *La Mere Educatrice*,[21] marking the naturalized relations between militarism, sacrifice, nationalism, and masculinity. These naturalized relations remain salient within discourses that criticize war, sacrifice, and militarism in Israel. In the case of women's literature, according to Szobel,[22] women poets used the binding of Isaac's myth[23] to subvert the taken-for-granted narrative, in which sacrifice of the son is an unavoidable fate of Jewish existence in Israel—suggesting, indeed, that retelling this myth could serve in repeating violence. Women poets in the 1930s and 1940s and later in the 1970s and 1980s, especially Leah Goldberg, wrote on poets' responsibility in showing humanity through aesthetic beauty and reflected on the cycles of historical violence without falling for its centripetal nationalist powers. Esther Raab[24] even offered an alternative critical reading of the anonymity of the sacrificed soldier, which could inform resistance to the narrative that justifies death and killing. These poems were written between the time when Stern wrote his poem on the unknown soldiers, in 1933, and Amichai's poem in 1969. Interestingly, they each signaled different possible narrative sequences; yet, neither entered the commemorative canon. We now turn to a short review of the ways the symbol of the unknown soldier is employed in popular culture in order to advance our understanding of its salience as a category that informs and, at times, helps justify death and killing in war.

Following are two examples of more recent application of the symbol. The first is when Israel withdrew from Lebanon in May 2000, and the newspaper *Yediot Ahronot* ran a two-page black-bordered spread on a Friday, listing the names of every fallen soldier, titled by Amichai's poem "We Do Not Have Unknown Soldiers." The second is when singer/songwriter Rona Keinan used Stern's poem from "When the Thorns Were Thorns" (recorded on her 2009 album *Songs for Yoel*) in a farewell to her father, Amos Keinan, who was a LEHI fighter, sculptor, and writer, and who later turned critical of revisionist ideas. These examples help understand an evolving character of commemorating discourse in Israel and how sacrifice for the sake of the country is viewed and acted upon by different groups. The first case is an apologetic account, which reacts to fierce discussion of the unnecessary deaths of soldiers in Lebanon. The second weaves the lamentation of times in which thorns were thorns, or the myth of sacrifice could putatively hold groups together—in both cases referring to Jewish dead men who were ready to sacrifice their lives in battle. We now turn to other uses of the symbol in Israeli culture.

THE ANONYMOUS GENTILE, AND DEAD RIGHT-WING POLITICIANS

In searching Parliament's (Knesset) recorded proceedings, the unknown soldier symbol was mentioned for the first time on February 19, 1985, having to do with a proposed law for the Holocaust Memorial Day. Non-Jews who saved Jews during the Holocaust were called then "unknown soldiers" by Yitzhak Artzi, who discussed the need of the State of Israel to support them forty years after the Holocaust.[25] In the same context of a Gentile who is given recognition or support from the Israeli nation, fallen soldiers who were not Jews were named unknown soldiers. This patriotic designation was mentioned in the proceedings in two other contexts: first, the memory of Avraham Stern, the author of the poem "Unknown Soldiers," on March 2000, sixty years after he was executed by the British. Second, and the most prevalent context for the usage of the unknown soldiers' symbol was about the Israeli General Security Service agents, whose actions and names are kept secret. In all cases, the soldiers are either forgotten or their identity concealed, are not necessarily Jews, and are always mentioned in a heroic context.

On October 24, 2001, in a Knesset meet-ing a week after the assassination of Knesset member and minister of tourism, Rechavam Zeevi,[26] Ariel Sharon, who was then Prime Minister, said, "He was a soldier of the State of Israel and the Zionist idea. Not about 'the unknown' but about people like him, Avraham Stern wrote in his poem the words 'only death will us sever.'" In 2012, when Yitzhak Shamir died, who was the leader of the LEHI para-military underground and Prime Minister of Israel between 1983–84 and 1986–92, Reuven Rivlin, the president, gave an obituary in the Knesset, "My sir: Prime Minister of Israel . . . and an eternal unknown soldier, in my name . . . and in the name of unknown soldiers in the service of the state and the paramilitary groups, we bow our head for you." In these last two instances, the reference to the deceased leader as an unknown soldier points to Stern's poem and is used to mourn the death of Stern's followers in the LEHI, within a political atmosphere that glorifies such sacrifice and adheres to the social and political convictions that came with it.

STRATEGIES OF REMEMBERING AND FORGETTING

The commemoration of fallen soldiers is performed in ceremonies for new monuments and in pop culture, from calendars and memorabilia to songs and poetry. Commemoration is also used in the construction of national consciousness through the creation of a national landscape of identification.[27] In this section, I examine the unknown soldier symbol as a prism through which cultural strategies of remembrance and forgetting have been used as a recruiting mechanism for missions of nation building that demanded various forms of sacrifice. Vinitzky-Seroussi and Teeger offer a helpful model through which to understand silence as a "complex and rich social space that can operate as a vehicle of either memory or of forgetting and can thus get used by various groups for different ends."[28] Vinitzky-Seroussi and Teeger discuss overt and covert silence. Overt silences are a literal absence of speech and narrative, while covert silences are silences that are covered and veiled by much mnemonic talk and representation. The Israeli unknown soldier is an example of both kinds: first, overt—the soldiers are unknown/forgotten, and this is lamented in the European model and in the case of citing Stern's poem. Then, by declaring that "we are those soldiers" (Stern) or "we do not have them" (Amichai), covert silence is added and used in the commemoration both of the forgotten fallen soldiers (named or not) and for the forgetting of unnamed ones. Thus, our case, in both its popular versions, is an example to a symbolic category that encapsulates both overt and covert silence for commemoration purposes that are also sources of identification.

Reciting Amichai, commemoration agents chose to negate a symbolic mechanism of modern nationalism because the "nationalization" of the fallen soldier, which in Europe reached its peak around World War I,[29] was strongly associated with the 1948 war in Israel by the sheer amount of lost lives among the Jewish population and by the very fact that many of them were, indeed, unknown and died almost immediately after arriving to Palestine, then to Israel from Europe.[30] In this way, Israeli Jewish culture, which recites Amichai's poem, has also separated itself from a distinct form of European remembrance and forgetting. The negation of the unknown soldier symbol is also a part of a larger discourse of personified Jewish remembrance of national catastrophes,[31] which demands that each of the dead be remembered as a named individual.

I suggest, then, that in this case, the Israeli Jews *negate the negation* of the name in modern European forms of national remembrance, claiming that its soldiers do not lose their names in dying. Indeed, they lose them before they die and regain them in dying.

Why has the Israeli Jewish commemoration culture had an ambivalent relationship with the European symbol of the unknown soldier? The right wing adopted it for the purposes of nation building. The center and center left, however, rejected it as a destruction of the memory of those who sacrifice their lives for the nation, underlining the same sacrificial mechanism. This mechanism is at work, for instance, in the Ministry of Defense department of soldiers' commemoration, titled "we will remember them all," a citation from a popular poem by Hayim Gouri from "The Friendship" (Ha'reut), which was the anthem of Palmach and is associated with socialist democratic values and Labor Party culture.

According to Sivan, the bulk of the remembrance effort is carried out in Israel through spontaneous activity of the civil society rather than by the state.[32] *Ad hoc* and later on, institutionalized commemoration by family, friends, relatives, and army comrades—separately or together with sports clubs, youth movements, kibbutzim, and schools—historically produced booklets dedicated to one or more fallen soldiers. They later also produced online platforms for these commemorational texts. According to Bilu and Witztum, material and textual commemoration has been produced and reproduced by state-authorized agencies such as the Department for the Commemoration of the Fallen Soldier within the Ministry of Defense.[33] Sivan[34] suggests that the form of textual commemoration through folk literature is more popular than monuments in Israel and that it tries to capture and preserve the individuality of the fallen.

However, the negation of the category "unknown" enabled a unique multidimensional commemoration that was not instructed by the state but has been nevertheless patrolled by cultural mechanisms shared by the Zionist society, to this day.[35] Accordingly, Nave[36] argues, the bereaved family was historically seen as the "silver platter"—they were the "ultimate," intensified Israelis, whose private disaster is transformed in the Israeli public discourse into a contribution, not a loss, and, ultimately, a presence and not a meaningless absence. Thus, the national community perceives itself as an extended grieving family, which loses sons who then are commemorated through inscription into the national memory by individualized means owned by the collective. As we will shortly see, this conviction changed since the 1970s.

Israel has separate cemeteries for soldiers and separate areas in civilian cemeteries for fallen soldiers. There is a standard structure and writing on soldiers' tombstones, which are built of Jerusalem stone in austere rectangular lines. The total standardization of remembrance historically left no room for individual commemoration. Bilu and Witztum[37] imply that the tension between collective and personal commemoration was most strongly manifested in the early 1990s in conflicts over epitaphs and the standardized writing that the state asked to keep formal in fallen soldiers' tombstones, and later agreed to allow variations in the tombstones' writing. This conflict was intensified around the long process of erecting a memorial to 73 soldiers who died in 1997 from the collision of two Air Force helicopters on their way to separate posts in Lebanon, in what Feige[38] termed the privatization of commemoration.

REMEMBERING AND FORGETTING INDIVIDUALS

In order to see how the symbol of the unknown soldier not only made sense to many publics in many periods but also how it was attached to other powerful symbolism, we return to a closer reading of Amichai's poem. There is a relation and a gap between the individual—the *one* who wants to remember—and the wreath, which is singular but composed of *many* flowers and the collective: soldiers, flowers, the dead, and names. This gap between the individual and the collective exposes Amichai's protest against the cyclic willingness to sacrifice life in war. However, it uses collective language as an allegorical reproach that also reads like a command of the proper singular way to remember. It is not clear who Amichai means by "we" (the nation? the state? those who remember? the dead?); the poem also does not imply if the unknown soldiers are already dead when "we" lack them. Both categories are unassailable—one does not challenge the reality of the "we" just as one does not question the ever presence of death.

I suggest that Amichai's poem offers two narratives. The first is the unknown soldiers as the frame story, told in the plural: "We do not have them." Later in the poem, "All the dead return home" and "They all have names." The second story, the inner one, is the fable of commemoration: it represents the fight between the individual and the collective through the prosaic national symbol of remembrance—flowers. The individual who remembers through a wreath of flowers is separated or "decomposed" from his or her collectivized identity and remains dismantled. Then the wreath itself becomes an object of commemoration activity: it is dispersed as if the flowers, the representatives of fallen soldiers, can be sowed and returned to life.

Following such a double reading of this text, the individual's total conscription to the nation does not question the latter's total power and is close in message to Stern's "Only death from our duty can us sever."

We can now ask whether by rejecting the symbol of the unknown soldier seen in the popularity of this poem, Israeli culture has actually denied a modern national statist European recruiting mechanism or if, instead, and perhaps counterintuitively, originated a more extreme recruiting vigor for the living, who would be willing to sacrifice their lives on the national altar knowing that by doing so they will "win" collective immortality—and that they, too, will be part of the wreath that is remembered and not forgotten. In other words, the ultimate recruiting power of the collective denies the individual's name while he or she is still alive. Therefore, in order to regain one's name, one should die (or "give one's life" as it is often put) for one's country and the safety of its citizens who are considered in the commemorative culture one's extended family.[39] This conviction was widely criticized in light of deaths due to terrorist attacks and families' conflicted relations with the state that led armed conflicts that are not easily justified.[40] Still, in looking at its remaining popularity in the Jewish commemorative cannon, Amichai's poem has offered the possibility for individual expression of the preferable way to commemorate by an individual, yet uses a collectivized voice that speaks for the collective and turns the message into a recruiting, paternalistic, and patriotic power.

According to Halbwachs,[41] collective memory is a form of individual memory, socially constructed and maintained by groups. The duration of collective memory is the duration of the group(s) producing it and their present social imaginary. Following Halbwachs, Winter and Sivan[42] claim that collective memory has a distinct "shelf-life"; after its "expiration," individuals and groups cease to share and express it unless it speaks to their experiences in the present. The negated symbol of the unknown soldier has had and continues to have a long "shelf-life" in Israel—precisely because of its firm obscurity. We now turn to discussing the resilience of this symbolic category in Israeli commemorative culture.

"DO NOT HAVE": REMEMBRANCE, SACRIFICE, AND MILITARISM

The rejection of the unknown soldier symbol became part of a future-oriented project of remembrance and forgetting, in which the individual—and especially the individual's willingness to kill and die—was created for ventures of nation building within a "nation-in-arms" narrative and then enlarged in a discourse on Jewish victimhood.[43] In its construction of memorials on battle sites inside the country's borders, the Israeli symbolic typology often negated other places of memory, other sites, which were not related to battle fields. In this sense, Israeli Jewish society negated continuity with the Jewish past, in which millions perished namelessly. Later on, in enlarging the narrative of sacrifice to include the Holocaust within a victimhood narrative, it included Holocaust victims in the memorial landscape and readings of known victims' names. In a 1991 project initiated by Yad Vashem, called "Unto Every Person There Is a Name," names of Holocaust victims are read aloud on the Holocaust Memorial Day in the Knesset, in cities and campuses in Europe, and in the United States on their Holocaust memorial day, defeat or liberation days, or on International Holocaust Memorial day, January 27.

Kimmerling[44] examined the place of the military and its meaning in Israeli society in relation to the conflicts between Israelis and Palestinians. According to him, the main platform for militarism in Israel is civilian militarism, in which the military plays a central role in the collective experience, especially through the centrality of mandatory conscription to the army. In this way, the whole of society is constantly preparing for war. Additionally, the public discourse prefers the terms "security" and "defense" to that of "military" and, thus, enlarges the legitimate scope of militaristic thinking and operation. Almog[45] traces militarism in Israeli society to the Sabra model, whose tough character on the outside is said to limit his expression of feelings (a reference to the attributes of a cactus, whose insides are softer and sweet). Sasson-Levi[46] shows how the Israeli civil outlook is dominated by the military service. According to her, military service, preferably in combat units, is the main expression of civil obligation. Until the mid-1990s, it excluded women, who, at that time, were not allowed to join combat units and Palestinians, who are not required under the obligatory conscription to serve. In recent years, Muslim and Christian Palestinians have been able to join combat units, and women have joined combat units in a manner that has enlarged the militaristic aspect of civic life.

In Amichai's poem, the commandment to remember individuals' names is accompanied by an example of a fallen soldier named Jonathan, which provides the poem an added sense of the personal and the individual. It proceeds with the following lines:

> And also to you, Jonathan,
> My pupil, whose name in the class list
> Is the same as your name in the dead list.
> My pupil as you were
> The name you had
> Your name.
> Please, even those who had not known him,
> Love him also after his death
> Love him: now a void,[47]
> A void that is its form–his form
> And its name—his name.

The lines that describe Jonathan's name "that is now a void" point to an additional duality to that life and death—the dead soldier's presence among a group of people who "knew him": his teacher and classmates and those to whom he is but another soldier—life and death, which exist in lists of school classes and fallen soldiers. According to Zerubavel,[48] patriotic sacrifice was a fundamental value in the Israeli culture before the State of Israel was established and in the first years of Israeli existence; however, it was challenged after the 1973 Yom Kippur war.[49] Hazan[50] claims, "The intergenerational conflict in Israel has been expressed mainly through the idea of 'abolishing the collective.'" Young Israelis have been involved in a quest for individualism since the early 1970s, especially after the Yom Kippur War, in 1973, which was perceived as a trauma.[51]

In the late 1960s, death became the subject of macabre humor, all in all from a perspective that sought responsibility from the state.[52] The gap between the heroic image of the Israeli fighter and the traumatic experience of unjustified wars was discussed through the memories and oral testimonies of soldiers. Political satires and plays expressed frustration about the state's choices in sending soldiers to wars. War criticism peaked after 1982 and the first Lebanon War.

Even so, public protest against militarism was and still is seen as a phenomenon that endangers the social order and the Israeli national interest.[53] For example, as Kimmerling noted,[54] "refuseniks" (soldiers who refused to serve in the occupied territories) never denied the civil importance of the military service; they still perceive it as an "Israeli experience" central to their Israeli identity. But the very act of refusal is viewed as a deviation away from the pure model of moral "military behavior." Another recent example of the centrality of army service in Israeli Jewish culture, even in pointing to ethical violations, is *Breaking the Silence*, veteran soldiers' movement who since 2004 (the second Intifada) collected anonymous testimonies of soldiers' actions during service in the occupied territories. They also do not resist universal conscription but do try to raise awareness of the moral corruption of the army service in the Israeli society that is inevitable in the tasks of the army as an occupying force.[55] We now turn from militarism back to sacrifice.

According to Rozental,[56] the Israeli bereavement ethos was based on three assumptions: grief is a "price" that should be paid for the continued existence of the Israeli people and the Israeli nation, public and individual griefs are tied, and bereavement is beyond political disputes. As this ethos was progressively challenged, competing acts of remembrance together with challenges to "remembrance authorities" emerged.[57] The hegemonic model, which can be viewed as reinforcing the importance of army service in Israeli society, has been challenged by different ethnic groups, for example, by some working class and Mizrahi Jews, and Ethiopian Jews who feel that they are not equal citizens and, therefore, that their military service is unfair and unjust.[58] These shifts in perceptions and representations of national sacrifice do not necessarily mean that sacrifice has ceased to be an important organizing principle in Israeli culture. Rather, the unknown soldier category seems to have survived these shifts, because it did not question Israeli mythological values and, at the same time, it negated or made obsolete unwanted values, therefore, preserving the readiness to be part of military conflict and war together with a collective promise of national commemoration.

UNKNOWN SOLDIERS

By definition, a soldier is an unknown person who bears an institutional status and whose main capacity is to serve in the army. However, in the case of soldiers dying in terror attacks and morally questioned wars since the 1970s, both Rozental[59] and Feige[60] claim that commemoration undergoes a process of privatization in which bereavement becomes personal and the national ethos of sacrifice for the nation is managed by national authorities that are detached from the bereaved and the bereavement process. It is, thus, worthwhile to examine the symbol of the unknown soldier at a time when we would not expect to encounter it, when collectivism and a one state/one ethnic group ethos are being challenged. The persistent popularity of the symbol can be explained by Ann Swidler's concept of "cultural repertoires"[61] that remained central as recruiting mechanisms, not only around the need to justify sacrifice in war. For instance, the discourse on the migration of Israelis to other countries moralizes those who have left Israel: (1) they are called "yordim," or descending, and (2) prior to leaving, they are asked to reconsider their choices by mention of the Holocaust and those who sacrificed their lives in war, a consideration that justifies and calls for further sacrifice. The unknown soldier symbol is, thus, also part of a powerful national ideology.

Ideology is constructed for and by individuals as subjects. The subject that is constitutive of ideology, according to Althusser,[62] only exists by creating concrete subjects as subjects and "concrete enough to be recognized, but abstract enough to be thinkable and [be] thought, giving rise to knowledge." The unknown soldier is an ideological mechanism that functions in such a way that it "recruits" (to use Althusser's language) subjects among the individuals and transforms the individuals into subjects. In order to see how the unknown soldier was utilized as a recruiting device, we have to ask whether we can think of a single unknown soldier, dead or alive, a question that Anderson[63] proposes. The answer is, "No." We can then ask: Is there a possibility of an unknown individual, dead or alive? The answer must be, "Yes." But their anonymity is not necessarily shaped by or for the collective. In most cases, the collective does not need their anonymity to recruit other civilians to perish for its persistence.

According to Anderson,[64] the Unknown Soldier Tomb symbolized not only the nation's tendency to erase individual names but also symbolized the deep relation with death, a characteristic that national projects share with religions. The relational connections between the Zionist project and the Jewish religion are deep and complicated, further ground for the necessity of a discourse on names, death, and the birth of the nation. The original World War I model of the unknown soldier was not flexible enough to endure different forms of sacrifice other than the fallen soldier who fought on remote fronts. This symbolism then was reworked in the Israeli case to connect to war at home, the pioneering ethos, and the high value of the name. By referring to unknown soldiers in memorial ceremonies, the mnemonic setting that considers their possibility becomes everlasting in national remembrance and, as such, has remained salient in both center-left and right-wing symbols of commemoration.

UNKNOWN AS FORGETTABLE

Sivan asks who have been forgotten and left un-commemorated.[65] The answer is the immigrants who arrived in 1948. They had a double disadvantage. First, they were less socially integrated when they joined the army upon arrival, migrating singly or as small families after the Holocaust. Second, they had a significant lower level of education as result of the interruption of schooling during the war years. According to Sivan,[66] the "1948 generation" is remembered as one made of native Israelis: the Sabra. Amichai's poem "We do not have Unknown Soldiers" also means avoiding the acknowledgment of this group that was erased from the heroic, victorious Israeli ethos, which has later also failed to include Mizrahi and Ethiopian soldiers as equal contributors. Interestingly, it was essential to stress that this group *remains* forgotten: "we" have forgotten that "*we*" *do* have soldiers who died unknown and that nobody literally remembers their names.

In the last three decades, this attitude toward Holocaust survivors has changed, and they have gained a place of honor in Israeli memory discourse. Feldman[67] shows in his analysis of the connecting path between Yad Vashem National Holocaust Memorial and the Mount Herzl National and Military Cemetery how the link constructed by Zionist commemorative culture between the Holocaust and the founding of the State of Israel has developed to include Holocaust survivors who died in the War of 1948 and, thus, reflects the changing attitudes toward national sacrifice. As Holocaust memory became more central to the ethos of sacrifice in Israeli Jewish society, it focused more on heroic aspects of everyday life as well as resistance. A proposal to grant Israeli citizenship to all those who died in the Holocaust was raised in the early days of the Israeli state. Zertal claims that this proposal produced a narrative of heroism that commenced not "over there," but "right here." The obligation to remember "here" in Israel is subordinate to a political community that included in its ethos the dead of other countries who were murdered before the state of Israel was established.[68]

THE UNKNOWN SOLDIER TOMB

According to Laqueur, in Europe, the mass killing of nameless soldiers led to a development of symbolism of *absence* through building cenotaphs and the Unknown Soldier Tomb. Both sites attracted and created strong, spontaneous responses of the people "to the infinite meaning of emptiness."[69] The unknown soldier was a distinctly modern way to create meaning: the concept becomes, in its universality, the cipher that can mean anything; itself, the sign of itself, and the sign of a half-million other selves. While in the case of Israel I do not subscribe to Laqueur's interpretation of the democratization of death through the equal erasing of names (it is an act of dehumanization that democracies could not afford after World War I), I do agree that there was indeed a mighty power of creating meaning through collective symbols of individual absence.

Laqueur[70] also points out that the unknown soldier was a precursor and signaled the opposite end of the commemorative strategy that is evident in the enumeration of names, as with the empty tomb, and represents the absence of a generic body. The tension between the physical body and its name is embodied in the topological zone of the unknown soldier memorial. In other words, prior to World War I, European society saw the importance of the name for the state and invented the category of the unknown soldier, a mechanism that enabled the return of the name after World War I and the later political activity around individual identities in democratic regimes.

The salience of the negated symbol in public representation of Israeli commemoration is part of the tradition of strong forgetful remembrance, paraphrasing Walter Benjamin's concept of insightful remembrance.[71] This notion records not only the missed potential for change in the past but identifies the forces that continue to repress this potential in the present.[72] According to Remmler,[73] insightful remembrance instills historical memory with the function of bearing witness to oppressive forms of collective remembering. The oppressive forms of collective remembrance encapsulated in the symbol of the unknown soldiers were voiced by women poets and activists, and in Lifshitz's ballad, with calls to cease violence—but have not been canonized. The "original" unknown soldier dissolved with respect to the living (though we remember the oppositional addressing by the unknown mother of the unknown soldier): he does not leave individual traces and often has no known burial site. As an unknown soldier who is part of an unknown collective, he cannot be really dead—he has no name and no singular existence, let alone death; he embodies and signifies the justified war.

"WREATH OF FLOWERS": COMMEMORATION CEREMONIES AND THE LEGACY OF THE LIVING

As I suggested earlier, soldiers' anonymity is embedded in their conscription. Their relations to their fellow soldiers and officers are vertical until the moment of death, which erases hierarchies and realigns those relationships as horizontal.[74] In the Zionist culture, the horizontal relationship exceeded the realm of myth, and the symbolic category of the friend (comrade, pal) was widely used. The "friend" is a Hebrew idiom and, as in socialist cultures, is a prefix connected to the person's first name. We encountered its centrality in the canonized poem by Haim Gouri "Ha'reut" (friendship, or camaraderie) in Israeli commemoration culture. In this section, I suggest that the same mechanism of anonymity was operative outside the battlefield in the sphere of friendship. The idiom "friend" is the most prominent symbol of Israeli Jewish collectivity and within this context, the use of friend as an idiom shifts the spotlight from the individual to the group. The category of "the friend" is divided into three interrelated subcategories: friendship, brotherhood, and camaraderie, which are briefly detailed here in their nuanced differences.

1. **Friendship** symbolizes an intimate relationship.
2. **Brotherhood** illustrates tribal-like connections between Israel's Jews. Calling a friend or a colleague "my brother"/ "my sister" also has a military lingo connotation that migrated into everyday Hebrew.
3. **Camaraderie** represents collective memory of war heroes and is best illustrated in the term *re'ut*, or friendship, between warriors.[75]

"Friend" is a mechanism that permits the formation of fluid boundaries because it has no immanent content. The concept is hierarchical and, therefore, denotes membership in various frameworks. At the bottom of the "friendship hierarchy" lies the Gentile who was referred to as *yadid* (pal or buddy) in Zionist discourse. Nonhierarchical relations were based on the emergence of the "native" Jewish Israeli Sabra. Hazan[76] suggests that "the image of the Israeli Jew who supposedly emerged from nowhere, drawing his strength from the elements of his old-new naturalized homeland, was epitomized in the construction of the fine figure of young warrior-cum-pioneer, whose collective memory did not extend beyond the horizons of his land." Such a figure of dual attribute recruited its symbolic apparatus from other nations' mythologies while adding to them local elements embedded in the specific context in which Zionism became and was sustained as a national movement in Israel.

CONCLUSION: "DISPERSING LEAVES," YOUTH, INDIVIDUALISM, AND NEW REMEMBERING GROUPS

The fallen soldier is usually a young person who, in the potential height of his or her life, happened to die in armed conflict. Youthfulness was the engine of the Zionist nation-building project (as well as of other nation-building projects). The relations between (1) being young, (2) having an eternal future, and (3) being unknown were, together, an unbounded recruiting force. The Zionist ethos was historically carried by youth pioneers. Youth socialization was extended through compulsory military conscription at age eighteen. In popularizing Amichai's poem, the negation of the unknown soldier symbol from the Israeli pantheon became a didactic attempt to offer a righteous voice to remember the fallen soldiers by their peers, while rejecting both the European nationalist and the Jewish revisionist models.

The recruiting power of the unknown soldier symbol has been expanded to include civilians over the years of the second Intifada (2000–2004), in which Jewish as well as Palestinian civilians have often been attacked, in a so-called Jewish majority "war" at home. Jewish civilians who were killed have been commemorated in the same manner as soldiers, on memorial plaques in public squares and remembered on the same day of remembrance for fallen soldiers. Since 1998, it is called "Memorial Day for the Fallen Soldiers of Israel and Victims of Terrorism." This designation of inclusion weakens the distinction between death in war and death in a terror attack, although the groups are still named as separated and are not simply "victims." This designation includes, in the narrative of national sacrifice of dead civilians, a move that is more often than not welcome in the Israeli Jewish society. Civilians and families whose members were injured or killed during terror attacks, like soldiers, are entitled to benefits.

I would like to conclude this exploration of anonymity in Israeli commemorative culture with two examples of refusal of the national sacrifice narrative. Mr. Hussein Abu Khdeir refused such inclusion. He is the father of the teenage Muhamad Abu Khdeir, who was kidnapped and murdered in July 2014 by three Israeli Jewish citizens as revenge for the kidnapping and killing of three Israeli Jewish teenagers in the West Bank (which started a 50-day war in Gaza). Abu Khdeir asked that his son's name not be inscribed on a Victims of Terrorism memorial in the Israeli memorial Pantheon on Mount Herzl, together with names of other, mostly Jewish, victims of terror attacks in Israel. This refused inscription illuminates the ways that anonymity is constructed unevenly by the state's commemorative acts to sectors of the Israeli and Palestinian society who can voice their resistance to it.

The second example is a group of former Jewish and Palestinian combatants named "Combatants for Peace." Since 2006, they and the Forum of Bereaved Families have organized an alternative Memorial Day for fallen soldiers. Mutual recognition and empathy for the other side in the conflict becomes a vehicle that the organizers and attendants of this ceremony hope to mobilize toward directly addressing the bereavement and loss on both sides, together with their past willingness to kill and die. This group also refuses the nationalist inscription that justifies sacrifice with disregard to national sentiment.

This essay has discussed the career and prominence of the unknown soldiers' symbol in Israeli Jewish commemoration culture. The symbol's eminence can be explained on both theoretical and historical levels. I claimed that it encapsulates overt as well as covert silence as tools to commemorate and elevate national sacrifice by different groups in Israel. I examined three versions of its use: the first, and most popular, by negation, in Amichai's poem "We Do Not Have Unknown Soldiers." The second celebrates and elevates sacrifice and occupation in Stern's "Unknown Soldiers." The last is in a poem that did not become popular in commemorative culture in Lifshitz's Ballad, which used the symbol so as to recruit many who will act to resist violence and destruction.

The historical explanation for the symbol's long "shelf life" considered the metamorphosis of criticism toward war and sacrifice in Israel, which still holds the army and military action as legitimate and central to the self-understanding of Jewish life in Israel. The recent return to performing Stern's song that glorifies sacrifice is an example of this explanation. For the hegemonic Israeli Jewish sector, collective as well as individual sacrifice was highlighted. For the national religious sector, which increasingly represents a significant proportion of Israeli soldiers and commanders (ever since the 1967 War), and a correspondingly significant proportion of the folk commemoration found in popular literature and the social imaginary, the Jewish command to remember—to make a written homage to the dead—was fulfilled as well. We are left with a small and currently marginalized number of groups that refuse this inscription into "national fame," which justifies war as sacrifice, and with the roads less taken, ones that may lead to civic action and commemoration that will be inclusive and center around life.

REFERENCES

1. In Hebrew, these words also mean to deconstruct, decompose, and dismantle—a triple, "secondary" connotation that points to the weaponry and memory of war.
2. First stanza from Yehuda Amichai's "We Do Not Have Unknown Soldiers," in *Akhshav Ba-ra'ash: Poems 1963-1968* (Jerusalem: Shoken, 1969), author trans. Amichai (1924–2000) migrated to Palestine from Germany and fought in the war of 1948; he was a teacher and one of Israeli's most acclaimed and translated poets and lived in Jerusalem. He received Israeli and international prizes for his work over his lifetime.
3. The translation of the Hebrew for "unknown soldier" is "nameless/anonymous soldier."
4. Avraham Stern (1907–1942) was a poet and an active member of the armed resistance movement, the "Irgun," a National Military Organization. His pen name and underground name in the Irgun was "Yair." In 1940, he formed a radical opposition group, known as LEHI (*Lohamei Herut Yisrael*), a Hebrew acronym for the Fighters for the Freedom of Israel, who fought the British Mandate. Stern's name is today commemorated in towns and street names in Israel.
5. Uri Zvi Greenberg (1898–1981) was a Hebrew and Yiddish poet, guerrilla "Irgun" fighter, revisionist party member, and member of the first Knesset.
6. Yaira Genossar, "On the Unknown Soldiers 1929–1932," *Iyunim Bitkumat Yisrael* 5 (1995): 497–524. Hebrew.
7. George L. Mosse, *The Fallen Soldiers: Reshaping the Memory of the World Wars* (Oxford: Oxford University Press, 1991).
8. Emmanuel Sivan, "Private Pain and Public Remembrance in Israel," in War and Remembrance in the Twentieth Century, ed. Jay Winter and Emmanuel Sivan (Cambridge: Cambridge University Press, 1999), 177–204.
9. Motti Neiger, Oren Meyers, and Eyal Zandberg, "Tuned to the Nation's Mood: Popular Music as a Mnemonic Cultural Object," *Media, Culture & Society* 33 no. 7 (2011): 971–87.
10. Hanna Nave, "Here I Pass. Stand by the Stone," in *Defusim Shel Hanzaha*, ed. Mati Meizel and Ilana Shamir (Tel Aviv: Misrad Habitachon, Publication/Ministry of Defense Publishers, 2000). Hebrew.
11. See, for instance, on the Ministry of Education website a discussion on teaching literature and poetry at times of war, accessed May 3, 2017, http://cms.education.gov.il/EducationCMS/Units/Mazkirut_Pedagogit/Sifrut/YetzirotSvivNose/Veichlizkor/sifrutLeaharMilhama.htm.
12. Kimmerling Baruch, "Military in Israeli Society," *Theory and Criticism* no. 4 (1993): 123–40; Kimmerling Baruch, *The Invention and Decline of Israeliness: State, Society and the Military* (Berkeley: University of California Press, 2001); Yoram Bilu and Eliezer Witztum "War-Related Loss and Suffering in Israeli Society: An Historical Perspective," *Israel Studies* 5 no. 2 (2000): 1–28, 4; Emmanuel Sivan, *The 1948 Generation Myth, Profile and Memory* (Tel Aviv: Maarachot, 1991); Orna Sasson-Levy and Gal Levy, "Combat is Best? Republican Socialization, Gender and Class in Israel," in *Militarism and Education*, ed. Hagit Gor Ziv (Tel-Aviv: Babel, 2005), 220–44.

13. Hannah Arendt, *The Human Condition* (Chicago: The University of Chicago Press, 1958); Maoz Azaryahu, *State Cults* (Kiriat Sede Boker: Machon Ben-Gurion, 1995) Hebrew; Don Handelman, *Models and Mirrors: Towards an Anthropology of Public Events* (New York: Berghahn Books, 1998); Haim Hazan, *Simulated Dreams: Israeli Youth and Virtual Zionism* (New York: Berghahn Books, 2001); Nissim Mizrachi and Hanna Herzog, "Participatory Destigmatization Strategies among Palestinian Citizens, Ethiopian Jews, and Mizrahi Jews in Israel," *Ethnic and Racial Studies* 35 no. 3 (2012): 418–35; Gershon Shafir and Yoav Peled, *Being Israeli: The Dynamics of Multiple Citizenship* (New York: Cambridge University Press, 2002); Yael Zerubavel, "Battle, Sacrifice, and Martyrdom: Changes, Continuity and Change in Patriotism Sacrifice in Israeli Culture," in *Patriotism in Israel*, ed. Avner Ben-Amos and Daniel Bar-Tal (Tel Aviv: Dyonon, 2004), 61–99. Hebrew.
14. Benedict Anderson, *Imagined Communities: Reflections on the Origin and Spread of Nationalism* (London: Verso, 1990); Thomas W. Laqueur, "Memory and Naming in The Great War," in *Commemoration: The Politics Of National Identity*, ed. John R. Gillis (Princeton: Princeton University Press, 1994), 156–67; Thomas W. Laqueur, "Names, Bodies and the Anxiety of Erasure," in *The Social and Political Body*, ed. Theodore R. Schatzki and Wolfgang Nattar (New York: The Guilford Press, 1996).
15. Avraham "Yair" Stern, "Unknown Soldiers," Anthem of the Fighters for the Freedom of Israel (LEHI), accessed January 10, 2017, http://www.saveisrael.com/stern/sternsoldiers.htm/. The translation is taken from a far-right website named "Save Israel" and located in Philadelphia.
16. Yaira Genossar, "On the Unknown Soldiers 1929–1932," *Iyunim Bitkumat Yisrael* 5 (1995): 497–524.
17. Yael Zerubavel, *Recovered Roots: Collective memory and the Making of the Israeli National Tradition* (Chicago: University of Chicago Press, 1995).
18. Zerubavel, "Battle, Sacrifice, and Martyrdom," 5.
19. Published in the literary pages of "Hashomer Hatzair," the socialist-Zionist secular Jewish youth movement, in 1940, and set to music by composer Stefan Wolpe.
20. Mona Siegel, "To the Unknown Mother of the Unknown Soldier: Pacifism, Feminism, and the Politics of Sexual Difference among French *Institutrices* between the Wars," *French Historical Studies* 22, no. 3 (1999): 421–51.
21. Ibid., 422.
22. Ilana Szobel, "'A Howl of Simple Words': The Akedah Motif in Hebrew Women's Poetry, 1930–70," *Jerusalem Studies in Hebrew Literature* (Mount Scopus, IL: Mandel Institute for Jewish Studies, 2008), 65–92.
23. Myth taken in the structuralist and post-structuralist tradition represented by Barthes and Levi-Strauss to be a narrative or story told within a community in which it stands for values that are shared by its members as natural. See Roland Barthes, *Mythologies* (New York: Hill and Wang, 2012, 1957) and Claude Levi Strauss, *Myth and Meaning: Cracking the Code of Culture* (New York: Schocken Books, 1979).
24. See Ilana Szobel, "In the Flowers of Spring and the Dead Son," in *Jerusalem Studies in Hebrew Literature* (Mount Scopus, IL: Mandel Institute for Jewish Studies, 2008), 84.
25. Yad Vashem, Holocaust Martyrs' and Heroes' Remembrance Authority, Jerusalem, has an "unknown righteous among the nations" memorial for Gentiles who saved Jews in the Holocaust.
26. Zeevi was a Major General in the IDF and later a politician. He founded the right-wing nationalist party "Moledet," which advocated forced expulsion of Palestinians from Israel.
27. Szobel, "A Howl of Simple Words"; Don Handelman and Lea Shamgar Handelman, "*The Presence of Absence*: The Memorialism of National Death in Israel," in *Grasping Land: Space and Place in Contemporary Israeli Discourse and Experience*, ed. Ben Ari, Eyal and Bilu, Yoram (Albany: SUNY Press 1997), 85–128.
28. Vered Vinitzky-Seroussi and Channa Teeger, "Unpacking the Unspoken: Silence in Collective Memory and Forgetting," *Social Forces* 88, no. 3 (2010): 1103–22.
29. Mosse, *Fallen Soldiers*.
30. Sivan, "*The 1948 Generation Myth*," cited in Bilu and Witztum, "War-Related Loss and Suffering."
31. A salient example is a famous poem by the Orthodox poet Zelda, "Unto Every Person There is a Name," which is recited and sung on various memorial days.
32. Sivan, "Private Pain and Public Remembrance," 179.
33. Bilu and Witztum, "War-Related Loss and Suffering," 1–28.

34. Sivan, "Private Pain and Public Remembrance," 177–204.
35. For example, the Ministry of Defense commemoration website lists the poem "Unto Every Person There Is a Name," by poet Zelda (a.k.a., Zelda Schneersohn Mishkovsky), among other poems that deal with personal loss and individual fallen soldiers, under the title of "We Will Remember Everyone," on an official government page of remembrance," accessed Jan 11, 2017, http://www.izkor.gov.il/.
36. Hanna Nave, "On Absence, Loss and Bereavement in the Israeli Reality," *Alpayim* 16 (1998): 85–120. Hebrew.
37. Bilu and Witztum, "War-Related Loss and Suffering," 1–28.
38. Michael Feige, "The Monument to the Helicopter Disaster and the Paradox of the *Privatization* of Commemoration of Fallen Soldiers," *Iyunim Bitkumat Yisrael* 20 (*2010*): 122–43. Hebrew.
39. The term "the family of bereavement" refers to relatives of fallen soldiers and blurs the boundaries between individual and collective mourning of those who lost their relatives and the rest of the Israeli society that support and identify with them.
40. Feige, "The Monument to the Helicopter Disaster."
41. Maurice Halbwachs, "The Social Frameworks of Memory," in *On Collective Memory*, ed. and trans. Lewis A. Closer (Chicago: University of Chicago Press, 1992), 37–167.
42. Winter and Sivan, *War and Remembrance*, 177–204.
43. Zerubavel, "Battle, Sacrifice, and Martyrdom."
44. Baruch Kimmerling, "Military in Israeli Society," 123–40.
45. Oz Almog, *The Sabra* (Tel Aviv: Am Oved, 1997). Hebrew.
46. Orna Sasson Levy,"Resistance within Suppression: The Construction of Gendered Identities in Female Masculine Duties," in *Will You Listen to my Voice? Representations of Women in Israeli Culture*, ed. Yael Azmon (Tel Aviv: Hakibbutz Hameuhad and Van Leer Publishers, 2001), 277–303. Hebrew.
47. In Hebrew, *hallal* means a fallen soldier and a void.
48. Zerubavel, "Battle, Sacrifice, and Martyrdom."
49. Ibid.
50. Haim Hazan, *Simulated Dreams*, 72.
51. Edna Lomsky-Feder, As If There Was No War: Life Stories of Israeli Men (Jerusalem: Magness Press, 1998). Hebrew.
52. Zerubavel, "Battle, Sacrifice, and Martyrdom"; Sivan, "Private Pain and Public Remembrance," 177–204.
53. Zerubavel, "Battle, Sacrifice, and Martyrdom."
54. Baruch Kimmerling, "Military in Israeli Society," *Theory and Criticism* 4 (1993): 137.
55. Tamar Katriel and Nimrod Shavit, "Between Moral Activism and Archival Memory: The Testimonial Project of 'Breaking the Silence,'" in *On Media Memory: Collective Memory in a New Media Age*, ed. Motti Neiger, Oren Myers, and Eyal Zandberg (London: Palgrave Macmillan, 2011), 77–87.
56. Rubik Rozental, *Is Bereavement Dead?* (Jerusalem: Ketter, 2001).
57. Vered Vinitzky-Seroussi, *Yitzhak Rabin's Assassination and the Dilemmas of Memory* (New York: SUNY Press, 2009).
58. Orna Sasson-Levy and Gal Levy, "Combat is Best? Republican Socialization," 220–44.
59. Rubik Rozental. *Is Bereavement Dead?*
60. Feige, "The Monument to the Helicopter Disaster."
61. Ann Swidler, "Culture in Action: Symbols and Strategies," *American Sociological Review* 51, No. 2 (April 1986): 273–86.
62. Louis Althusser, *Essays on Ideology* (London: Verso, 1984), 47.
63. Benedict Anderson, *Imagined Communities*, 48–59.
64. Ibid., 9.
65. Sivan, "Private Pain and Public Remembrance," 177–204.
66. Ibid., 193.
67. Jackie Feldman, "Between Yad Vashem and Mt. Herzl: Changing Inscriptions of Sacrifice on Jerusalem's 'Mountain of Memory,'" *Anthropological Quarterly* 80, no. 4 (Fall 2007): 1147–74.
68. Idit Zertal, *Israel's Holocaust and the Politics of Nationhood*, trans. Chaya Galai (New York: Cambridge University Press, 2005), 9–58.
69. Laqueur, "Memory and Naming in The Great War," 157.
70. Ibid., 163.
71. Walter Benjamin, "Theses on the Philosophy of History," in *Illuminations*, trans. Harry Zohn, ed. Hannah Arendt (New York: Schocken Books, 1985).
72. Karen Remmler, *Waking the Dead: Correspondences between Walter Benjamin's Concept of Remembrance and Ingborg Bachmann's Ways of Dying* (Riverside, CA: Ariadne Press, 1996), 2.
73. Ibid., 7.
74. Thanks to Ross Poole for illuminating this point.
75. Danny Kaplan, *The Men We Loved: Male Friendship and Nationalism in Israeli Culture* (New York:

Berghahn Books, 2006); Irit Dekel, "'The Void Keeps Growing': Traumatic Space in the Transformation of the Peace and Democracy Watch from Elite to an Enclave," in *Trauma's Omen: Israeli Studies on Identity, Memory and Representation,* ed. Nadav Davidovitch, Michal Alberstein, and Rakefet Zalashik (Tel Aviv, IL: Hakibbutz Hameuchad–Sifriat Poalim Publishing Group, 2016). Hebrew.

76. Haim Hazan, *Simulated Dreams: Israeli Youth and Virtual Zionism* (New York: Berghahn Books, 2001), viii.

Why Religious Discourse Has a Place in Medical Ethics: An Example from Jewish Medical Ethics

Ira Bedzow

Abstract

This article will lay out the different rhetorical strategies that exist in religious discourse on topics related to medical ethics. In demonstrating that religious ethicists use different rhetorical strategies, depending on their goals and audiences, this essay attempts to show how recognition of the different strategies is a first step to finding practical tools to assist in dialogue between individuals and groups in multicultural settings. By understanding how to account for these different rhetorical strategies when considering arguments from different religious groups and in negotiating norms and values in the public square, public discourse related to medical ethics can be enriched, and, importantly, ways to avoid or at least ameliorate ethical conflict or tension between people and groups in a multicultural environment may be found.

Religious arguments in multicultural environments have enormous potential to enrich the larger society, yet religious and secular ethicists frequently suffer from an inability to converse due to cultural and ethical differences as well as from a lack of receptivity on both sides to the arguments made by others. Increased division and fractious communication easily occur when differences are not heard. The problem of the lack of receptivity partially stems from the fact that religious ethicists use different rhetorical strategies and advance different positions, depending on the audiences whom they are addressing. The different strategies and positions are not due to duplicity on anyone's part; rather, they result from the different ways that values and norms are prioritized for internal or multicultural audiences.

My argument for the importance of religious discourse in medical ethics, therefore, does not pertain to cultural humility as it relates to understanding the beliefs and values of a particular patient, nor is it an attempt to engage in interfaith dialogue or introduce theology into bioethics. Rather, my argument is methodological. Different cultural systems express their beliefs according to the value premises that undergird ethical arguments, and religious ethicists will utilize different rhetorical strategies based on their tradition and the audience they are trying to persuade. By understanding each of these strategies of ethical argumentation, public discourse related to medical ethics can be enriched, since, by knowing the motivation for positing different arguments, we can account for them when negotiating norms and values in the public square as part of a multicultural compromise. At the very least, we might be able to find certain ways to avoid or at least ameliorate ethical conflict or tension between people and groups in a multicultural environment.

I plan to demonstrate the value of religious discourse in medical ethics, first by explaining select strategies utilized by cultural-religious groups living in multicultural environments and, second, by showing how they can be utilized in public debates. Finally, I will explain how unveiling value premises held by different groups can add to the public conversation about healthcare. While this approach can be utilized for any number of different cultural-religious groups, I will demonstrate its efficacy with examples from the Jewish tradition, and I propose that philosophers and ethicists in different traditions can and should provide examples from their own traditions. The reason for limiting my examples to the Jewish tradition is twofold. First, as someone who is fully immersed in Jewish legal and ethical scholarship, I am able to understand the internal motivations behind using these strategies of argument and to appreciate the important implications of their use. Second, as a medical ethicist, I recognize the need for religious-cultural arguments to be presented in such a way that they can be accepted within public discourse.[1] In other words, these assertions must be translated into a form that can be understood by other traditions.[2]

The reason for this need for "translation" is that different religious or philosophical traditions are grounded in different value premises and exegetical priorities. Therefore, two moral arguments, each from a different religious-philosophical tradition, may be logically sound within their own frameworks yet unsound when seen within a different framework. The consequence of this reality is that rival arguments cannot challenge the logic of each other's claims nor can anyone argue effectively against holding different first premises on which either argument's conclusions rely, since no rational way of weighing first premises exist. When public discourse does not recognize or acknowledge this limitation, what results is an intellectualized "pep-rally" between rival claimants, each side asserting its premises as the correct ones to follow.[3] In order to avoid relativism or perspectivism in public moral discourse,[4] advocates within the public conversation who want to introduce ideas or methodologies from their respective traditions must be conversant in their tradition and the traditions of those with whom they seek to communicate. When people come together from different religious traditions in multicultural communities and each introduces ideas from particular traditions in a way that can be heard by others, the greater intellectual community can create a common space outside of each tradition, into which scholars from each group may bring tools and additional perspectives from their unique histories. As the space enlarges, the people who occupy this mutual arena develop their own tools, and the space becomes independent of the separate traditions. In this space, concepts are understood differently than from within the respective traditions; it is not that each tradition simply understands the concepts in a new way.

In this essay, I will not show how such a public space can be created, since the creation of such a space can only occur when scholars from different traditions actually engage in intercultural conversation for the purpose of finding concrete ways to live and converse together. This is as much a social and political endeavor as a moral one. Creating a common space for social discourse does not occur when an individual engages in comparative ethics or theology as an academic exercise. The purpose of this essay, then, is to show how scholars living in a multicultural community do not engage in ethics—especially in a public forum—from an objective standpoint that is independent from the norms and values of their respective traditions. Rather, as this essay attempts to make clear, the desire to live faithfully among others is an underlying motivation for how religious philosophers discuss ethics and for which rhetorical strategies religious philosophers will use and when. In other words, how they explain a norm or justify a value will depend on the audience being addressed and the point they are trying to make.

Before I provide examples of how philosophers in the Jewish tradition make medical ethics arguments, I want to first distinguish between Jewish medical law/medical halakha and Jewish medical ethics, as it pertains to this discussion. Medical halakha determines what a patient or a doctor who adheres to Jewish law can or cannot do. It is a question of both jurisprudence and practical detail. Writings of medical halakha attempt to justify particular actions with a sense of immediate relevancy; that is, they exemplify what is acceptable or obligatory to do in a given case. They justify those actions within coherent jurisprudential explanations, but they do not seek to build a grand schema that puts those positions into a greater philosophical context. Jewish medical ethics, on the other hand, attempts to uncover or provide—depending on the strategy—the values communicated through practical halakhic decision-making. In other words, it is the result of philosophical engagement with medical halakha, where the ethicist recognizes the underlying assumption that halakha, as a normative system, will contain information about the world (facts) and obligations for how to interact in that world (norms).[5] Jewish medical ethics can contribute to the broader questions of medicine and health care as they pertain to living in a multicultural environment when ethicists communicate those values in a language that is understood, not only by those who adhere to halakha but also by the broader public.

STRATEGIES OF DISCOURSE

Three major strategies that religious philosophers use when communicating an ethical stance are the pragmatic, the patriotic, and the personal. Use of each particular strategy will depend on the argument the philosopher is putting forth, the audience to whom he or she is speaking, and the people for whom the position applies.

Pragmatic Jewish Medical Ethics

The pragmatic strategy of communicating Jewish medical ethics attempts to use sources in the Jewish legal tradition to persuade society to allow for religious freedom. In this particular strategy, one recognizes that information and obligations can be interpreted in different ways,

given the exegetical perspective with which one approaches the law. Therefore, the pragmatic Jewish medical ethicist will give ethical explanations of halakhic facts and norms, yet not with the intention to explain the law as part of a coherent philosophical perspective. Rather, the intention is to give reasons for why observance of halakha should be permitted in a multicultural society.

Since the purpose of a pragmatic strategy is to normalize Jewish law so that the broader multicultural society is motivated to allow Jews to live in conformity with their tradition, pragmatic Jewish medical ethicists are "giving reasons for commandments." However, they are not "reasoning from the commandments." Providing reasons for commandments imposes reasons onto halakha that the greater community can both express and understand from its own context. In other words, pragmatic ethicists give reasons from a perspective that is outside their internal tradition; that is, they use the values of the greater society to justify why the position is persuasive. Reasoning from the commandments, on the other hand, is to apply moral reasoning to halakha, using halakha as a data set to uncover moral values that serve as premises for halakhic norms.[6] A Talmudic example of pragmatic Jewish ethical reasoning can be seen by the following anecdote:

A certain heathen asked Rabbi Yohanan ben Zakkai, "These rituals [of the red heifer] that you perform appear like witchcraft. You take a cow, burn it, pound it, and take its ashes. If one of you becomes impure from a dead body, you sprinkle upon him two or three drops, and say to him, "You are pure!" Rabbi Yohanan answered him, "Have you ever . . . seen a person possessed by the demon of madness?' Said the heathen, "Yes." "What do you do for him?" "We bring roots, and make them smoke under him, and sprinkle water upon the demon to exorcise it." Said Rabbi Yohanan, "Let your ears hear what you utter with your mouth! The spirit of impurity is exactly like this demon. . . . Water of purification is sprinkled upon the person made impure by contact with a corpse, and the spirit flees." When the heathen had left, Rabbi Yohanan's disciples asked him, "Our master! Him you dismissed with a flimsy excuse [Heb. *kaneh*], but what explanation do you offer us?" He said to them, "By your lives! It is not the corpse that makes one impure, nor the water that makes one pure. Rather, the Holy One, Blessed be He, declared, 'A chukka I have enacted, a decree I have issued; you may not violate my decree,' as it is written, 'This is the law [Heb. chukka] of the Torah' (Num. 19:2)."[7]

Rabbi Yohanan used a pragmatic strategy to justify the practice of the red heifer because he was faced with a challenge to its legitimacy on the grounds that it was not rational. The heathen did not seek to understand why the ritual was established in the first place; therefore, no response that sought to justify the rationality of the ritual within the Jewish theological-philosophical framework would satisfy. In order to persuade the heathen not to take offense to the practice Rabbi Yohanan had to explain it in terms with which the heathen was both familiar and valued as legitimate.

A contemporary example is when Jewish ethicists defend circumcision against anti-circumcision groups by justifying the ritual because of its health benefits. The protest against circumcision is oftentimes on the grounds that circumcision is cruel to infants and that the state has a responsibility under *parens patriae* to protect children from the religious whims of their parents. Any response claiming that God commands such "cruelty" to children will either be incomprehensible or stoke the coals of criticism. However, a response that includes data that circumcision has health benefits, including decreased risks of urinary tract infections, sexually transmitted diseases in men, and penile cancer, would serve to justify the "instrumental cruelty" for the sake of beneficence. Of course, the reason for circumcision in the Jewish tradition is because God commanded such, but mentioning the health benefits allows for a pragmatic justification for its acceptance by those parts of society that might question it.

The cost of employing a pragmatic strategy is that halakha becomes limited in its authority of enforcement and in the realm of its relevance, since its legitimacy has become dependent on its acceptance by the majority. When the majority does not accept halakha's legitimacy in a certain area of law, it will no longer have authority in that area. For example, since before the destruction of the Temple by the Romans and the loss of Jewish autonomy in the Land of Israel, Jewish law lost the authority to establish courts that preside over cases of criminal law.[8] This means that from that time onward its adherents must rely on different legal systems, namely, those of the states in which they live, to set the agenda for criminal law. Similarly, for a more contemporary example, the cost of allowing Jews in the United States to settle disputes through their own system of adjudication, such as the Beth Din of America, was to limit the Beth Din of America's authority by subordinating it to US civil law. As a court of arbitration, the Beth Din of America must conform to American civil law procedures. It also cannot rule in a way that is contrary to public policy or shows manifest disregard for US law;[9] otherwise, its decisions will be vacated by the courts.

Patriotic Jewish Medical Ethics

The patriotic strategy of communicating Jewish medical ethics attempts to enter the public conversation to promote Jewish values that the religious philosopher believes are also shared by the greater public. In this strategy, one recognizes that the Jewish tradition is both particular to the Jewish people and is universal through the institution of the Noahide laws,[10] so that certain values are meant to be promoted broadly.

The cost of employing a patriotic strategy is that halakha, in this case, also must be limited in its authority due to external considerations, albeit for different reasons. Certain values have different practical ramifications, depending on whether they are embedded in a Jewish legal framework or a broader one that includes both Jews and non-Jews. The reason for the differences would be that the value must fit within a broader social view and cannot be appreciated independently of its relationship to other facts and norms within a system. Because Jewish law is particular to the historical development and theological goals of the Jewish people, values embedded within it will be related to each other through priorities that differ in both kind and order from those adopted in the Noahide system, which applies to humanity as a whole. For example, Jewish laws of lineage are strictly social in nature.[11] Therefore, when a non-Jewish person converts to Judaism, halakhically, they are considered as not having any relatives. A consequence of this is that according to Torah law, if a brother and sister both convert, they may marry each other, since they are not considered to be related. However, the rabbinic position recognizes that this exception to the prohibition of incest occurs because the situation is so rare, and law, while a delimiting set of principles and regulations, does not account for every situation but rather provides a general set of norms that apply to the reasonable person in probable situations. Therefore, knowing that this exception might raise ethical concerns for the broader public, there is a rabbinic decree that two siblings who convert may not be married, for fear that people might say that "they came from a place of greater holiness to a place of lesser holiness."[12] When the rabbis instituted this decree, they did not subordinate their values to the values of the greater public; rather, they promoted Jewish social values and their application of them to a case where they were not explicitly mandated. In doing so, however, they looked to the outside world in their consideration of an internal affair.

The need to consider external viewpoints when employing a patriotic strategy also creates a difficulty in applying shared values that have conflicting ramifications when seen through both Jewish and Noahide law. This gives rise to situations in which, when addressing the general public, the patriotic Jewish ethicist could be forced to promote a position that is different from the one he or she would be obliged to affirm within an internal Jewish ethical discourse. For example, the jurisprudential analysis of abortion with respect to Noahide law is different from the one affirmed within Jewish law. To explain, the Talmud cites Rabbi Yishmael that a Noahide who aborts a fetus has the legal status of a murderer,[13] and Maimonides codifies the law in accordance with the view of Rabbi Yishmael.[14] Among the legal commentators, there is a debate as to whether making abortion a capital offense implies that a fetus is a person with rights under Noahide law or whether the offense relates not to the severity of the crime but rather to a policy of stringency with respect to punishment under Noahide law. The former position would disallow even therapeutic abortions.[15] However, in halakha, there are times when therapeutic abortions are permitted.[16] Given this jurisprudential difference, what policy should patriotic Jewish medical ethicists promote? If they were to promote a position that disallows even therapeutic abortions, they would be advocating a position that is in conflict with Jewish law and hinders a pragmatic strategy. If they were to promote a position that allows for therapeutic abortions, they would be advocating a position that they think is contrary to universal values, or at least norms, as prescribed by Noahide law. Of course, advocating a discriminatory policy that differentiates between Jews and non-Jews is not an option, since it contradicts the principle of substantive justice that is held so highly in our multicultural environment, which promotes equality and consistency of treatment for everyone, regardless of race or creed.

As this case demonstrates, a further consideration that must be taken with respect to promoting a patriotic strategy relates to whether Jewish law obligates Jews to promote universal values as dictated by Noahide law, or whether Jewish law just requires Jews to adhere to such values when their application is in line with halakha. The relevance of this consideration does not concern the question whether to take a patriotic stance at all, but rather when—such as in the case of abortion—taking a patriotic stance would be pragmatically detrimental for the Jewish internal position. Within the Jewish legal tradition, there is a difference in one's obligation to enforce or impose Jewish law upon Jews and the lack of obligation to enforce or impose Noahide law upon non-Jews.[17] However, it is nonetheless seen as meritorious to persuade non-Jews to follow Noahide law.[18] If promoting universal values is meritorious but not an obligation, then a patriotic Jewish ethicist can promote pragmatism at the legal level and persuasion at the level of civil society.

In the contemporary American debate over abortion, which is a good example of a topic where there is little if any common ground of discourse between opposing sides, the Jewish medical ethicist can provide a strategy for public policy that allows for compromise. While currently each side of this debate is starkly drawn, leaving little room for dialogue, a normative Jewish social position may be promoted that allows for nuance without imposing its own internal belief system. Instead of using legislation to enforce unilaterally one's position regarding the ethics of abortion, the debate over abortion should start with respecting the fact that both positions are firmly rooted in a moral or legal tradition, and each tradition starts with different and opposing value premises. If neither side can convince the other of its conclusions—because they start with different premises—then the positions of both sides should be respected as a pragmatic decision and legitimized by the law. In practice, the law should provide a safe means for women to make choices, yet communities should recognize that no person lives without influence from neighbors and friends. Those who want to reduce the number of abortions that occur in this country should look to inform individuals for whom they care and with whom they live rather than attempt to make changes by legislative fiat. In the multicultural society in which we live, policy choices and legislation should take into account what is possible to achieve, given any opposition between traditions, both in terms of respecting the traditions themselves and in finding a common ground where open dialogue can be persuasive, rather than relying on legislation that can be viewed as oppressive and ignored.

Personal Jewish Medical Ethics

The personal strategy of communicating Jewish medical ethics does not attempt to enter the public conversation in order to promote Jewish values in society directly, but rather seeks to reinforce those values in those who adhere to Jewish law. It seeks to find ways to meaningfully integrate those values into everyday life and not allow for observance of them to devolve into routine, unreflective habit. The value of this approach for the sake of advancing public discourse is to encourage Jewish ethicists to have a strong sense of cultural heritage and understanding of their tradition as well as to develop the depth and confidence needed to promote its values in the public sphere.

Jewish ethicists will rely on each of the above strategies, depending on context and the audience they are addressing. Therefore, it is important to understand each strategy and know when each is being used and, importantly, how each strategy relates to informing discussion in the public sphere. If one looks at all religious arguments as having the same strategy, then contradictory claims or reasons can come across as incoherent. However, if one knows which strategy is being used, then one can determine how relevant the argument is in terms of weighing the normative claim and the reasons given to justify it.

Moreover, when creating a common space for discourse, recognizing differences in perspective can provide context and counterpoint in the public debate over issues in health care. Providing context and counterpoint, however, is different from engaging in the creation of a public space for discourse. It is, nevertheless, a first step, since it shows how different traditions reveal others' value premises when they must explain themselves to others. Below, I will give two examples to show how this occurs when a Jewish perspective on an issue is juxtaposed with views from other traditions.

CONTEXT AND COUNTERPOINT

Withholding and Withdrawing Care

Even though withholding and withdrawing care are still referred to as distinct concepts in conversations regarding end-of-life care, US law and the American Medical Association (AMA) Code of Ethics state that there is no ethical or legal difference between withdrawing and withholding a medical therapy, which includes, among others, mechanical ventilation, renal dialysis, chemotherapy, antibiotics, and artificial nutrition and hydration. The distinction between the concepts of withholding and withdrawing care originates in Catholic moral theology, and the underlying premise for the distinction is that there is a difference between actively doing something that facilitates death and passively allowing nature to take its course. Jewish medical ethics, on the other hand, like US law and secular ethics, does not distinguish between withholding and withdrawing care, except for certain circumstances outside the scope of this analysis, yet it arrives almost at the opposite conclusions than that of US law and medical ethics. Jewish medical ethics conceives withholding and withdrawing as morally objectionable in most cases where US law and secular medical ethics would not. However, understanding the Jewish medical ethics view can better clarify the US legal and the AMA's positions than continuing only to contrast the position with one that makes a distinction between action and passivity.

The philosophical justification for not distinguishing between withholding and withdrawing in secular medical ethics and law is explained through the equivalence thesis:

1. If it would have been morally permissible to have withheld therapy (that was in fact already started), then it is now morally permissible to withdraw that therapy.
2. If, in the future, it would be morally permissible to withdraw a therapy (that has, in fact, not yet been started), then it is now morally permissible to withhold that therapy.

The first point assumes that ethical analysis begins at the current moment without any consideration with what has already occurred. The second point assumes that a potential future decision should retrofit into current decision-making. The equivalency thesis does not give moral weight to continuing the status quo if one is currently treating a person.

Jewish law does not make a distinction between passive and active in this case, as either can be an abrogation of one's duty, though it does recognize gradations in causality. There is, however, a Jewish jurisprudential principle that advocates passivity when there is a conflict between two legal directives. This rabbinic concept allows one to override a Torah law passively when it is necessary to ensure broader Torah observance. For example, Jews do not blow the shofar when Rosh Hashanah is on the Sabbath for fear of carrying it in a public domain, which is a Torah prohibition. This principle does not simply promote passivity in contradistinction to action. In being passive, one is upholding a principle or a duty. Therefore, passivity, in this case, should be seen as actively refraining from performing an obligation in deference to another obligation. The consequences of passivity and activity are weighed against each other. With respect to withholding and withdrawing care, the moral question is not simply what would be the consequences of acting or not acting. Rather, the question begins with laying out what are the duties to treat, whether treatment would be efficacious or simply prolonging the process of dying, and how causative would one's actions or inaction be in facilitating death given one's duty. Unlike the equivalence thesis, this view is temporal in analysis, since it does give moral weight to continuing the status quo of currently treating a person.

The similarity between the secular and the Jewish approach is that moral obligation or accountability does not rest solely with the actions or passivity of the physician. Rather, in both frameworks, ethical deliberation begins with the question, "What is the relationship between physician and patient, and what obligations does that relationship entail?" In secular medical ethics, the physician's obligations are contingent on the contractual nature of the patient-physician relationship; therefore, it is morally permissible to withhold or withdraw care both in the event that care is medically non-beneficial and in the event that the patient terminates the relationship. In the Jewish medical ethics framework, on the other hand, because physicians have an independent obligation to treat that is not contingent on a formal patient-physician relationship, withholding and withdrawing care in many cases is morally permissible when the duty to treat has been annulled for medical reasons only and not because the patient wants to terminate the patient-physician relationship. By attempting to show how the Jewish view provides context for the secular view of withholding and withdrawing, I am not advocating for paternalism or medical battery. Rather, I am trying to show how the secular view—that the ethics of withholding and withdrawing are determined in light of the patient-physician relationship and not solely from the actions of the physician—can be more fully understood when also compared to a Jewish framework that shares the premise that decisions should be seen in light of the patient-physician relationship rather than when explained solely by contrasting the equivalence thesis with a position that distinguishes between withholding and withdrawing.

Reproductive Autonomy versus the Traditionalist View

The World Health Organization defines reproductive rights as follows: "[R]eproductive rights embrace certain human rights that are already recognized in national laws, international human rights documents and other consensus documents. These rights rest on the recognition of the basic right of all couples and individuals to decide freely and responsibly the number, spacing and timing of their children and to have the information and means to do so, and the right to attain the highest standard of sexual and reproductive health. It also includes their right to make decisions concerning reproduction free of discrimination, coercion and violence, as expressed in human rights documents."[19] In line with this definition, reproductive rights commonly include the right to legal and safe abortion; the right to birth control; freedom from coerced sterilization, abortion, and contraception; the right to access good quality reproductive healthcare; and the right to education and access, in order to make free and informed reproductive choices. As the examples attest (though the definition can be read otherwise), reproductive rights are traditionally seen as negative rights (that is, the right to have someone not interfere) and not as an entitlement right (the right for society to give a person the ability to have a child if he or she currently cannot). Similarly, US Supreme Court cases that established legal thinking about procreative liberty and autonomy seem to interpret reproductive rights as a right to be protected against interference. For example, *Griswold v. Connecticut* (1965) was a landmark case that affirmed the "right to marital privacy." *Eisenstadt v. Baird* (1972) extended the right of marital privacy to unmarried people, permitting them to use contraception on the same basis as married couples. *Planned Parenthood of Southern Pennsylvania v. Casey* (1992) upheld the constitutional right to have an abortion. Nevertheless, the question of whether reproductive rights should be considered as negative rights or entitlement rights creates diverging attitudes towards artificial reproductive technology.

One view that looks at reproductive rights as entitlements advocates unlimited procreative liberty. From this perspective, people should have the right to produce children in any manner that they see fit, have the right to produce the type of children that they want, and be able to create any type of family they want, as well as to expect that society has an obligation to provide them with means to be able to do so. The state's concern with preserving a certain image of the family does not justify prohibition of non-coital, collaborative conception. This view is also rooted in the notion that individuals have a right to choose and live the kind of life that they find meaningful and fulfilling and that the purpose of society is to provide the ability for people to achieve it.[20]

The traditionalist view, on the other hand, conceives of human procreation, though seemingly an exclusively private act, as having a profoundly public meaning. This view considers how procreation determines the relationship between one generation and the next; how it shapes identities, and creates attachments and responsibilities for the care and rearing of children (and the care of aging parents or other needy kin). Moreover, this view sees procreation as a way to accept, rather than reshape, engineer, or design the next generation. It emphasizes the idea that a child is not a possession to be created based on the parents' wishes.[21] Rather, parental love should be founded on a sense of "natural humility," by which is meant restraining from changing the natural world to suit social desires. In this perspective, people are not entitled to reproduce and cannot demand society to assist them; rather, reproduction is a gift and a responsibility incumbent on people.

However, others cannot take away that individual's responsibility; doing so would be a violation of his or her negative liberty to be free from outside interference.

In the Jewish tradition, reproduction is considered a great commandment (mitzvah), not a right; yet, the community still has an interest in providing means to assist people with difficulty having children. Also, the Jewish tradition upholds that it is proper at times to manipulate nature for the betterment of humankind. However, the determination of what is "better" is not a matter of individual or even social choice but rather is based on the duties set forth by Jewish law.[22] This view can be seen as a counterpoint position for both those who uphold reproductive autonomy and those who propose traditionalism, because it shares values that are affirmed by each perspective. It shares the view with the traditionalists that life is sacred and should not be manipulated "willy-nilly." With those who advocate for reproductive autonomy, it shares the value of human genetic improvement, even though it would define what is considered "better" in terms of its own internal framework. Introducing the Jewish view as another voice in public discourse on this topic can provide an avenue to begin creating a common space outside of the two opposing positions, since it can show how the values of each position can be appreciated so that there is mutual understanding for compromise.

CONCLUSION

In providing these examples, my goal is not to show how Jewish medical ethics compares to other forms of ethical decision-making in healthcare. Rather, my goal is to show how introducing voices into public discourse and knowing the strategies those voices use in promoting their positions might enable us to appreciate the complexity and nuance of multicultural compromise. To change public dialogue from being a cacophony of voices to one that allows for people to hear each other and find a common language in which to communicate is a very different and much harder enterprise than simply giving other voices an opportunity to speak (though this, of course, is necessary). However, creating a common space is possible if we recognize its importance and understand how and why different voices promote their positions. Only when we recognize from where each of us is coming can we search together for solutions.

REFERNCES

1. The Jewish tradition recognizes and provides canonical support for differentiating between internal and external modes of communicating values that lie at the foundation of Jewish law. From an internal Jewish perspective, the sages proffer that there are seventy ways to understand the Torah (Numbers Rabbah 13:15.), which indicates that they recognize that concepts in the Torah can survive different paradigms and languages of explanation, and that there can be diversity within a unified people. From an external perspective, the sages state that every single word that God spoke was split into seventy languages, corresponding to each of the seventy nations of the world (BT Shabbat 88b; see also Exodus Rabbah 5:9). Multilingual communication is not for Israel's benefit in gaining a deeper understanding through linguistic distinctions, since that type of benefit is proffered by the first rabbinic source; rather, it is to provide a means for universal acceptance of certain values, albeit in a different mode than is found within the internal Jewish tradition. This dual notion is supported by the sages' explanation of the second time the Israelites received the Torah, which occurred during the last weeks of Moses' life and before their entrance into the Land of Israel. The verse that introduces Moses' repetition states, "On the other side of the Jordan in the land of Moab, Moses began explaining this Torah, saying..." (Deut. 1:5). The sages understand the word "explain" to mean that Moses expounded the Torah in the seventy languages of the nations of the world (Midrash Tanhuma, Devarim 2; Genesis Rabbah 49:2). Moreover, after he finished explaining the Torah to the people, the Torah records Moses commanding the people to erect stones, coat them with plaster, and inscribe upon them all the words of this Torah, well clarified (Deut. 27:1–8). Because the words "explain" and "clarified" are linguistically related in Hebrew, the sages understood that the inscription on the stones was also written in seventy languages (BT Sotah 32a). The giving of the Torah by Moses to the Israelites was modeled after the giving of the Torah on Mount Sinai. Translations of the Torah were given for the nations of the world so as to provide a means for them to learn the lessons the Torah provides.

2. Translation is not only a process of converting a word from one language to another; it can also mean converting something from one form of discourse to another.

3. For a more in-depth analysis of this claim, see Alasdair C. MacIntyre's *After Virtue: A Study in Moral Theory*. Bloomsbury Revelations (London: Bloomsbury, 2014).

4. Alasdair C. MacIntyre, *Whose Justice? Which Rationality?* (Notre Dame, IN: University of Notre Dame Press, 2008), defines the relativist challenge as a denial that rational debate between, and rational choice among, rival traditions is possible. Relativism exists because each tradition has its own internal characteristic modes of justification; therefore, no tradition can deny the legitimacy of another. The perspectivist claim, as perceived by MacIntyre, is that each rival tradition is a mutually exclusive way of understanding the same thing; therefore, the rival traditions are just complementary perspectives for one and the same truth.

5. Laws, as normative reasons for acting, must possess both explanatory and descriptive reasons as well as normative ones. This is because the normativity of a normative reason depends on a person recognizing the facts that the normative reason entails. Therefore, normative reasons must be able to describe the reality of a situation properly, to explain why the situation contains a normative aspect, and to explain why a particular response is appropriate.

6. For a more in-depth explanation of reasoning as recognizing and responding to legal reasons, see Ira Bedzow, "An Alternative View of Reasons and Reasoning," in *Maimonides for Moderns: A Statement of Contemporary Jewish Philosophy* (Cham, CH: Palgrave Macmillan, 2017). 157–90.

7. Numbers Rabbah 19:8.

8. BT Sanhedrin 41a; JT Sanhedrin 1:18a.

9. Federal Arbitration Act, 9 USC §10(a) (2002).

10. The Noahide laws are normative for non-Jews and were prescriptive for Jews before the giving of the

Torah (BT Hullin 100b). The Noahide legal system consists of seven general instructions concerning adjudication, idolatry, blasphemy, sexual immorality, bloodshed, robbery, and the eating of a limb torn from a living animal (Tosefta, Avoda Zara 8:4–6; BT Sanhedrin 56a–b); and they are identified as being within the first commandment given to the first human being, "And Hashem Elohim commanded regarding the man saying, 'Of every tree of the garden you may certainly eat.' (Gen. 2:16)." Even though the laws were given to the first human being, they are still called the "Noahide laws," since mankind is considered to be descended from Noah after the Flood. The general nature of the Noahide laws allows for the existence of differences in moral temperament across different societies, even if the broader ethical outlines are the same. Given a certain location, customs may develop that may be different from those in other places due to the constraints of geography, demography, and economy. With varying customs will come varying social perspectives and, hence, different nuances in moral temperament. The relationship between law and ethics is, therefore, easier to see through a more comprehensive legal system such as Jewish law than through a more general one.

11. Shulhan Arukh, *Even HaEzer* 1–4.
12. BT Yevamot 22a; Shulhan Arukh, *Yoreh Deah* 269:1.
13. Sanhedrin 57b.
14. Maimonides, Hilkhot Melakhim 9:4.
15. This is in accord with certain positions on abortion in both the Catholic and Natural Law traditions.
16. Rabbi I. Y. Unterman, *Noam* VI (1963): 1–11; Rabbi Moshe Feinstein, *Iggrot Moshe, Choshen Mishpat* 2:69; Rabbi Eliezer Waldenberg, *Tzitz Eliezer* 13:102, 14:101.
17. *Tur, Yoreh Deah* 158:1; Beit Yosef *Yoreh Deah* 158 s.v. *rebenu umekol makom, Hoshen Mishpat* 425; *Bach* on *Tur, Yoreh Deah* 158 s.v. *umekol makom; Drisha* on *Tur, Yoreh Deah* 158:1, *Sema, Hoshen Mishpat* 425:15–19; *Darkhei Moshe He'Arukh Yoreh Deah* 158 s.v. *ain moredim;* Shulhan Arukh, *Yoreh Deah* 158:1–2; *Shach, Yoreh Deah* 158:2; *Taz, Yoreh Deah* 158:1.
18. *Book of Jonah* 3:1–10. Rabbi Menachem Mendel Schneerson, "Sheva Mitzvot Shel Benei Noah," *HaPardes* 59, no. 9 (1985), 7–11.
19. WHO, "Guiding principles: human rights and gender equality," in *Consolidated Guideline on Sexual and Reproductive Health and Rights of Women Living with HIV.* Geneva: World Health Organization; 2017. Licence: CC BY-NC-SA 3.0 IGO: chap 1.42, accessed June 27, 2017, http://apps.who.int/iris/bitstream/10665/254885/1/9789241549998-eng.pdf?ua=1/.
20. John A. Robertson, "Procreative Liberty and the Control of Conception, Pregnancy, and Childbirth," *Virginia Law Review* 69 (1983): 405–64.
21. Leon R. Kass, *Human Cloning and Human Dignity: The Report of the President's Council on Bioethics* (Washington, DC: Public Affairs, 2002), accessed September 3, 2017, https://bioethicsarchive.georgetown.edu/pcbe/reports/cloningreport/preface.html/.
22. This can be seen by the statement of Rabbi Akiva, "God did not give the commandments because He wants them for His own need but in order to refine the Jewish people." As King David says in Tehillim (18:31), "The saying of God is [for the purpose of] refinement."

החופה בספרות חז"ל – סמל בתהליך שינוי

ניסן רובין

מבוא

במשך דורות רבים ועד ימינו החופה היא סמל מרכזי בטקס נישואים יהודי. החופה המקובלת עשויה יריעת בד מתוחה על ארבעה מוטות. מתחתיה החתן מארס תחילה את הכלה בברכות אירוסים; אחר-כך מקדש אותה בטבעת; ומסיים בברכות נישואים הידועים כ"שבע ברכות".

בספרות תנאים אנו מוצאים תהליך שונה של התקשרות בני זוג. תהליך זה נעשה בכמה שלבים: תחילה נערכו אירוסים בבית אבי-הכלה, שכללו קידושים וכתובה. השלב הבא היה טקס העברת הכלה לבית אבי-החתן. השלב המסיים את תהליך ההתקשרות בין בני הזוג היה טקס הנישואים, שתחילתו בכניסת הזוג לחופה. כבר עתה אציין שמלכתחילה לא היתה החופה מרכיב עקרוני בטקס הנישואים, ורק מתקופה מסוימת, שידובר בה להלן, תפסה בו החופה והכניסה לחופה, מקום מרכזי.[1]

במאמר זה אני מבקש לעקוב ראשית, אחר תהליך ההתגבשות של החופה כסמל מרכזי בנישואים. שנית, להבין את השינויים במרכיבים הסמליים שלו. שלישית, להסביר את הרקע החברתי לשינויים במשמעויות של הסמל.

בדרך-כלל עוסק המחקר הסוציולוגי והאנתרופולוגי בחברות בנות זמננו. בחברות הללו יש לחוקרים נגישות בלתי אמצעית לחברה הנחקרת באמצעות מתודות שונות, כשאלוני-מחקר, ראיונות, תצפיות ועוד. אבל, כאשר המחקר עוסק בחברה מסורתית-היסטורית, כמו החברה היהודית בתקופת המשנה והתלמוד, הנגישות לחברה הנחקרת אינה ישירה, אלא בעיקר, באמצעות חקר של קורפוס נתונים קיים: התלמודים והמדרשים, הספרים האפוקליפטיים והאפוקריפיים, מגילות מדבר יהודה, כתבי פילון האלכסנדרוני, האוונגליונים, היסטוריונים יהודים ונוכרים ועוד. במאמר זה אני בודק את מנהג החופה רק מתוך התלמודים והמדרשים, המייצגים תקופה של מאות שנים שבוודאי מתחוללות בה תמורות. כי הרי גם בחברה מסורתית, שנתפסת כחברה סטאטית בעיני עצמה, קורים בהדרגה שינויים שיש לחשוף את גורמיהם. אולם, כאשר חוקרים תהליכי שינוי אין להסתפק בהצגת השינויים אלא להציע הסברים לתמורות שהתגלו. באמצעות מתודה

מבנית-סטרוקטורלית אני מבקש להתקדם לקראת הסבר התופעה. מתודה קלאסית זו שמקשרת בין תופעות חברתיות שונות, ראשיתה באמיל דורקהיים ואחרים[2] והמשכה בפרנן ברודל והיא משמשת כאמצעי לניתוח שינויים במשך-זמן היסטורי ארוך (longue durée).[3] מתודה זו מבודדת את מרכיבי המבנה החברתי ובודקת אם קיים קשר בו-זמני בין שינוי שחל במרכיב אחד של המבנה לבין מרכיב שני.[4] במקרה שלפנינו אני מבקש, כאמור, לבדוק את ה"חופה" כסמל במבנה החברתי. למרות שהמושג חופה הוא סמל עתיק ונזכר במקרא, תוכנו הלך והשתנה, ויש לבדוק לאילו תמורות במבנה החברתי קשור שינוי זה. אך לפני שנדון בכך, נברר תחילה את מהותה של החופה.

מהות החופה

חופה כמבנה יציב

החופה נזכרת הרבה במקורות חז"ל, אך לא תמיד מתקבלת תמונה אחידה על מהותה. מספר חוקרים חשובים כבר בירררו את המושג; נלך בעקבותיהם ונוסיף את מה שיהיה לנו להוסיף. בפירוט דנו בזה קרויס והרשברג[5] ואחריהם ביכלר,[6] שהשיג עליהם. טענתו היתה שקרויס והרשברג אינם מבחינים בין זמנים ומקומות של המקורות שאליהם הם מתייחסים, וממילא עולה מהם תמונה שאינה תואמת לחיים האמתיים.

נברר תחילה את המושג "חופה". המובן המקראי של חופה הוא חדר: "יצא חתן מחדרו וכלה מֵחֻפָּתָהּ" (יואל ב ט').[7] לכאורה, המקביל לחדר החתן הוא חופת הכלה. אבל מהפסוק "והוא כחתן יוצא מֵחֻפָּתוֹ" (תהלים יט ו'), משתמע כי חדר החתן הוא שנקרא חופה. מתקבל על הדעת ששניהם, החתן והכלה, ישבו בחדר שנקרא חופה, ורק לצורך הצורה הפיוטית השתמש הנביא יואל במילים נרדפות – "חדר" ו"חופה". ביכלר דוחה בצדק את קביעתו של הרשברג הטוען כי החופה היא מעין כילה של בד סביב המיטה; מקורות; שנציגם להלן – מלמדים שהחופה היתה סוג של מבנה, כנראה זמני, אבל יציב. כבר עתה יש לומר, כי לא בכל זמן ובכל מקום היתה נהוגה חופה. במקום

שנהגו, יש שהיו מקימים את החופה בתוך חדר גדול, ויש שהיו בונים אותה סמוך לבית. החופה, שהייתה מעוטרת, הייתה משמשת את הזוג גם לשינה. בחופה נערכה ברכת החתנים (או "שבע ברכות") הראשונה – לפני החתן והכלה יחד. נראה כי בשאר שבעת ימי המשתה, כאשר בירכו ברכת חתנים, לא הייתה הכלה נוכחת בחופה בעת הברכות. אבל החתן היה מקבל שם את אורחיו כל שבעת הימים, כשהוא מוקף בשושביניו וב"בני החופה" (חברים המלווים את החתן ויושבים אתו בחופה. על המושג – להלן). בה בעת ישבה הכלה בחדרה, בנפרד מהחתן, עם הנשים וחברותיה שבאו לכבדה.

המשמעות הסמלית של החופה גלויה לעין. בחברה פטריארכלית ופטרילינאלית (שהייחוס עובר בה רק הזכרים בלבד) הכלה באה לגור עם בעלה בקרב המשפחה הרחבה של בית-האב שלו. לכן טקס הנישואין הוא בבית-האב של החתן, וטקס זה מבטא את מיזוג הכלה בביתו. זאת לעומת טקס האירוסין, שנערך בבית-האב של הכלה, שממנו היא יוצאת, והוא טקס ניתוקה מבית אביה.

חברה חקלאית מבוססת בדרך-כלל על משפחות רחבות עם משקי בית הכוללים את משפחת האב ומשפחות בניו הנשואים, כפי שהיו במקומות ובזמנים מסוימים בארץ-ישראל. במשפחה הגרעינית של הבנים בתוך המשפחה הרחבה, אין את מידת האינטימיות שיש במשפחות גרעיניות עצמאיות המנותקות מבית-האב, כי המשפחה הרחבה מעורבת באופן אינטנסיבי ביומיום של המשפחה הגרעינית. למרות האמור, החופה, המיועדת לחתן ולכלה למשך שבעת ימי המשתה של החתונה, מגדירה באופן זמני את הזוג כיחידה אינטימית בתוך המשפחה הרחבה. כי החופה היא מבנה של חדר סגור העשוי ממחיצות עמידות יחסית, אבל אינו מבנה של קבע. חופה זו היא, מצד אחד, חדר אינטימי שמסמל לאינטימיות; אבל, מצד שני, מבנה ארעי לפריצה על-ידי המשפחה הרחבה. החופה מקבלת אפוא, מעמד זמני של טריטוריה משותפת ובלעדית לכלה ולבעלה בתוך בית-האב של בעלה, אפילו עם זכות-יתר מסוימת לכלה כמקום אינטימי משלה. זכות זו מתבטאת בהסברו של ר' יוחנן (דור שני לאמוראי ארץ-ישראל): "למדתך תורה דרך ארץ שאין חתן נכנס לחופה [לקיום יחסי אישות] עד שתהא כלה נותנת לו רשות [למרות שהמקום הוא רכושו]. הדא הוא דכתיב [זהו שכתוב]: 'יבא דודי לְגַנּוֹ וְיֹאכַל פְּרִי מְגָדָיו' (שיר השירים ד ט"ז). ואחר-כך: 'בָּאתִי לְגַנִּי אֲחֹתִי כַלָּה' (שיר השירים ה א')" (ויקרא רבה ט ו, עמ' קפה). לאחר שבעת הימים הם עוזבים את חופתם ומתמזגים כזוג בתוך המשפחה הרחבה. נראה שדפוס כזה היה מצוי בראשית ימי תקופת המשנה, כשמשק בית של משפחה רחבה היה שכיח. סביר שדפוס זה המשיך להתקיים בקרב משפחות עירוניות מהמעמד הבינוני ובקרב משפחות

עירוניות עשירות גם בשנים מאוחרות יותר, כשהמשפחה החקלאית הרחבה נעשתה נדירה.

הדים לחופה כמבנה יציב נשמעים מכמה מקורות. המשנה אומרת: "לעולם היא [בת ישראל המאורסת לכוהן] ברשות האב [ואינה אוכלת תרומה], עד שתיכנס לחופה" (משנה, כתובות ד ה). הירושלמי אומר על משנה זו: "לא סוף דבר לחופה אלא לבית שיש לו חופה בעי [צריך]" (ירושלמי, כתובות ד ד, כח ע"ד). כלומר, אין צורך שתיכנס לחופה כדי לאכול בתרומה; די שתיכנס לבית שיש בו חופה. בהמשך עולה מדברי ר' אלעזר שאם יש לבית טרקלין וקיטון, חופה וקיטון ונכנסה לטרקלין – היא נחשבת לנשואה לעניין ירושה, גם אם לא נכנסה לחופה. מדובר אפוא, לפי דברי האמוראים, בחופה שהיא חדר לעצמאי.

מסוף תקופת התנאים מצוי הסיפור הבא: "רבי עבד ליה הלולא לר' שמעון ברבי, כתב על בית גנגא: עשרין וארבעה אלפין ריבואין דינרין נפקין על בית גנגא דין ולא אזמיניה לבר קפרא [רבי יהודה הנשיא עשה חתונה לר' שמעון בנו, ולא הזמינו את בר קפרא, כמחאה כתב בר קפרא על החופה (=בית גנגא): 'עשרים וארבעה אלפי ריבוא דינרים יצאו על חופה זו ובר קפרא לא הוזמן']" (בבלי, נדרים נ ע"ב). מבנה שהושקע בו סכום עתק כזה, ושאפשר גם לכתוב עליו כתובת מחאה, ודאי שאינו כילת מיטה.[8]

דוגמא נוספת לכך שחופה היא מבנה, מצויה במדרש, שאומרו הוא מראשית תקופת האמוראים בארץ-ישראל:

אמר ר' הושעיא: למה הדבר דומה? לכלה שהייתה עומדת בתוך חופתה ונתפחמו ידיה. אם מקנחת היא אותם בכותל – הכותל מתפחם וידיה אין מתנקות; ואם בפסיפס – הפסיפס מתפחם וידיה אין מתנקות; ואם מקנחת היא בשערה – שערה היא מתנאה וידיה מתנקות. (דברים רבה, וילנא, א י)

מדרש זה המתאר את מבוכת הכלה, מאשש את הנאמר לעיל שהחופה הייתה מקום אינטימי של הכלה בימי שבעת ימי המשתה.

גם משני מדרשים מאוחרים יותר נראה שכך הבינו את הדבר. הראשון הוא של אמורא ארצישראלי מהדור הרביעי: ר' פינחס אמר: למלך שהיה משיא בנו ועשה לו חופה, סיידה וכיירה וציירה, כעס המלך על בנו והרגו, נכנס בחופה התחיל לשבר בקנים ומכפיע בחצאות ומקרע בילאות [ולשבר מחיצות ולקרוע וילונות]. אמר: בני אבד ואילו קיימין?

(בראשית רבה כח ו, עמ' 265)

בחופה זו יש "קנים", יש מחיצות, וגם וילונות. הרס כמתואר במשל חייב להיות בדבר יציב, כי המשל מעניד

את המת הנעדר מול החופה הקיימת, שאותה הוא הרס. הרס של כילה רופפת לא היה משאיר את הרושם שהמשל מבקש להטביע. המדרש השני מעביר אותנו אל גניבה בבבל, שהיה בדור השלישי לאמוראים. זו אותה חופה המתוארת במשל של ר' פנחס הארצישראלי:

גניבה ורבנין גניבה אמר למלך שעשה לו חופה, סיידה וכיירה וציירה, ומה היה חופה חסירה, כלה שתכנס לתוכה.

(בראשית רבה י ב, עמ' 85).

מהמדרשים הללו וממקורות הלכתיות שהוזכרו למעלה, מובן מאליו שבבית-האב מקימים את החופה לבן. אבל במדרש אחר נמצא משל יוצא דופן, המדבר על חופה שהאב עושה דווקא לבתו. מאוד מתקבל על הדעת שהמדרש הוא ביטוי למציאות מוכרת לדרשן. המדרש הוא מפי ר' יונתן, דור שלישי לאמוראי ארץ-ישראל, בן זמנם של הדרשנים שהוזכרו קודם, ר' פנחס ור' גניבה:

ר' יונתן אמר למלך שהשיא את בתו ועשה לה חופה ובית וסיידה וכיירה וציירה וראה אותה וערבה לו. אמר: בתי, בתי הלווי [הלוואי] החופה הזו תהא מעלה חן לפני בכל עת כשם שהעלית חן לפני בשעה הזו.

(בראשית רבה ט א, עמ' 69)

מגניבה למדנו על האפשרות שהאב יכין את מבנה החופה לבנו, עוד לפני שמצויה לו כלה. מר' יונתן למדנו על האפשרות שהאב נותן לבתו בית כנדוניה ובנוסף לכך מכין את החופה בביתו. משמעות הדבר הוא שהנישואין הם בבית הכלה ולא בבית החתן. דבר זה מלמד על שינוי במבנה המשפחה – ממשפחה רחבה למשפחה גרעינית.[9] אז, אם לאבי הכלה יש אמצעים כלכליים (במשל של ר' יונתן אבי-הכלה הוא "מלך", כלומר, בעל אמצעים) ולאבי החתן אין, החופה יכולה להיעשות בבית הכלה. ייתכן שהמדרשים המאוחרים על חופה בבית החתן, ממשלים משלים על-פי מציאות של מבנה משפחה שכבר לא קיים, או קיים רק במקצת מקומות ובמקצת משפחות. ייתכן גם שהממשלים נבנו לצורך הנמשל, ואינם משקפים מציאות היסטורית עכשווית.[10] המקורות המוקדמים יותר על חופה בבית החתן בוודאי מייצגים מציאות היסטורית של זמנם. כך, לדוגמא, משלו של ר' יהושע בן קרחה, מהדור הרביעי לתנאים באמצע המאה השנייה: "לאדם שעשה חופה לבנו והתקין מכל מיני סעודה. לימים מת בנו, עמד ופזר את חופתו" (בבלי, סנהדרין קח ע"א). אין פירוש הדברים שבמאות המאוחרות יותר לא היו חופות בבית החתן. וודאי שהיו. אולם המשבר הכלכלי הגדול באימפריה הרומית של המאה השלישית היה בין הגורמים לשינויים במבנה

המשפחה, כך שניתן למצוא דפוסי משפחה שונים באותה חברה. לפיכך, מי שהאמצעים בידיו עושה חופה, או – כמו שמקובל בכל מקום – שני הצדדים משתווים ביניהם על ההוצאות, ומקימים החופה במקום שמחליטים.

"קושרי חופה" ו"בני חופה"

החופה הייתה, כאמור, יציבה אבל ארעית. זאת ניתן ללמוד ממעשה הגג שלה, שהיה גג ארעי, מעין סכך של סוכה, שחבריו החתן היו מתקינים: "רבי אמי ורבי אסי הוו קא קטרין ליה גננא לרבי אלעזר, אמר להו: אדהכי והכי איזיל ואשמע מלתא דבי מדרשא, ואיתי ואימא לכו [ר' אמי ור' אסי היו קושרים את חופתו של ר' אלעזר. אמר להם: בין כך וכך אלך ואשמע דבר בבית המדרש ואחזור ואומר לכם]" (בבלי, ברכות טז ע"א).[11] משתמע מסיפור זה שחבריו החתן באו לקשור את ענפי הסכך של חופתו, ואולי גם לקשטה, ולחתן לא נתנו להשתתף במלאכה. במקום לשבת בטל הלך לבית המדרש ושם, כמסופר בהמשך הסיפור, שמע דבר הלכה מר' יוחנן, וחזר ומסר תוכנו לחבריו שהעידו לו ואמרו: "אילו לא באנו לשמוע אלא דבר זה דיינו". נראה שהיה זה נוהג מקובל לסכך בבדי הדס.[12] כך, לפחות, אנו שומעים ממקורות בבליים על

הנהו בני גננא, דגזו להו אסא [אותם בני חופה שגזמו להם (גויים) הדס] ביום טוב שני. לאורתא שרא להו רבינא לאורוחי בהו לאלתר [לערב, במוצאי יום-טוב שני, התיר להם רבינא להריח מהם מיד עם צאת החג]. אמר ליה רבא בר תחליפא לרבינא:[13] ליסר להו מר [יאסור עליהם מר], מפני שאינן בני תורה! – מתקיף לה רב שמעיה: טעמא [הטעם] – דאינן [שאינם] בני תורה [ועשויים לזלזל בחג], הא [אבל אם הם בני תורה שרי [מותר]? והא בעינן [והלא צריכים אנו] בכדי שיעשו [להמתין במוצאי החג אותו פרק זמן הדרוש להכנת הדבר שנעשה בחג]! – אזלו שיילוה [הלכו ושאלו] לרבא, אמר להו [להם]: בעינן [צריכים אנו] בכדי שיעשו.

(בבלי, עירובין מ ע"א)

קושרי חופות אלה היו "בני חופה" (חבריו החתן) שלא-יהודים קצצו להם ענפי הדס ביום שני של חג לקישוט הסוכה. כיוון שנקצצו בחג, אסר רבינא להריח אותם עד צאת החג, כי היה עליהם להמתין "כדי שיעשו". כלומר, בצאת החג היה עליהם להמתין פרק זמן הדרוש לקיצוץ ההדסים ורק אז להריחם. לאחר דין ודברים התקבלה דעתו של רבא, שיש להמתין "כדי שיעשו" ולא להריח מיד.[14]

להדסים ששימשו לקישוט החופה, יש משמעות מיוחדת בתרבות היהודית. כבר ראינו אותם כאן, בחופה, ואנו

פוגשים בדי הדס גם בריקודים לפני הכלה, בעת שמעבירים אותה מבית אביה לבית בעלה;[15] ולהבדיל, הדסים שימשו גם להנחה על ארון המת וכבשמים לפני המת. כידוע, ההדס הוא מארבעת המינים – לולב, אתרוג, הדס וערבה – הניטלים בחג הסוכות. על משמעותו בטקס היהודי נוכל ללמוד מהמדרש. המדרש מנגיד את הערבה להדס: ענפי הערבה כמשים מיד לאחר שקוצצים אותם מהאילן, ואילו ההדסים ממשיכים ללבלב ללא מים במשך זמן ניכר. כך אומר המדרש: "'וענף עץ עבות' [הדס], זה יעקב, מה הדס זה רחוש בעלים, כך היה יעקב רחוש בבנים. וערבי נחל, זה יוסף, מה ערבה זו כמושה לפני שלושה מינין [מתייבשת לפני שלושת המינים] הללו, כך מת יוסף לפני אחיו" (ויקרא רבה ל י, עמ' תשח). לפי נגה הראובני,[16] יש להדס כמה תכונות שמכשירות אותו כסמל מעבר בחתונה. הוא ראשית לכל סמל לילודה – הוא "רחוש" בעלים, ומלבלב זמן רב ללא מים – ולכן יש לראות בו סמל לחיוניות ולהצלחה בנישואים. ההדס עמיד באש, ויותר מזאת, כאשר שורפים אותו הוא נעשה להדס "משולש", כלומר, בדיו מצמיחים שלושה של עלים במישור אחד. זהו ההדס המהודר שר' יהודה ממליץ להשתמש בו למצוות ארבעת המינים בחג הסוכות (בבלי, סוכה לב ע"ב). תכונות אלה של נצחיות, יכולת עמידה ואפשרות תחייה, עושות את ההדס כמתאים לשמש בטקסי נישואין וגם בטקסי אבל, כאשר מבקשים להדגיש את חיי הנצח ואת התקווה לתחייה.

גם מדרשי האגדה משתמשים במושג "קושר חופות". למשל, כשהם מתארים את הזיווג שעשה האל בין אדם וחוה בגן עדן:

ר' לוי בשם ר' חמא בר חנינא: שלוש עשרה חופות קשר להם הקב"ה בגן עדן, הוא דכתיב: "בעדן גן אלהים היית כל אבן יקרה מסֻכָתֶךָ אֹדֶם פִּטְדָה ויהלם תרשיש שהם וישפה ספיר נֹפֶךְ וברקת וזהב מלאכת תֻפֶּיךָ ונְקָבֶיךָ בָּךְ ביום הִבָּרַאֲךָ כּוֹנָנוּ" (יחזקאל כח י"ג). ריש לקיש אמר: אחת עשרה [חופות]; ורבנן אמרי: עשר. ולא פליגי [חולקים]: מאן דאמר [מי שאמר] שלש עשרה – עבד [עשה] "כל אבן יקרה מסוכתך" – תלת [שלוש המילים 'כל אבן יקרה'] מייצגות שלוש חופות, תשע האבנים הטובות המנויות בפסוק והזהב – מייצגות עשר חופות]; ומאן דאמר אחת עשרה – עבד לההן חדא [עשה את שלוש המילים כחופה אחת]; ומאן דאמר – עשר לא עבד חד מנהון [לא חשב אותן כחופות].

(קהלת רבה, וילנא, ח א)

במקור מקביל בבראשית רבה (יח ב עמ' 160-162), באים דברי ר' אחא בר חנינא ש"עשה כתלים של זהב ותיקריות של אבנים טובות ומרגליות... אפילו קורקסים

[קרסים] שלזהב עשה לו". גם אם במציאות לא היו חופות פאר מעין אלה, המתאימות לשליט או למעמד האצולה, ניתן ללמוד מכך שהחופה היתה מבנה מיוחד, שקישטו אותו לכבוד האירוע בחפצים היפים ביותר ותלו על קירותיו סדינים מיוחדים, כפי שנראה להלן, שאותם חיברו בקרסים.[17] אם נוסיף לאגדות אלה את משלי החופה של המלך ש"סיידה, כיירה וצירה", הרי לפנינו מבנה שהאגדות, לפחות, מתארות אותו כדבר שהשקיעו הרבה כדי להכינו לתפקידו.

קישוטי החופה

מדרש זה קושר אותנו לקישוטי החופה. ודאי שכל אדם מקשט החופה לפי יכולתו, ואפילו למעלה מיכולתו. דבר רגיל הוא בטקסים מעבר שרבים נוטים בהם לצריכת ראווה, כי הטקס מייצג את הסטטוס החברתי-כלכלי, ומי שחושש לדימוי הסטטוס שלו נוטה להוציא הוצאות על-פי המעמד שהיה רוצה להשתייך אליו. כיוון שכך, כל חתונה, גם חתונת עניים, תפגין שפע. גם במקורות חז"ל מעלים תיאורי הקישוטים של החופה, ושל החתן והכלה, תמונה של שפע. בתוספתא, סוטה טו ט, מסופר כי ב"פולמוס אחרון [בימי מרד בר-כוכבא][18] גזרו על חופת חתנים. אילו הם חופת חתנים? אלו של זהב.[19] אבל עושה הוא אפיפיירות[20] ותולה בה כל מה שירצה". מובן שלאחר כישלון מרד בר-כוכבא, כשגזרו על החופה, לא גזרו לבטל חופה בכלל, אלא ביקשו להמעיט בפאר ולא להכניס לחופה קישוטי זהב. יש לשער שגזירה זו לא החזיקה מעמד זמן רב, מפני שבעלי יכולת אינם יכולים שלא להפגין עושרם, ואחריהם מחזיקים כולם.[21] על כל פנים, המקבילות התלמודיות של התוספתא מתארות מהם אותם קישוטים שגזרו שלא ייכנסו לחופה; משמעות של גזירה נהגו לקשט בהם. לפי הירושלמי "אלו הן חופות חתנים? סדינים מצויירים ושהרוני זהב תלויין בהם" (ירושלמי, סוטה ט טז, כד ע"ג). לפי הבבלי: "זהורית המחתבות" (בבלי, סוטה מט ע"ב). לפי המסורת שבירושלמי תלו על הקירות "סדינים מצוירים"; אלה הם הסדינים שהמשנה (כלים כד יג) קוראת להם "סדינים של צורות", אותם תלו על הקירות לנוי.[22] כן תלו בחופת החתן "שהרוני זהב", שהם תכשיטים בצורת ירח (סהר), וכך גם נקראו במקרא (למשל: "העכסים והשביסים והשהרונים" ישעיהו ג י"ח). המסורת שבבבלי, "זהורית המחתבות", מפורשת על-ידי רש"י כ"טלית צבועה שני, ובו קבועין טסי זהב, עד שמעמידין אותה כמן כיפה". רש"י מסביר "זהורית", בעקבות "לשון של זהורית" שבראש השעיר המשתלח לעזאזל (משנה, שבת ט ג) שהייתה עשויה מאריג בצבע שָני, שהוא אדום עז.[23] "מחתבת", מוסיף רש"י, הם לוחות דקים של מתכת ("טס", לפי משנה, כלים יג ו) שקובעו בתוך האריג האדום ויצרו מעין נברשות בצורת

כיפה. קשה לשער למה בדיוק כיוון רש"י בפירושו, אבל קרוב לשער לפי העניין שהיו אלה נברשות נוי שתלו בגג הסוכה.

כשביטלו "בפולמוס האחרון" את קישוטי הזהב בחופה, קישטו בתחליפים זולים יותר. לפי התוספתא והמקורות המקבילים, "עושה הוא אפיפירות ותולה בה כל מה שירצה". האפיפירות,[24] לפי ליברמן, הם חבלים עשויים פפירוס, שעליהם תולים כל מה שרוצים, פרט לתכשיטי זהב. דוגמא למיני דברים שתולים ניתן לקבל מברייתא בשמחות, העוסקת בלוויה של צעירים וצעירות שנפטרו לפני שהספיקו להינשא. כיוון שלא נישאו, קוראת להם הברייתא "חתנים" ו"כלות":

עושין חופות לחתנים ולכלות [שנפטרו], ותולין בהן אחד דברים שהביאו אוכל ואחד דברים שלא הביאו אוכל, דברי רבי מאיר, ורבי יהודה אומר אין תולין בהן אלא דברים שלא הביאו אוכל; אלו דברים שתולין בהן, אגוזים שלא הביאו אוכל, ורימונים שלא הביאו אוכל, גלוסקאות שלא הביאו אוכל, ולשונות של ארגמן ולגינין צלוחיות של שמן המר [המור].[25] ואלו דברים שאין תולין בהן, אגוזים שהביאו אוכל, ורימונים שהביאו אוכל, וגלוסקאות שהביאו אוכל, ולגינין צלוחיות של שמן מתוק. כללו של דבר כל התלוי בחופה אסור בהנאה.

(שמחות ח ב)

המחלוקת בין ר' מאיר ור' יהודה היא אם תולים או לא תולים דברי אוכל שראויים לאכילה. לפי ר' מאיר – תולים בין ראויים ובין שאינם ראויים לאכילה; לפי ר' יהודה – תולים רק דברים שאינם ראויים לאכילה. לדברי הכל, מינים ש"הביאו אוכל" אסורים בהנאה, אך המחלוקת היא אם יש איסור של איבוד אוכלין בדברים ש"הביאו אוכל". ר' מאיר אינו חושש, ובחופת "חתן" או "כלה" שנפטרו מתיר לתלות הכל. מסתבר אפוא שבחופה רגילה גם ר' יהודה מתיר לתלות דברים ראויים לאכילה. אולי חשב ר' יהודה על דמיון בין מות צעירים, לבין אגוזים ורימונים שנקטפו בעודם בוסר, ולכן התיר רק אלה בחופת צעירים שנפטרו.

כאן המקום לברר מושג סתום. בבבלי, סוטה יב ע"ב יש מחלוקת תנאים בדרשת פסוק: "[ותפתח ותראהו את הילד] והנה נער בֹּכה" (שמות ב ו'). קרי ליה "ילד" וקרי ליה "נער"?! תני: הוא ילד, וקולו כנער, דברי ר' יהודה. אמר לו נחמיה: אם כן עשיתו למשה רבינו בעל מום? אלא מלמד שעשתה לו אמו חופת נעורים בתיבה. אמרה שמא לא אזכה לחופתו". המושג "חופת נעורים", או "חופת נערים" (במקבילה בשמות רבה א כז, עמ' 77) הוא יחידאי. אולי התכוון ר' נחמיה לומר שאמו עשתה לו חופה מעל לתיבה מפני שחששה שלא תזכה לראות בחתונתו. הרי ראינו שהיו

עושים חופה לבחור ולבחורה בלוויה שלהם, אם נפטרו כשהם עדיין רווקים.

חופה בקיטון

עלינו לברר עוד מקור אחד, מהמאה השלישית בארץ-ישראל, אשר ממנו משתמע שהחופה לא הייתה מבנה חיצוני זמני, אלא בנו אותה בקיטון, שהוא חדר שינה, או חדר הפונה לטרקלין.[26] ברייתא בענייני ירושה אומרת כי אב שהשיא את בנו בבית ומת האב, זכה הבן בבית. שאל ר' חגי את ר' יוסי: "היתה חופתו בקיטון ועשה לו היסב בטרקלין, מהו [האם מקבל הבן את שני החדרים לרשותו]?" (ירושלמי, בבא בתרא ט ג, טז ע"ד). לדעת ביכלר, לא עשו חופה בקיטון וזו היתה רק שאלה היפותטית הקשורה בבעיה מורכבת של ירושה. יתכן שביכלר צודק, אבל אני חושב שהיתה אפשרות שיבנו חופה בתוך הבית שיועד לחתן, שנקרא "בית חתנות".

כך אנו קוראים במשנה: "המוכר מקום לחבירו לבנות לו בית וכן המקבל מחבירו לבנות לו בית חתנות לבנו ובית אלמנות לבתו בונה ארבע אמות על שש דברי רבי עקיבא" (משנה, בבא בתרא ו ד). משנה זו קובעת תקן לשטח הדירה של "בית חתנות". המוכר בית, או קבלן הבונה בית, מתחייב לפחות לשטח כזה לבית חתנות. ממשנה זו אנו גם למדים על מקרים שאלמנה חזרת לגור בבית אביה, מפני שהיא חייבת לעזוב את בית בעלה המת. זאת, קרוב לוודאי, כשלא היו לה בנים ולא המשיכה את קו בית-האב של בעלה. התלמוד שואל, מדוע אין המשנה מדברת על בית חתנות לבנו ולבתו? והתשובה, שלפי שיטתנו מובנת מאליה, היא: "דלא דרכה דחתנא למידר בי חמוה [אין דרך החתן לגור בבית חמיו]" (בבלי, בבא בתרא צח ע"ב). כי הרי האשה היא שעוברת למשק הבית של בית-האב של בעלה, ואין הבעל משתלב בבית-האב של אשתו. בית חתנות בתוך הבית עשוי להיות פתרון לחתונה בימות הגשמים כשלא ניתן לבנות חופה מחוץ לבית מחמת הגשמים. במקרה זה החופה היתה קטנה ולא רבים נכנסו לתוכה, ואת הסעודה, ה"היסב", עשו בטרקלין. נראה שבדרך-כלל היתה החופה ליד הבית.

החתן והכלה ישבו בחופה בשבעת ימי המשתה. בתוך החופה עמדה מיטת בני הזוג שהייתה מחופה בכילה וקראו לה "כילת חתנים". הכילה ניתנה לפירוק, כדי שאורחים יוכלו לשבת שם. מקורות מסוף תקופת התנאים ומימי האמוראים מעידים על כך: "אמר שמואל משום ר' חייא: כילת חתנים מותר לנטותה ומותר לפורקה [בשבת]" (בבלי, שבת מה ע"ב – מו ע"א). מלאכה זו מותרת בשבת מפני שהכפּילה – העשויה מאריג בד הפרוש על מוט מאחז שנתמך על גבי שני כלונסאות מאונכים לצדי המיטה,

ומשתפל כאוהל משני צדי המיטה – אין לה גג ברוחב של טפח ולכן לא חל עליה דין אוהל.[27] מסיבה זו התיר שמואל לישון בכילת חתנים בסוכה, "לפי שאין לה גג" (בבלי, סוכה יא ע"א).[28]

"אשקא דריספק"

לסיום דיוננו על החופה, מעניין לעיין בעוד מקור אחד, בעל אופי פולקלוריסטי. מקור זה נמצא בין אגדות החורבן של ירושלים בבבלי, גיטין נז ע"א:

אשקא דריספק חריב ביתר, דהוו נהיגי כי הוה מתיליד ינוקא שתלי ארזא, ינוקתא – שתלי תורניתא, וכי הוו מינסבי, קייצי להו ועבדו גננא. יומא חד הוה קא חלפא ברתיה דקיסר, אתבר שקא דריספק, קצו ארזא ועיילו לה, אתו נפול עלייהו מחונהו. אתו אמרו ליה לקיסר: מרדו בך יהודאי! אתא עלייהו. [על יצול של עגלה חרבה ביתר. שהיו נוהגים (בביתר) כאשר היה נולד תינוק – היו שותלים ארז, תינוקת – שותלים תורנית, וכאשר היו נישאים היו קוצצים את העצים ועשו מהם חופה. יום אחד עברה שם בתו של הקיסר, ונשבר יצול העגלה שלה. קצצו ארז, והכניסו לה. באו אנשי ביתר והתנפלו עליהם. באו ואמרו לקיסר: מרדו בך יהודאים! בא עליהם במלחמה].

לפי מקור זה בנו את החופה מקורות של שני עצים שונים, שניטעו בעת לידת החתן והכלה. הארז – המייצג גבריות; והתורנית (ארון כנראה) – המייצג נשיות. שני העצים שניטעו על-ידי משפחות שונות במקומות שונים, נעקרים ממקומם ומתאחדים יחד לשם בניית חופה. העצים עצמם נגדעים ומתים, אך החופה שנבנתה מהם מבטאת חיים חדשים. כמותם, גם בני הזוג ניתקים ממשפחות המוצא הגרעיניות שלהם, ובונים משפחה גרעינית חדשה. הכריתה והבנייה, הניתוק והשילוב של העצים, הם מטאפורה לכל אחד מבני הזוג על עזיבת בית אחד וכניסה לבית חדש. אמירה מנוגדת כזו היא שפה שבאמצעותה מציגה התרבות את מצבי המעבר ואת דרכי ה"פתרון". עוד נשים לב שהמדרש מספר לנו כי בתו של הקיסר ישבה בעגלה; בת קיסר, כמו בנות מלכים או עשירים, או נשים בכלל, מייצגת במשלים ובאגדות את הצד החלש. העץ שקצצו לשם תיקון ציר העגלה שלה היה ארז – המייצג את החתן, את הצד הזכרי – ולא תורנית, המייצגת את הכלה. הרכב זה של הסמלים מעצים את תחושת החורבן בחברה שערכיה הם פטריארכליים. כי למקרא האגדה מתקבל הרושם שאישה חלשה גרמה למרד, תוך שהשפילה את הארז הגברי השמור ליום נישואיו: היא כרתה אותו ושמה אותו כיצול בעגלתה.

הכניסה לחופה

החופה ביהודה לפני ואחרי מרד בר כוכבא

החופה, כמוזכר למעלה, ידועה במקרא ונזכרת גם במקורות תנאיים קדומים יחסית. אולם מעיון במקורות חז"ל עולות השאלות אם החופה היתה תמיד אביזר הכרחי, ואם היתה חלק מהותי של הטקס, או שמא היתה רק מנהג מקומי. אם החופה לא היתה חלק עקרוני של הטקס, אזי, במקום שנהגו להקימה היא שימשה כסמל לכניסת האשה לבית הבעל.

במאמרו היסודי על החופה הראה אברהם ביכלר[29] שבמקורות של תנאים, בירושלים שלפני החורבן וביהודה שלפני ימי מרד בר-כוכבא, אין התייחסות למושג חופה בהקשר של הכנסת הכלה לבית בעלה. המונח השכיח הבא לציין את הנישואים הוא הפועל כ.נ.ס. כך, למשל, המשנה אומרת כי סכום הכתובה של בתולה הוא מאתים וזל אלמנה – מאה; רצה החתן להוסיף – מוסיף. ממשיכה המשנה:

התאלמנה או התגרשה – בין מן האירוסין בין מן הנישואין – גובה את הכל [כולל התוספת]. רבי אלעזר בן עזריה אומר: מן הנישואין – גובה הכל; מן האירוסין – בתולה גובה מאתים, ואלמנה מנה [מאה זח], שלא כתב לה [את התוספת] אלא על מנת לכנסה [שתיכנס לרשותו].

(משנה, כתובות ה א)

דהיינו, כשכתב את סכום הכתובה בעת הקידושין, התכוון לכך שיסתיימו בנישואים, ומשלא היו נישואים אינה גובה את התוספת. בבבלי, הדן בעניין, מעלה האמורא רבין (דור שלישי-רביעי בבבל, שלמד בארץ-ישראל והביא מתורתה לבבל) את השאלה: לפי שיטת ר' אלעזר בן עזריה "נכנסה [הארוסה] לחופה ו[עדיין] לא נבעלה – מהו, חיבת חופה קונה או חיבת ביאה קונה" (בבלי, כתובות נו ע"א). השאלה העקרונית היא: האם הנישואים נעשו מוחלטים בעקבות הכניסה לחופה, או בעקבות יחסי האישות שלראשונה מתקיימים בחופה ("דסתם חופה לביאה קיימא")?[30] בבבלי כבר לא מדובר ב"כניסה" סתם, אלא ב"כניסה לחופה". על-כל-פנים, לפועל "כנס" (עם חופה או בלי חופה), אין משמעות של יחסי אישות, אלא של כניסה לרשות הבעל (בבלי, כתובות נז ע"א).

אכן, בכמה אירועים שהתלמוד מספר עליהם ושהתרחשו לפני מרד בר-כוכבא, אנו מוצאים את השימוש בפועל כ.נ.ס. בלבד, ללא הקשר של כניסה לחופה. שם בדרך-כלל הכוונה היא של כניסה לבית הבעל, או כניסה לרשותו. אנו קוראים:

מעשה שמתה אשתו של ר' טרפון, עד שהוא בבית הקברות אמר לאחותה היכנסי וגדלי את בני אחותך. אף-על-פי-כן כנסה ולא הכירה עד שעברו עליה שלשים יום.
(ירושלמי, יבמות ד יא, ו ע"ב).[31]

בבבלי (מועד קטן כג ע"א) מסופר סיפור זה על יוסף הכהן. אולי היו אלה שני מקרים שונים שהעורך ניסחם באופן דומה. הירושלמי מספר על בת אחותו הקטינה של ר' אליעזר שלא רצה לשאתה, על-פי שיטתו שאין לשאת קטנה. לאחר שהפצירה בו לשאתה "כנסה ולא הכירה [לא קיים עמה יחסי אישות]" (ירושלמי, יבמות יג ב, יג ע"ג).[32]
כך אנו שומעים גם מדברי הלל הזקן:

דרש הלל הזקן לשון הדיוט [הלל דרש את הלשון העממית, לשון ההדיוטות, כאילו הייתה לשון חכמים]: כשהיו בני אלכסנדריא מקדשין נשים, אחר בא וחוטפה מן השוק. ובא מעשה לפני חכמים, בקשו לעשות בניהן ממזרין. אמר להם הלל הזקן: הוציאו לי כתובת אמותיכם. הוציאו לו וכתוב בה: 'כשתכנסי לביתי תהוי לי לאנתו [תהיי לי לאשה] כדת משה וישראל'.
(תוספתא, כתובות ד ט)

לפי מקור זה, היו באלכסנדריה שנהגו לחטוף אשה מאורסת שכבר נעשו בה קידושין. מאורסת דינה כאשת-איש, ובניה שילדה לחוטף הם ממזרים. ביקש הלל כתובות של אנשים אחרים מאלכסנדריה כדי לראות את נוסח הכתובה.[33] הוא מצא שכתוב שם "כשתכנסי לביתי תהי לי לאשה" ודרש הלל מלשון זו שהקידושין היו על תנאי שתיכנס לבית האיש שקידש אותה, ואין דין אישות תופס באשה עד שתיכנס לביתו. אם לא נכנסה, בטלו הקידושין למפרע. בנוסח זה שבתוספתא לא מדובר על כניסה לחופה. כן לא מדובר על כך בשתי מקבילות שבירושלמי (יבמות טו ג, יד ע"ד; כתובות ד ח, כח ע"ד – כט ע"א), שבהן הנוסח הוא כמו בתוספתא, דהיינו, "כשתיכנסי לביתי". אבל הנוסח בבבלי,[34] אומר ביכלר, שונה:

אנשי אלכסנדריא היו מקדשין את נשותיהן, ובשעת כניסתן לחופה היו באין אחרים וחוטפים אותם מהן, ובקשו חכמים לעשות בניהן ממזרים. אמר להן הלל הזקן: הביאו לי כתובת אמכם. הביאו לו כתובת אמן, ומצא שכתוב בהן 'לכשתכנסי לחופה הוי לי לאינתו [הוי לי לאשה]', ולא עשו בניהן ממזרים.
(בבלי, בבא מציעא קד ע"א)

לפי ביכלר, המקורות הקדומים לא דיברו על כניסה לחופה, אך עורכי הבבלי ניסחו את הברייתא על-פי מה שהיה

מקובל בזמנם. ובאמת, אומר ביכלר, מצאנו במשנה: "העיד רבי נחוניא בן גודגדא על החרשת שהשיאה אביה שהיא יוצאה בגט ועל קטנה בת ישראל שנשאת לכהן שהיא אוכלת בתרומה ואם מתה בעלה יורשה" (משנה, עדיות ז ט). כנראה יש לקרוא ר' יוחנן (ולא ר' נחוניא) בן גודגדא, כפי שהוא במקבילה במשנה (גיטין ה ה) כי ידוע לנו שר' יוחנן בן גודגדא שימש במקדש כלוי יחד עם ר' יהושע בן חנניה,[35] והמקורות ההיסטוריים שבידינו הם אמינים.

ובכן, הוא העיד שקטנה, שבדרך כלל אינה ראויה ליחסי אישות, הנשואה לכהן, אוכלת בתרומה כאילו הייתה אשתו, והוא גם יורשה אם נפטרה. כניסה לחופה, אין במשנה זו. אבל במשנה אחרת בעדויות אנו קוראים: "העיד רבי יהודה בן בבא ורבי יהודה הכהן על קטנה בת ישראל שנשאת לכהן שהיא אוכלת בתרומה כיון שנכנסה לחופה, אף על פי שלא נבעלה" (משנה, עדיות ח ב). ר' יהודה בן בבא חי בדור השלישי והרביעי של התנאים ועבר מיבנה לאושא לאחר מרד בר-כוכבא. ביכלר סבור שמלכתחילה המילים "כיוון שנכנסה לחופה" לא היו בעדותו של ר' יהודה בן בבא, והן נוספו באושא, כי בגליל – שלא כביהודה – נהגו בחופה.

הלכה זו חולקת על עמדתו של ר' אליעזר בן הורקנוס, שמתנגד לנישואי קטינה, כפי שהדבר בהמשך של תוספתא מקבילה: "העיד ר' יהודה בן בבא ור' יהודה הכהן על בת כהן שנישאת לכהן שכיון שנכנסה לחופה אף על פי שלא נבעלה, שר' אליעזר אומר וכן תיבעל וכן היה ר' אליעזר אומר לא ישא כהן אשה עד שתגדיל" (תוספתא, עדויות ג ב).[36] ההשערה של ביכלר היא שעד מרד בר-כוכבא, ביהודה נהגו כמו שנקבע ביבנה, שקטנה נכנסת לבית בעלה, ולא נהגו שתיכנס לחופה. רק אחרי המרד (137 לספירה) נהגו לפי תקנות אושא בגליל, שקטנה נכנסת לחופה.

לביכלר הוכחה נוספת לכך שכניסה לחופה היא מושג גלילי, שנכנס בהדרגה למקורות שלפני ימי בר-כוכבא. המקורות מדברים על ההבדל בין יהודה לגליל בענייני השושבינין, שהיו מלווי החתן מצד משפחתו ומלווי הכלה מצד משפחתה, מהאירוסים ועד הנישואים.[37] לפי הירושלמי "אמר ר' יודה: ביהודה בראשונה היו מעמידין אותן שני שושבינין אחד משל כלה ואחד משל חתן. אף-על-פי-כן לא היו מעמידין אותן אלא בשעת נישואין. ובגליל לא היו עושין כן" (ירושלמי, כתובות א א, כה ע"א). בבבלי הנוסח הוא: "ביהודה בראשונה היו מעמידין להן שני שושבינין, אחד לו ואחד לה, כדי לשמש את החתן ואת הכלה בשעת כניסתן לחופה, ובגליל לא היו עושין כן" (בבלי, כתובות יב ע"א). בתוספתא: "ביהודה בראשונה היו מעמידין שושבינין שנים, אחד משל חתן ואחד משל כלה, ואף-על-פי-כן לא היו מעמידין אותן אלא לנישואין. ובגליל לא נהגו כן" (תוספתא כתובות א ד). אמנם, ברישא של הברייתא בתוספתא נזכרת החופה: "בראשונה ביהודה היו מפשפשין את החופה... היו

מיחדין את החתן ואת הכלה שעה אחת קודם לחופה", אבל חסר כאן הביטוי כניסה לחופה. מהשוואת הנוסחאות למד ביכלר שההתייחסות לחופה השתנתה במקורות בהדרגה: הנוסח הקדום יותר הוא בירושלמי, אחריו בתוספתא, שבה יש התייחסות חלקית לחופה, ולבסוף בבבלי – המדבר על כניסה לחופה.

בהשוואה של מקורות ארציישראלים אחרים עם מקורות בבבלי אנו מוצאים דברים דומים. בשמחות (ז טו) אנו קוראים על חתן ש"טָבַח טבחו ומת אביו או חמיו, הרי זה כונס ובועל בעילת מצוה ופורש לאחר שבעת ימים". לעומת זאת, הבבלי אומר שבמקרה זה "מכניסין את המת לחדר ואת החתן ואת הכלה לחופה ובועל בעילת מצוה ופורש ונוהג שבעת ימי המשתה ואחר כך נוהג שבעת ימי אבלות" (בבלי, כתובות ג ע"ב – ד ע"א).

לכאורה השערתו של ביכלר מתקבלת על הדעת, דהיינו שיש להבחין בין מקורות קדומים יותר, שלפיהם הכניסה לבית הבעל מציינת את סוף תהליך הנישואין, לבין מקורות מאוחרים יותר, שבהם החופה מציינת שלב זה.[38] זאת ועוד, יש מקורות תנאים שמשתמשים במושג קרוב לזה: "כניסה לרשות הבעל". כך אנו קוראים במשנה (כתובות ד ה): "לעולם היא ברשות האב עד שתיכנס לרשות הבעל לנישואין".[39] הכניסה לרשות הבעל מתחילה משיצאה מרשות האב (או מרשות שליחיו) ונמסרה לרשות הבעל (או לרשות שליחיו). אף-על-פי שהאשה עוד לא נכנסה בגופה לבית הבעל, היא כבר נחשבת לאישתו, גם אם לא קיים אתה יחסי אישות. כך אומרת המשנה: "הבא על אשת איש, כיון שנכנסה לרשות הבעל לנישואין, אף-על-פי שלא נבעלה, הבא עליה – הרי זה בחנק" (משנה, סנהדרין יא ו). חכמים נזקקו למושג "כניסה לרשות", מפני שבין יציאתה מבית אביה לכניסתה לבית בעלה יכולים להיות מצבי ביניים: האחד, שכבר הזכרנו, יציאה מבית-האב ומסירתה לידי הבעל או לידי שלוחיו. זה יכול להיות במקרה שהחתן גר במרחק רב מהכלה ואין אפשרות לערוך תהלוכתה של הכנסת כלה. במקרה כזה, הבעל או שליחיו באים לקבל את הכלה מבית אביה. במקרה השני, הכלה כבר נכנסה לבית הבעל או לחופתו, אך טרם קוימו יחסי אישות, החותמים סופית את מעשה הנישואים.

אירועים שקורים בין שתי התחנות – היציאה מבית-האב, הכניסה לבית הבעל וקיום יחסי אישות – עשויים לעורר שאלות הלכתיות בדבר מעמדה של הכלה. המושג "כניסה לרשות" פותר בעיות הקשורות למצבים גבוליים. למשל:

היו בה מומין [ולכן מיקחו מקח טעות] ועודה בבית אביה [וירצה (החתן) לגרשה ואביה תובע ממנו את כתובתה]

האב צריך להביא ראיה שמשנתארסה נולדו בה מומין הללו, ונסתחפה שדהו. נכנסה לרשות הבעל [וירצה לגרשה בלי כתובה], צריך [הבעל] להביא ראיה עד שלא נתארסה היו בה מומין אלו והיה מקחו מקח טעות. דברי רבי מאיה.

(משנה, כתובות ז ח)[40]

הכניסה לרשות הבעל יוצרת סטטוס של נישואים עוד לפני הכניסה לבית ולפני יחסי האישות. כך פותר מושג זה שאלות הקשורות בירושת האשה ובכתובתה; בהפרת נדריה; במעמדה בתקופת האירוסין, אם מת בעלה בתקופת האירוסין ובשאר זכויות שיש לאב בבתו הקטנה והנערה,[41] אם מתה בין היציאה מבית-האב לבין הכניסה לבית הבעל.[42]

אך הקושי בהבחנה החדה של ביכלר בין תקופות נובע מכך שאנו מוצאים במקורות תנאים את המושג "כניסה לחופה" לצד המושג "כניסה", בלא שנוכל להפריד באופן ברור בין מקורות של יבנה למקורות של אושא. לא סביר לפרש, כפי שהציע ביכלר, שכל "כניסה לחופה" במקור תנאי היא תוספת של תקופת אושא, כשם שפירש את המקורות של ר' יהודה בן בבא ור' יהודה הכהן. נשווה, למשל, את המקורות הבאים, שהיו לפני ביכלר:

בת ישראל פקחת שנתארסה לכהן פקח ולא הספיק לכונסה עד שנתחרש, אינה אוכלת בתרומה... אין אוכלת בתרומה עד שתכנס לחופה לשם נישואין ותבעל לשם אישות.

(תוספתא, יבמות י א)

בת ישראל פקחת שנתארסה לכהן פקח ונכנסה לחופה לשם נישואין ולא הספיק לבועלה עד שנעשה פצוע דכא וכרות שפכה, הרי זו אוכלת...

(תוספתא, יבמות י ב)

בת ישראל פיקחת שנתארסה לכהן לא הספיק לכונסה לחופה של נישואין עד שיחרש הוא או עד שנתחרשה היא, אינה אוכלת בתרומה.

(ירושלמי, יבמות ו א, ז ע"ב)

באותו מקור בתוספתא נעשה שימוש מקביל ב"לכונסה" סתם וב"שתכנס לחופה של נישואין". במקבילה בירושלמי "לכונסה לחופה של נישואין", ובמשנה אנו קוראים "בית דין שלאחריהן אמרו: אין אשה אוכלת בתרומה עד שתכנס לחופה" (משנה, כתובות ה ג).[43] אגב, בעניין אכילת תרומה של אשה שהתקדשה לכוהן, אין אנו מוצאים את הביטוי "כניסה לרשות". המקורות מנסחים, בדרך-כלל, כניסה לחופה (פרט לרישא בתוספתא יבמות י א, שהוחזרה

למעלה), אולי מפני שהכוהנים ביקשו להגן על זכויותיהם ולא להאכיל נשים בתרומה לפני שתהליך הנישואין שלהם הסתיים סופית. במשנה אנו מוצאים בית-דין שלאחריהן שאמרו: "אין האשה אוכלת בתרומה עד שתיכנס לחופה" (משנה, כתובות ה ג).[44]

על-כל-פנים, הביטוי "כניסה לחופה" מצוי במקורות תנאיים ראשונים. מצאנו שבית הלל אומרים שאדם יורש את אישתו הקטנה "משתכנס לחופה" (בבלי, יבמות פט ע"ב). משנה אומרת: "שנים שקדשו שתי נשים ובשעת כניסתן לחופה החליפו [בטעות] את של זה לזה ואת של זה לזה, הרי אלו חייבים משום אשת איש [שכל אחת היא אשת חברו]" (משנה, יבמות ג י).[45] וכך במקורות נוספים.[46] אגב כך למדנו מהלכה זו כי אולי היו מקרים שהחתן והכלה לא ראו זה את זו עד כניסתם לחופה, כי השידוך נעשה על-ידי הורי הצדדים, ולכן החתנים לא הרגישו בהחלפה.

דחוק מאוד לומר שכל המקורות המדברים על "כניסה לחופה" הם מתקופת אושא ואילך. מצאנו שגם התוספתא מדברת על "כניסה לשם נישואין", ואילו מקבילה בבבלי על "כניסה" סתם. המקורות דנים בשאלה למי שייכים דמי הכתובה, אם האישה המקודשת יצאה מרשות אביה אך מעשה הנישואין לא הסתיים. למשל, בתוספתא: "מסר האב [את בתו] לשלוחי הבעל או שמסרו שלוחי האב [את הבת] לשלוחי הבעל, או היתה לה[47] חצר בדרך ונכנסה ולנה בתוכה או שנכנסה לחופה לשם נישואין ומתה, אף-על-פי שכתובתה אצל אביה, בעלה יורשה" (תוספתא, כתובות ד ד). ובבבלי: "מסר האב לשלוחי הבעל, או שמסרו שלוחי האב לשלוחי הבעל, או שהייתה לו חצר בדרך ונכנסה עמו לשום נישואין, אף-על-פי שכתובתה בבית אביה, מתה – בעלה יורשה" (בבלי, כתובות מח ב). כאן אי-אפשר לומר שערוך מאוחר של הבבלי שינה לפי הנהוג בגליל.

החופה כיסוד בנישואים בהתאם לתנאים החברתיים המשתנים

אכן, הרושם הוא שבמקורות האמוראים אנו מוצאים תדיר את הביטוי "כניסה לחופה", יותר מאשר את הביטוי "כניסה" סתם, הן בעניני הלכה[48] והן בעניני אגדה.[49] אבל לאחר סקירת כלל המקורות על החופה, אני מציע השערה שונה קצת מזו של ביכלה. המושג חופה הוא, כאמור, מושג מקראי עתיק והיה ידוע ביהודה בימי הבית השני ואחריו. המקורות משתמשים במושג "כניסה" או "כניסה לבית", ולא "בכניסה לחופה", לא מפני שהמושב לא היה ידוע להם או לא היה בשימוש, אלא מפני שלא תמיד נהגו בחופה, מהסיבה דלהלן: כאשר התנאים מאפשרים את צירוף משפחת הבן למשק הבית של אביו, אזי הכניסה של האשה לביתו היא הביטוי האולטימטיבי של הקנין, ואין צורך

בחופה. די בכניסה לבית כדי להתחיל את תהליך הנישואים, שסופו בקיום יחסי אישות. אכן, היו גם מי שעשו חופה, שהיא אלמנט קישוטי חגיגי המסמל את הכניסה לבית, אך החופה אינה יסוד בנישואים.

אבל, כאשר התנאים הכלכליים משתנים, אין אפשרות למזג את משפחת הבן עם משפחת האב והזוג גר בנפרד, נעשית החופה לסמל חשוב המציין את כניסת האישה לרשות הבעל. בונים אפוא חופה לחתן ולכלה בבית אבי החתן, לשבעת ימי המשתה, ושם החתן מכניס את הכלה לרשותו. בחופה הם מקיימים לראשונה יחסי אישות, והנישואים נעשים סופיים.[50] נראה שמתקופת בר-כוכבא ואילך, כאשר תנאי המחיה הלכו והורעו, הפכה החופה לסמל עיקרי של הנישואים – יותר מאשר הכניסה לבית.

החופה הייתה מנהג עתיק, אך ביהודה, עד ימי מרד בר-כוכבא, כנראה לא נהגו להקים אותה בכל מקום. ביהודה ביטאה תחילת מעשה הנישואים הכניסה לבית הבעל. מאוחר יותר נעשתה החופה סמל לכניסה לבית הבעל והפכה לחלק מן הטקס. "בראשונה" ביהודה, במקום שנהגו שהחתן פגש את ארוסתו בבית הכלה ואפילו קיים אתה יחסי אישות, לא היתה החופה סמל חיוני. אולם כאשר השתנה המבנה החברתי-כלכלי – ובעיקר בחברה עירונית, שבה הפיקוח על הנשים הדוק יותר – היתה החופה מקום המפגש הראשון של החתן והכלה, ולכן נעשתה סמל מרכזי. כבר ראינו במשנה ביבמות שכלות הוחלפו בטעות בעת כניסתן לחופה, כנראה מפני שהחתן והכלה לא הכירו זה את זו לפני כן.

בזמנים ראשונים היתה הכלה יוצאת "בהינומא וראשה פרוע" (משנה, כתובות בא) שפירשו שיצאה בליווי הימנונות [hymenaios, שיר ביוונית] ושירה ושערה פזור על כתפיה (אמוראים בארץ-ישראל פירשו "הינומא" כ"פריומא", אפיריון; ואמוראי בבל פירשו כ"נמנומא", צעיף לכתובות,[51] אך לא פירשו ככיסוי לפנים) והכלה לא כיסתה פניה. הסיבה היא כנראה שהכלה כבר היתה בקשר עם החתן בתקופת האירוסין הארוכה והם התראו מדי פעם. אבל כשהמפגש החופשי בין החתן לכלה נעשה פחות מצוי, עלה הנוהג שהכלה מכסה פניה עד כניסתה לחופה. על כך אנו שומעים במדרש אמוראי, מר' יהושע בן לוי: "מה כלה זו כל ימים שהיא בבית אביה מצנעת עצמה ואין אדם מכירה, וכשבאת ליכנס לחופתה היא מגלה פניה..."[52] (שמות רבה מא ה). הווה אומר: בארץ-ישראל בדור ראשון של האמוראים נהגו שהכלה מכסה פניה עד כניסתה לחופה.

באופן עקרוני האישה היא "קרקע עולם" (בבלי, סנהדרין עד ע"ב), דהיינו, היא פסיבית כקרקע הנכנעת לחורשיה. כמו שבקרקע ובנכסי דלא ניידי שהאשה מביאה אתה יש לבעלה אך ורק זכויות שימוש בקרקע והנאה מהפירות, אך

הנכסים נשארים בטריטוריה של בית אביה ("נכסי מלוג"), כך גם היא עצמה "קרקע" ה"שייכת" לטריטוריה של בית אביה, אבל זכויות ה"שימוש" בה והזכויות בפירות – בילדים – שייכים לבעל. החופה, שלמעשה שייכת לחתן או לבית אביו, נעשית לתקופת טקס הנישואין גם לתחום זמני של האשה, אך לא לטריטוריה קבועה שלה. היא אין לה בעלות על המקום, אלא רק זכות פיקוח זמני, שבמסגרתו היא נותנת לבעלה זכויות בגופה, כנזכר לעיל: "אמר ר' יוחנן: לימדתך תורה דרך ארץ, שאין חתן נכנס לחופה [לקיום יחסי אישות] עד שתהא כלה נותנת לו רשות" (ויקרא רבה ט ו, עמ' קפה).[53] החופה נעשתה לסמל חשוב מפני שבתוכה התקיימו לראשונה יחסי האישות. הבבלי אומר: "דסתם חופה לביאה קיימא [שסתם חופה עומדת לשם ביאה]" (בבלי, כתובות נו ע"א); ובמקום אחר אנו קוראים: "אמר רבי חנן בר רבא: הכל יודעין כלה למה נכנסה לחופה, אלא כל המנבל פיו אפילו חותמין עליו גזר דין של שבעים שנה לטובה – הופכין עליו לרעה" (בבלי, שבת לג ע"א).[54] כשחכמים ביקשו לבטא מעשה מבחה הם תיארו מצב בו הכלה נתפסת בקלקלתה ערב חופתה או בחופתה ממש: "למה [חטא בעל פעור] הדבר דומה? לבת מלך שנתקשטה ליכנס לחופה לישב באפיריון ונמצאת מקלקלת עם אחר, שנתרפו ידי אביה וקרוביה" (במדבר רבה כ כד). או ביטוי חריף אחר: "אמר ר' שמעון בן חלפתא עלובה היא הכלה שמקלקלת בתוך חופתה" (שיר השירים רבה ח ב, עמ' קסט).

סיכום

מהמקורות למדנו על התמורות במשמעות הסמלית של החופה בזמנים ובמקומות שונים. החופה מוזכרת במקרא, אך אנו רק מבינים שמשמעותה היא חדר שבו ישבו החתן והכלה, ותו לא. מקורות תנאים מיהודה עד מרד בר כוכבא, מדברים על "כניסה" של הכלה לבית החתן, או על "כניסה לרשותו" ופחות על "כניסה לחופה", כי כן נהגו לעשות חופה ביהודה. לא מפני שלא הכירו מנהג עתיק זה, אלא משום שלא היה צורך בחופה שתסמל כניסה לרשות החתן. הסיבה היא במבנה החברתי שהשתנתה: ביהודה עוד היו משקי בית של משפחות רחבות שבהן הכלה עוברת מבית אביה לבית המשפחה הרחבה של אבי החתן, ואז כניסת האישה לביתו הוא הביטוי הקנייני (בנוסף לשלושת דרכי הקניין בכסף, בשטר ובביאה), ללא צורך בחופה כסמל לקניין. היו, כנראה, מי שעשו גם חופה, אבל החופה לא הייתה יסוד בנישואים. יתר-על-כן, ביהודה החתן והכלה התראו לפני הנישואים ופעמים עברה הכלה לגור בבית החתן והייתה להם אפשרות לפגישה אינטימית, לכן, לא דרושה חופה כמציינת מקום שבו הזוג מתייחד לראשונה. לעומת זאת, בגליל, במקום

שלא נפגשו החתן והכלה בין אירוסים לנישואים, וביהודה לאחר החורבן בעקבות מרד בר כוכבא, בנו חופה לזוג והחופה נעשתה לסמל מרכזי. מכאן ואילך בדורות אמוראים, המקורות בדרך-כלל מדברים על "כניסה לחופה" ומזכירים פחות "כניסה" סתם או "כניסה לרשות".

REFERENCES

1. ראו אתנוגרפיה על טקסים אלה: ניסן רובין, שמחת החיים: טקסי אירוסים ונישואים במקורות חז"ל: תל אביב: הקיבוץ המאוחד, 2004.

2. Emile Durkheim, *The Rules of Sociological methods*, New York 1938; Max Weber, *The Methodology of Social Sciences*, New York 1947; Claude Levi-Strauss, New York 1963.

   דיון על המתודה ראו: ניסן רובין, "תיאוריות סוציולוגיות-אנתרופולוגיות כמסגרת לפרשנות טקסטים". בתוך: אבינועם רוזנק (עורך), הלכה, מטה-הלכה ופילוסופיה: עיון רב-תחומי. ירושלים תשע"א, עמ' 98 – 121.

3. פרנן ברודל, הים התיכון: מרחב והיסטוריה. ירושלים תשס"ב.

4. איני נכנס כאן לגישות שונות בדיון האקדמי בשאלת שינויים והתחדשות במסורת. אזכיר רק כמה מהם: Eric Hobsbawm and Terence Ranger (eds.) *The Invention of Tradition*. Cambridge 1983; Hans-Georg Gadamer, *Truth and Methods*, New York 1989; Daniel Boyarin, *Intertextuality in Reading Of Midrash*. Bloomington and Indianapolis, IN 1990;

   אבי שגיא, אתגר השיבה אל המסורת. ירושלים 2006: רחל שרעבי, התחדשותה של מסורת: חגיגות הסהרנה בישראל, תל-אביב 2016.

5. Samuel Krauss, *Talmudische Archëologie* II: Leipzig, 1911, p.1; אברהם ש' הרשברג, "מנהגי האירוסין והנישואין בזמן התלמוד", העתיד ה, תרפ"ג, עמ' 75 – 104.

6. Cf. Adolf Büchler, "The induction of the bride and bridegroom into the chuppa in the first and second centuries in Palestine," in: *Livre d'homage a la mémoire du Samuel Poznański*. Varsovie: Comitè de la grande synagogue, 1927, pp. 82-132.

7. על-פי פסוק זה אומרת המשנה, סוטה ח ז: "במלחמת מצווה הכל יוצאין, אפילו חתן מחדרו וכלה מחופתה". השוו תוספתא סוטה ז כד. במטבע לשון זו משתמש רב כשהוא מסביר את חטאו של אסא מלך יהודה: הוא הוציא חתן מחדרו וכלה מחופתה לשם אנגריא, בלי להתחשב בתלמידי חכמים (בבלי, סוטה י ע"א).

8. בויקרא רבה הסיפור הוא על ר' שמעון ברבי שעשה סעודה לחתונת בנו, ובר קפרא כתב מחאה על השעה ראו גם: קוהלת רבה א ג.

9. על השינוי ממשפחה רחבה למשפחה גרעינית, ראו ניסן רובין, קץ החיים: טקסי קבורה ואבל במקורות חז"ל, תל אביב: הקיבוץ

המאוחז, 1977, עמ' 93 – 102. בספר זה הראיתי שבעקבות שינויים פוליטיים וכלכליים שהתחוללו בארץ-ישראל אחרי הכיבוש הרומי, הוחרמו אחוזות וקרקעות על-ידי השלטונות הרומאים והוטלו מסים כבדים על בעלי הקרקעות. כמו כן משבר כלכלי במאה השלישית באימפריה הרומית האיץ את תהליך פרוק המשפחות הרחבות למשפחות גרעיניות (בעל, אישה וילדיהם הלא נשואים), כל משפחה גרעינית לעצמה.

10. על התאמת הסיפור לנמשל ראו: עפרה מאיר, "נושא החתונה במשלי המלכים באגדות חז"ל", בתוך: *פרקים בחקר מנהגי חתונה*, ירושלים: מאגנס, תשמ"ו, עמ' טז.

11. ראו הסיפור המקביל בירושלמי, ברכות ב ה, ע"א.

12. במקום אחד אנו שומעים על אסון שהתרחש בגלל אש שאחזה בחופה והחתן נספה בתוכה. ראו: בבלי, יבמות קטו ע"א.

13. רבינא זה הוא כנראה ר' אבינא, בן הדור השלישי לאמוראי בבל, בן זמנו של רבא (רבה) בר תחליפא ושל רבה, המשתתפים בדיאלוג במקור זה. על רבינא זה ראו: חנוך אלבק, *מבוא לתלמודים*, תל-אביב: דביר, תשכ"ט, עמ' 274. אבל אלבק סותר עצמו כאשר בעמ' 310 בספרו הוא קובע של ר' אבא בר תחליפא הוא בעצם ר' אחא בר תחליפא, שהוא בן זמנו של רבינא, כשהוא עצמו קובע שרבינא הוא ר' אבינא! אבינעם כהן מוצא שיש לקרוא כאן ר' אחא בר תחליפא ורבינא, וקשה להכריע. ראו: אבינועם כהן, *רבינא וחכמי דורו*, רמת גן: אוניברסיטת בר אילן, תשס"א, עמ' 68.

14. ראו בבלי, שבת קנ ע"ב, שאין להחשיך על התחום בשבת "למיגזא ליה אסא", לחתור ענפי הדס לחופה.

15. על ריקודים עם ענפי הדס לפני הכלה בעת העברתה לבית החתן, ראו: רוביו, *שמחת החיים* (לעיל, הערה 1), עמ' 192 – 198.

16. נגה הראובני, *טבע ונוף במורשת ישראל*, נאות קדומים: השמורה הלאומית של טבע וארץ במקורות ישראל, 1980, עמ' 82-83. ראו על ההדס בטקסי האבל: רובין, *קץ החיים* (לעיל, הערה 9), עמ' 125.

17. ראו עוד נוסח בבבלי, בבא בתרא עה ע"א. ראו גם איכה רבה ג יט על מלך שנשא מטרונה ואמר לה "כך וכך חופות אני עושה לך" שהוא משל רחוק מהמציאות (ובמקבילה: פסיקתא דרב כהנא יט ז, עמ' 305 – 306 .). יש עוד מדרשים על חופות אגדיות מפוארות, אך אלה אינן חופות חתנים דווקא, כמו שבע החופות של המשיח (פסיקתא רבתי לז, קסג ע"א); החופה לעתיד לבוא של ר' שמעון בן חלפתא (רות רבה ג ד); חופה ל"בעלי המצוות" לעתיד לבוא (ויקרא רבה כה ב, עמ' תקע), ועוד.

18. שמכונה במקורות "פולמוס אחרון". ראו ליברמן, *תוספתא כפשוטה* לסוטה, ניויארק: בית המדרש לרבנים שבאמריקה, עמ' 769 – 770.

19. בכתב-יד ארפורט "אילו זהוריות המחתבות". כך גם בבבלי המובא להלל. בירושלמי דלהלן עטרת חתנים מפורש כזהוריות מחתבת.

20. ראו להלן הערה 23.

21. על הקלה בגזרות ראו דברי ראשונים שמצטט ליברמן (לעיל, הערה 18), עמ' 767 והערה 48 שם. ראו גם רוביו, *שמחת החיים* (לעיל, הערה 1), עמ' 189 – 190 על ביטול הגזרה על האפיריון, ושם עמ' 294 – 296 על מנהגי "זכר לחורבן".

22. המשנה מונה שלושה סוגי סדינים: לשכיבה, לווילון ושל צורות. חנוך אלבק בהשלמות והוספות לעדיות ד י, עמ' 481, מסביר מהם מיני הסדינים האלה.

23. "אי זהו אדמדם שבאדומים – זה זהורית עמוקה (ירושלמי, סוכה ג ו, נג ע"ד).

24. כך בירושלמי, אבל בבבלי "פפיריות" ובכתב-יד מינכן "פירפיריות". ראו ליברמן (לעיל, הערה 18), עמ' 770. אברהם אבן שושן, *המלון החדש*, ירושלים: קריית ספר, 1974, ערך "אפיריות" מפרש: "מקלעת של קנים על גבי עמודים לאורך שורת צמחים לשם הדליית שריגיהם" על פי משנה, כלאים ו ג. לפי זה יתכן שעשו מעין מתקני קנים לתליית קישוטים. וכן תרגם מרכוס יאסטרוב במילונו.

25. בבלי, מגילה י"ג ע"א: "מאי שמן המור? רבי חייא בר אבא אמר סטכת, רב הונא אמר שמן זית שלא הביא שליש. תניא, רבי יהודה אומר: אנפקינון – שמן זית שלא הביא שליש, ולמה סכין אותו – שמשיר את השיער ומעדן את הבשר".

26. "בקיטוניות הפתוחות לטרקלין", בבלי, יומא פו ע"ב.

27. ראו גם בבלי, שבת קלח ע"א-ע"ב; ביכלר (לעיל, הערה 6), עמ' 89 – 90.

28. ראו גם דיון בין אביי לרב יוסף בבבלי, סוכה יט ע"ב.

29. ביכלר (לעיל, הערה 6).

30. לא כאן המקום לדון בשאלה אם חופה עצמה קונה, על-כל-פנים בימי רב הונא בבבל נהגו שחופה קונה. ראו: בבלי, קידושין ה ע"א. ראו גם רוביו, *שמחת החיים*, לעיל הערה 1, עמ' 111 ודיון נרחב אצל גלעד גייבל "על שייכות וביתיות: עיון בסוגיית חופה קונה". *אסיף* ג, תשע"ג.

31. ראו מקבילה בשמחות ז טו. בכתבי-יד אחדים הנוסח בשמחות הוא "לא בא עליה אפילו לאחר שלושים יום" ראו:
D. Zlotnik (ed. and tr.), *The Tractate Mourning*. New Haven and London: Yale University Press, 1966, עמ' 17 בטקסט העברי ועמ' 55 בטקסט האנגלי.

32. מקבילה באבות דר' נתן, נו"א, טז, והסיפור שונה: "נטל ממנה רשות וקדשה ובא עליה", אך זה בניגוד לשיטתו של ר' אליעזר. ראו: בבלי, יבמות פט ע"ב.

33. ראו הפירוש הקצר של ליברמן לתוספתא, כתובות, על אתר לשורות 30 ו-33.

34. ראו ביכלר (לעיל, הערה 6), עמ' 94-95.

35. ספרי במדבר קטז, עמ' 132; תוספתא, שקלים ב ד; בבלי, ערכין יא ע"ב.

36. ביכלר (לעיל, הערה 6), עמ' 114-117.

37. על תפקידי השושבינים ראו רוביו, *שמחת החיים* (לעיל, הערה 1), עמ' 225 – 233..

38. מלבד המקורות שהובאו יש מקורות תנאים נוספים המעידים על כך, למשל: משנה, כתובות ז ותוספתא, כתובות ז י ("כנסה סתם ומצאו עליה נדרים"); כתובות יג ה ("אדמון אומר: יכולה היא שתאמר:'...או כנס או פטר"); בבלי, מועד קטן יח ע"ב ("מארסין [במועד] אבל לא כונסין") ובזבחים מג ע"א.

39. בכתב-יד קיימברידג', ובכתב-יד מינכן הנוסח הוא "עד שתיכנס לחופה". וראו משנה, כתובות ה ג. ראו השלמות ותוספות של אלבק למשנה כתובות ד ה.

40. ראו גם: ירושלמי, כתובות ז ט, לא ע"ג; קידושין ב ה, סב ע"ה.
41. ראו המשנה: "האב זכאי בבתו בקדושיה בכסף בשטר ובביאה. וזכאי במציאתה ובמעשה ידיה ובהפרת נדריה. ומקבל את גיטה ואינו אוכל פירות בחייה. נשאת – יתר עליו הבעל שאוכל פירות בחייו וחייב במזונותיה בפרקונה ובקבורתה" (כתובות ד ד).
42. בעניין ירושה וכתובה: משנה, כתובות ד ה; תוספתא, כתובות ד ד; בבלי, כתובות מח ע"ב. בעניין הפרת נדרים: משנה, נדרים י ה; ספרי במדבר קנד, עמ' 204-205; בבלי, כתובות מט ע"א; יבמות פז ע"א וראו מה שכתב על בר ביכלר (לעיל, הערה 6), עמ' 109. בעניין שומרת יבם: תוספתא, נדרים ו ה; ירושלמי, נדרים יז, מב ע"א.
43. ראו תוספתא, כתובות ד ג: "שהאשה אוכלת בתרומה כיון שנכנסה לחופה אף-על-פי שלא נבעלה". ברם, לפי ספרי, במדבר קיז (עמ' 137) נראה שבת ישראל המאורסת לכוהן אוכלת בתרומה אפילו לא נכנסה לחופה.
44. וכן ירושלמי, כתובות ה ב, כט ע"ה. ראו הנוסח בתלמוד ירושלמי כתב-יד ליידן, מהדורת יעקב זוסמן, ירושלים: האקדמיה ללשון העברית, תשס"א, עמ' 982: "בית דין שלאחרון". השוו גם משנה, עדויות ח ב.
45. השוו למקבילה תוספתא, יבמות ה ט. הם חייבים בחטאות, משמע שההחלפה היתה בשוגג.
46. תוספתא, סוטה ה א; ירושלמי, יבמות ו ו, ז ע"ב; יבמות יג א, יג ע"א; בבלי, כתובות מח ע"ב.
47. בכתב-יד ארפורט "היתה לו". ראו ליברמן, *תוספתא כפשוטה*, כתובות, עמ' 235.

48. למשל: בבלי, יבמות נז ע"ב; כתובות נו ע"א; כתובות מח ע"ב; סנהדרין נז ע"ב.
49. למשל: בבלי, שבת לג ע"א; ויקרא רבה כ ג, עמ' תנב (ובמקבילות: פסיקתא דרב כהנא כו ב, עמ' 387 וקוהלת רבה ב א); ויקרא רבה ט ו, עמ' קפה (ובמקבילות: פסיקתא דרב כהנא א א עמ' 1, שיר השירים רבה ד לא, עמ' קכה; שמות רבה מא ה; במדבר רבה כ כד; דברים רבה י ד).
50. בירושלמי, כתובות ג ה, כז ע"ב פוטר ר' שמעון את האונס נערה מתשלום צער (מלבד בושת, פגם וקנס), מפני שהמעשה "דומה לחותך יבלת חבירו ועתיד לחתכה". הוא יוצא מתוך הנחה שוביניסטית שהנאנסת אין לה צער ואולי אפילו נהנית, מה עוד שהבתולים בין כה וכה עמדו להסרה, כמו יבלת. על כך ענו לו: "לא דומה נבעלת באשפה לנבעלת בחופה".
51. ירושלמי, כתובות ב א, כו ע"ג; בבלי, כתובות יז ע"ב. על ההינומא ראו: רובין שמחת החיים, לעיל הערה 1, עמ' 199.
52. השוו דרך ארץ זוטא (מהדורת שפרבר ז ב), עמ' מט-נ (במהדורת היגר, מסכתות זעירות, עמ' 89). במדרש שבשיר השירים רבה ד כב (עמ' קיט) דברים דומים משם ר' שמעון בן לקיש: "מה כלה זו יושבת בפוריא [אפיריון] ואומרת: 'ראו שאני טהורה חז [השמלה עם הבתולים] עדותי מעדה עלי', כך תלמיד חכם צריך שלא יהא בו דבר של דופי...". ענייני כיסוי וגילוי הפנים אינו מחכר במדרש זה.
53. במקבילות: שיר השירים רבה ד לא (עמ' קכה). בפסיקתא דרב כהנא א א עמ' 1 הדברים הם משם ר' חנינא; בבמדבר רבה יג ב בשם ר' חוניא ובתנחומא נשא כ, משם ר' אבהו.
54. בבבלי, כתובות ח ע"ב המאמר בשם ר' חנן בר רב.

Jon D. Levenson, *The Love of God: Divine Gift, Human Gratitude, and Mutual Faithfulness in Judaism* (Princeton: Princeton University Press, 2016), 235.

Review by James A. Diamond, Joseph and Wolf Lebovic Chair of Jewish Studies, University of Waterloo, Ontario

Biblical scholarship has largely viewed covenantal love between Israel and God in the Hebrew Bible in terms of a political relationship. William Moran's classic study of Deuteronomic love, in 1963, set the stage by showing that it is modeled after ancient Near Eastern Suzerain-Vassal treaties.[1] As such, it delineates the obligations on the part of a subordinate "lesser king" for the grace and protection bestowed upon him by the "greater king." To this way of thinking, the act of loving a king is not a subjective disposition, but rather a pact calling for steadfast loyalty and allegiance. However, the Hebrew Bible suggests something more when that king is God, sanctioning that love with the command to love God "with all your heart, with all your soul, with all your might" (Deut. 6:5). Subsequently, rabbinic Judaism elevates it to a cardinal theological value by memorializing it liturgically in the *Shema* prayer. The renowned Bible scholar Jon Levenson[2] argues for a biblical conception of love of God that, while certainly built on this mundane political dimension, also transcends it. Political fealty is far from the only one that mattered to the biblical authors when it came to God. In a study that mirrors its subject matter in its passion, lyricism, and sensitivity, Levenson reintroduces the romance the love of God demands, which has heretofore been critically drained.

Levenson methodically teases out those essential elements that are unique to the covenantal love of the Bible. First, as opposed to other ancient Near Eastern law codes, is its "placement of law within a covenantal framework" (p.14). Second, if love of God entails actions rather than pure emotions, as opposed to what most in the modern world would immediately think, there is another love that comes to mind beyond the romantic kind. It is one that encompasses far more than feelings. Drawing on biblical metaphors of parental rather than spousal love, what the parent *does* for the child is surely an essential component of that love. Third, as Levenson notes, is that the feeling of love can be *generated* by deeds such as a "ritualized remembering" (p. 32) of revelation. This resolves the problem of how emotions can be commanded. Fourth, God's love for Israel is gratuitous—a "gift, not a reward" (p. 46). As such, it is in a sense built into Israel's "DNA" and passed on generationally rather than earned. Fifth, and here, perhaps, is its crucially unique dimension according to Levenson: God's love is irrevocable. However, that does not mean His love is unconditional, in that it does require some type of compliance and observance on the beloved's part. On the other hand, while disobedience can only disrupt, alienate, and sour the relationship, non-observance or rebellion can never definitively terminate it.

God's covenant with Abraham is unconditional and arbitrary as far as the narrative advises us. That said, the arrangement also grounds the subsequent Sinaitic communal covenant with the nation Israel, which conditions it on further obligations and commandments. Betrayal of the covenant is always portrayed as a temporary "rupture" (p. 114) between an idyllic past and a rehabilitated future that is certain and promised by God to arrive. Levenson demonstrates this in what I found to be the strongest and most insightful part of the book, by examining closely the marriage and erotic metaphors of the love between God and Israel as they are worked out in Hosea, Jeremiah, Ezekiel, and, finally, in the Song of Songs. Hosea's adulterous wife and Jeremiah's equally promiscuous spouse signify Israel's idolatrous breach of her marriage vows to God. As such, the law that governs human beings would have demanded an inexorable divorce. However, the love that grounds the covenant between Israel and God ensures the covenant's or marriage's, if you will, survival, despite any infidelity. That love also surmounts Ezekiel's graphically depicted whoring women and the death of his wife, both representing defilement of the Temple and its destruction. Temple reconstruction and cultic restoration will inevitably occur, supported by the guarantee that "the unavailable lover will return" (p. 125).

As far as the "Song of Songs," Levenson, surprisingly, but with cogent reasoning, finds classic midrashic readings of the lovers—as stand-ins for Israel and God—to be actually more in line with its intended meaning. This runs counter to the general scholarly trend, which views this kind of interpretation as allegorical. An intense love between a lover and a beloved, the elusiveness of the male lover, and external forces that threaten the relationship, line-up with the shaky romance between God and Israel described elsewhere in the Bible. Ironically, the biblical book that is totally absent of any mention of God is actually all about God. When read in the larger context of the Bible as a whole rather than in isolation, it, as Levenson insightfully notes, "places both the marriage metaphor of the prophets and the poems of erotic longing in the Song of Songs within a new framework, in which love is again the central term, the essence, in the relationship of God and Israel" (p. 132).

Though Levenson's reading of the Song of Solomon and, more generally, his exposition of the biblical love of God, are convincing, there are, as one would expect, questions remaining and alternative readings equally plausible. His narrow focus on Deuteronomic love, which ignores the larger context of the canonical scriptures that comprise the Hebrew Bible, is problematic. Surely, a study that deals with an aspect of *Jewish theology* (i.e., the approach of rabbinic Judaism throughout its long history) rather than merely *biblical* theology (i.e., the attempt to understand the theology of the Bible in its original context) must encounter the text holistically in its final redacted version. Such is the way Jewish theology has evolved during the entire history of rabbinic Judaism for two millennia. Indeed, that is the very way Levenson asks us to read the Song of Songs—as part of the entire biblical corpus in which it is set, and what we would expect of a book that purports to examine a key concept within *Judaism*.

Would it not be instructive to examine the various human love affairs in the Bible characterized by the same term for love (*ahv*) for other clues as to what love of God might entail? Could the fact that virtually every one of these loves ends in disaster, familial disintegration, or death (Isaac and Rebekah, Jacob and Rachel, Jacob and Joseph, Samson and Delilah, and Michal for David, to name a few) suggest a negative view of love between earthly beings. The bond between David and Jonathan, a love so intense as to garner the phrase mentioned only one other time ("being [*nefesh*] bound up with being"), illustrates best this deleterious view of human love in terms of its effects on Jonathan. In his blinding, self-abnegating love for David, he surrenders his royal prerogative as crown prince and, therefore, extinguishes his future. His alliance with David against his father, Saul, turns his back on his past. Jonathan risks impending death to protect David, imminently exposing his present to obliteration. In fact, his actual ensuing death on the battlefield is instrumental in clearing the way to David's ascendancy to the throne. Perhaps the message is that the Bible wishes human beings to displace their own loves in favor of the love of God.

Hence, the Song of Songs could even be read in light of this narrative account of love to render a reading antithetical to Levenson's. Taking the lovers in their most evident sense as simply human lovers (instead of allegorizing them as God and Israel) may very well poetically capture the Bible's advocacy of love of God over love of human beings. The book's sole objective meditation on love by its author, detached from its protagonists, reveals or points, if you will, to the message as a general human phenomenon (Song of Songs 8:6–7) and is a key concept. Though Levenson cites this passage as "most memorable," he fails to explain precisely why. It is significant that love is almost exclusively cast in morbid metaphors: It is first analogized to "death." It then likens love to "Sheol," a kind of posthumous purgatory. It further deepens love's ominous features by comparing its consequences to "darts of fire." The last analogy, *Reshef* (darts), conjures a common biblical sense as an instrument of devastation, war, and plague, as well as its ancient Near Eastern connotations of a netherworld deity. Love is then placed alongside "jealousy," a term most often associated with violence and anger, heightening its devastating force. Taken all together—the lesson might be that human love is damaging and explains why the beloved, in the ultimate verse of the book, pleads for her lover to "run away." She does so because she is not willing to surrender to its injurious consequences.

This message may not appeal to our modern maudlin sensibilities but that is no reason to reject it as an overarching biblical idea. In fact, it may be vital to our understanding of the binding of Isaac, the *akedah*, where the term love (*ahavah*) appears for the very first time in the final redacted chronology of the biblical canon. Abraham's love for Isaac sets the stage for the trial.

Could the *akedah* provide the most graphic form of the Bible's deprecation of human love as a threat to the love of God? Abraham's love for Isaac threatens to usurp the love of God, which the Bible holds supremely vital to human life. God demands that Abraham vanquish his love for another human being, his son, in favor of loving Him. Abraham's willingness to sacrifice his parental love for God demonstrates that human love must be subordinate to the love of God.

When Levenson moves from the biblical age to the Middle Ages, his eagerness to locate a medieval rationalist such as Maimonides on a biblical trajectory leads to mischaracterization. For example, Levenson argues that despite Maimonides' intellectualism, he promotes a publicly committed life, and his ideal lover "is hardly a monk or a hermit" (p. 170). In that sense, Levenson claims, Maimonides veers away from Greco-Roman and Islamic philosophical influences and toward "the covenantal theology of the Hebrew Bible to a high degree." However, even though Maimonides is notorious for being subject to diametrically opposing interpretations, Maimonides' description of his ideal lover, which Levenson cites in support of this assertion, is anything but an endorsement of the active life so prominent in the Bible. Maimonides' portrayal of the very highest sate of intellectual perfection achieved by Moses, which is also an ideal love of God, is the point where he "talks with people, and is occupied with bodily necessities, while his intellect is wholly turned toward Him" (*Guide for the Perplexed*; 3:51). In fact, the only thing that is really active in this "lover" is the mind. The philosopher/lover retreats into himself, with his own mind and inner-self replacing the proverbial cave. His external actions are disembodied acts, attributed to him only in the sense of an automaton. It is, in fact, a hermetic existence sealed off from what is merely a façade of public life. He is always with God because his essential self, which for Maimonides is the intellect, is with God and not with people. This reinvention of Moses, as paradigmatic of the Maimonidean ideal, is unrecognizable in the Bible.

Though Levenson's book purports to deal with the theology and practice of love of God "developed over the millennia" (p. xiii), its predominant focus is on the Bible, unsurprisingly for an outstanding scholar who has dedicated his life to the study of the Hebrew Bible. Even when Levenson moves to the Middle Ages of Bahya and Maimonides and onto the modern period of Buber and Rosenzweig, it is to show the idea's consistencies with its origins in the ancient Near Eastern context. And so, in the chapters dealing with the medieval, Levenson's preferences, are for Bahya ibn Pakuda's eleventh-century ethical tome *Duties of the Heart* and Joseph Albo's (1380-1444) *Sepher Ha-'Ikkarim*, since they allow for greater traces of the divine biblical romance involving a personal, reactive God possessed by a suprarational love of Israel. Levenson emphasizes their continuity with the Bible on love *of* and love *by* God as "striking" and "remarkable" 165, 178). Likewise, Rosenzweig is the clear winner in the contest with Buber for the soul of Jewish theology. Buber's rejection of essential elements of the biblical God as a lawgiver and as a lover of community, both of which undermine his "contentless" individualistic I-Thou encounter, rule him out as an authentic bearer of the biblical tradition. Accordingly, Levenson literally grants Rosenzweig the very last words in the book, which allows the divine lover's commandment "Love Me" to resonate with the "genuine tone of the ancient commandment."

Notwithstanding the inevitable criticisms and questions raised by any review of a learned work, Levenson's fine study is a noteworthy contribution to the understanding of a difficult and central theological concept. It should be a staple for any course dealing with Jewish theology or the love of God in religion. Like its topic, it is a lovely book. Levenson's work also provides a sorely needed antidote to current expressions of a love of God that perversely motivates so much death and destruction. Suicide bombers declare such love the instant before murdering scores of innocent people in its name. On the contrary, to abide by the divine law "Thou shalt not kill," and to preserve life, as the rabbis understood the overarching principle governing all mitzvoth of "You shall live by them," captures Levenson's characterization of Rosenzweig's notion of loving God. It is to take "a principled stance of openness to the Torah as the medium for encountering the loving and commanding God of Israel" (p. 192).

REFERENCES

1. William L. Moran, "The Ancient Near East Background of the Love of God in Deuteronomy." *Catholic Biblical Quarterly* 25, no. 1 (1963): 77–87.
2. Jon D. Levenson is the Albert A. List Professor of Jewish Studies at the Harvard Divinity School, Cambridge, MA.

Todd M. Endelman, *Leaving the Jewish Fold: Conversion and Radical Assimilation in Modern Jewish History* (Princeton: Princeton University Press, 2015), 367.

Review by Sylvia Barack Fishman, Joseph and Esther Foster Professor of Judaic Studies, Department of Near Eastern and Judaic Studies, Co-Director, Hadassah-Brandeis Institute, Waltham, MA

Some Jews have chosen to disassociate from their inherited ethnoreligious culture for diverse reasons and in very different contexts over the past millennia. Todd M. Endelman[1] demonstrates this perplexing but complex phenomenon in his recently published masterful and comprehensive volume. Effectively synthesizing historical research by scores of scholars in addition to his own impressive work, Endelman's global narrative is both detailed and panoramic, portraying Jews who chose conversion or radical assimilation, or both, from the Middle Ages to the present day.

A number of draconian episodes in history decimated Jewish communities, such as the Spanish and Portuguese Inquisitions and the defeat of Muslim forces, leading up to the expulsion of Jews from the Iberian Peninsula. Christian triumphalism "seemed to some converts to prove the truth of the church's claim that God had abandoned the Jews and consigned them to endless exile and punishment," Endelman posits. The resulting almost complete lack of confidence in Judaism among many *conversos* changed the face of worldwide Jewry forever. While many Sephardic Jews who settled across the Ottoman Empire immersed themselves in Jewish religious as well as communal life and culture, former converts who made their way to Western Europe "attached themselves to the [Jewish] community for social and economic reasons primarily." Some converted emigres in Amsterdam, London, and elsewhere "stood apart from the community altogether." New Christians in Venice and Southwestern France "moved uneasily between Jewish and Christian communities" (see pp. 54–56 for these citations). In the aftermath of these cataclysms, Sephardic Jewry declined numerically worldwide and Ashkenazi Jewry rose proportionately.

Until the onset of modernity, it was seldom appropriate to consider pre-modern conversions "voluntary," Endelman warns, because religiously neutral space was virtually non-existent, and the "imbalance in power relations between Judaism and Christianity" was profound (p. 30). Some Jews switched religions reluctantly and sorrowfully, others eagerly, and still others out of fear or pragmatism; but religious and pragmatic motivations were typically entangled vis-à-vis the different impacting internal and external pressures. In most locales, desperately impoverished Jews were the most likely to convert to Christianity, while Jews of average or secure means and social status were much less likely to leave the fold. Records of conversions often refer to Jews in particularly miserable circumstances, including "battered women who were trapped in abusive marriages, . . . convicted criminals who were sentenced to die and wanted to save themselves, and beggars" (p. 31), who eked out a living by traveling from town to town and repeatedly converted to collect the fees the church offered to new immigrants.

In Catholic Poland and Italy, coercion continued from medieval through early modern times. In sixteenth-century Italy, onerous conditions for the Jews were exacerbated by the forceful spread of involuntary ghettos, further restrictions on Jewish economic activities, and repeat public burnings of the Talmud and other Hebrew books. Converts out of Judaism were primarily poor young men in their twenties, escaping these grim conditions; fewer poor women converted, some of them single/unmarried and some fleeing unhappy marriages to older Jewish men. Some converts to Christianity became priests or nuns, while others simply accepted clothing and money. In the early eighteenth century, the Polish church became interested in converting Jews, and religious institutions for that purpose were established. Tragically, they were to be filled by the "kidnapping of Jewish children." Endelman details how "the children were subject to both the carrot and the stick, including flogging and starvation. Once [these] children submitted to baptism, parents were powerless to obtain their return" (p. 45). When Polish Jews experienced the cataclysmic Chemielnicki massacres in 1648, about 1000 of them converted to the Orthodox Church. Far greater numbers were slaughtered or enslaved. Memories of these hideous sufferings in the collective Jewish psyche were not unrelated to later crises of faith in the wake of the charismatic leaders Shabbetai Tsevi (1626–1676) and Jacob Frank (1726–1791), whose disastrous endings precipitated spasms of conversions among the community.

The Protestant Reformation did not produce a friendlier attitude toward Judaism, but it did precipitate newly energetic but less violently coercive approaches to conversion. Protestant leaders in seventeenth-century England and Germany and elsewhere in Northern Europe believed that converting Jews into their putatively purified Christianity would speed the Second Coming. Persuasion rather than coercion was utilized also because increasing notions of religious tolerance emerged from "the splintering of Christian unity and the inability of any one denomination to monopolize power," Endelman notes (p. 33). Offers of education and employment were sweet enticements for Jewish baptism, and conversions increased somewhat. But the results were often disappointing; many converts discovered that their apostasy removed them from the Jewish community still without giving them viable economic tools or the social integration tools to survive in the Christian community. Moreover, because they had accepted economic enticements, the Christian community often suspected Jews of converting for impure motives. This pervasive mistrust was exacerbated by the continuing and understandably persuasive/intimidating practice of allowing condemned Jews to escape the gallows through conversion. As a result, even sincere converts often found that their professions of a newly embraced faith were "not as powerful as the negative sentiments about Jews that had accumulated over the centuries and become embedded in Western ways of feeling and thinking." Despite their conversions, they continued to be considered Jews, and, thus, "the quintessential Other" (pp. 36–37).

Conversion to Christianity became attractive to broader segments of Jewish society in the eighteenth century as the ideals of the Enlightenment (the Age of Reason) began to emerge, and attempts at political emancipation of the Jews gained momentum: Jewish communities became modernized, Westernized, and secularized. But, that said, the likelihood of conversion differed significantly from country to country. In Western European Jewish communities like Holland, France, and England—and later America—Jews were relatively well-integrated. Many found that affluent, well-educated, ambitious Jews could progress tolerably as Jews, and rates of conversion remained low. However, in Russia, Hungary, Prussia, and Austria, where anti-semitic attitudes escalated, permeating society and cruelly restricting Jewish occupational and social upward mobility, progress was tantalizingly just out of reach and conversion often seemed the only answer.

Endelman describes how the distancing of Jews from their roots increased on immigrations to different countries:

> Economic prosperity, immersion in Western culture, familiarity with non-Jewish society, and indifference to religious tradition were no longer the experience of the few. By the end of the [19th] century, Jews who were "candidates" for conversion—that is, who were susceptible to the attractions of shedding their Judaism by virtue of their social and economic position—numbered in the hundreds of thousands. As one Zionist writer in Vienna quipped in 1902, when a Viennese Jew reached his first hundred-thousand kronen, conversion became de rigueur (p. 90).

Quite realistically, these Jews viewed conversion as the necessary entrance ticket into the modern Western world, with all of its opportunities and advantages. Not surprisingly, under these conditions, youth and career ambitions were importantly connected to the likelihood of conversion. Large numbers of young men converted in order to get into universities or in order to obtain appropriate employment after completing their studies.

Young women converted too, often motivated by social ambitions or by individualistic yearnings for self-fulfillment. In some locales, women were numerically more likely to convert than men; for example, nearly two-thirds of Jewish converts to Christianity in Berlin from 1770–1805 were female. Endelman describes the larger patterns:

> [W]omen were no more likely than men to leave the fold *when their levels of acculturation and integration were similar*. However, since notions of gender structured female education, work, and social interaction [had arrived,] . . . Jewish women experienced acculturation earlier than Jewish men, usually because they received little religious schooling, and their exposure to secular culture was not considered a threat to their faith (p. 134).

The intensity of Jewish religious experience in one's life—or the lack of it—was connected to whether conversion was acted upon; those who did convert to Christianity were usually "the least firmly attached to Jewish practice or rooted in Jewish social networks" (p. 117). Endelman recounts particularly poignant specific cases in prominent secularized Jewish families: "Simon Dubnov's younger daughter Olga, swept up in the revolutionary events of 1905, fell in love with a Ukranian worker, . . . bore him twin sons, and then converted in order to marry him. While studying law at the University of Rome, Rachel Ginsberg, the daughter of Ahad Ha-Am (1856–1927), became the lover of a fellow émigré (p. 123).

Despite a rising number of converts, even secular families often followed the Jewish custom of cutting off children who defected to Christianity, sometimes leaving converts to comprise their primary social circles with other converts, since many Christians were not eager to socialize with former Jews. Indeed, as more Jews converted, their new Christianity was often regarded with increasing suspicion by their non-Jewish neighbors. Jewish "radical assimilation" (p. 171) often precipitated envy and opposition more intense than their traditional differences had aroused. Gradually, realizing that no matter how hard they tried to rid themselves of Judaic "defects" (p. 177), they continued to be disdained and many converts became deeply disillusioned. For some, this disillusionment was one more impetus for emigration to America.

Until contemporary times, even the most disparate motivations, contexts, and conditions usually produced very similar results—an estrangement from Jewish life for converts and their descendants. While the alternative religious identifications to which they fled or succumbed, usually, were not as hospitable to new converts as their threats or enticements had promised, the children or grandchildren of converts were typically deeply embedded in non-Jewish religious culture, society, and life in general, with little consciousness of—and little interest in—their fading Judaic lineage.

This picture changes when Endelman brings his sweeping overview up to the present time, roughly in the middle of this volume. He discusses how, especially, in America, an "extraordinary shift in sentiment was made possible by the *destigmatization* of Jewishness, itself one part of a broader turn toward the toleration of difference and the emergence and validation of segmented forms of identity" (p. 214). Endelman dutifully presents both *pessimistic* and *optimistic* schools of sociological interpretation (p. 215), including the argument of some contemporary social scientists in the United States today who depart from prior historical understood patterns. Such observers point to dramatic levels of American-Jewish "pride" (p. 214), even among intermarried Jews who are not raising their children as Jews by religion. Their data show that adult children of intermarriage today who have some attenuated Jewish background—unlike most in the past—may be motivated to seek out and reclaim their Judaic heritage. However, Endelman demurs from the optimistic view: "As American Jews grew closer to other white middle-class Americans, the forces of secularization undermined their most distinctive traits—their religious customs." He adds—foreshadowing his own later comments—"The only Western society in which a secular Jewishness was successfully transmitted over several generations was that which emerged in the twentieth century in the Land of Israel, because there alone Jews were no longer a minority" (p. 219).

Rather than moving directly from this depiction of contemporary Western environments to his concluding remarks, Endelman interposes several fascinating chapters on cases of Jewish converts who experienced spiritual life transformations and on the fate of Christianized Jews in the aftermath of their religious change. By inserting these, Endelman breaks his developed narrative momentum, which might have been interpreted as progress to a happy ending otherwise.

Instead, in his concluding chapter, Endelman characterizes his story as a "dispiriting tale" of "radical assimilation" (p. 365). He then sets a curious juxtaposition before his readers: Today, deeply ingrained essentialist anti-semitic attitudes may have diminished, but they have not disappeared. They have, however, been reinforced by a deep-seated mistrust for Jewish nationalism and a profound negativity with which many academics and many liberals regard Zionism. In some Jewish circles, as well, it is normative to celebrate the creativity and "the resourcefulness of diaspora Jews," but it is "wildly unpopular" to celebrate the Jewishness that emanates from the Jewish State or to suggest that the Jewish State and diaspora Jewry may at the very least depend on each other for Jewish vitality (pp. 360-67). After the massive evidence across history presented and Endelman's assembly of the centuries-long attempts to make Jews into something other than Jews, some readers may feel challenged to probe whether negativity toward the very existence of the Jewish State is yet another essentialist hatred of things Jewish and the newest episode in the attempt to eradicate Jewishness.

REFERENCES

1. Todd Endelman is the William Haber Professor of Modern Jewish History at the University of Michigan, Ann Arbor, MI.

Moshe Halbertal, *On Sacrifice* (Princeton: Princeton University Press, 2012), 134.

Review by Zev Garber, Los Angeles Valley College, Valley Glen, CA

On Sacrifice is a brief tome, a philosophical treatise on the give and take of Scripture and liturgy that is manifested so frequently in today's headline news, embodying acts of religion, terror, suicide, and war, seen in Moshe Halbertal's context as contributions to the public governance—as a sacrificial community. The gleanings from Halbertal's[1] *On Sacrifice* reflect the multi-faceted idea and practice of sacrifice within theistic Judaism (e.g., *korbanot* [animal offerings] and *kiddush ha-Shem* [acts of martyrdom]) and its implications in historic and contemporary ethics, politics, and religion. In the religious domain, the sacrificial offering is given in the context of a hierarchical relationship—acceptance, rejection, drama, and trauma thereof are appropriately discussed.

Self-transcendence for the sake of higher commitments and values is central in the moral and political arenas. Positive and negative dimensions of self-sacrifice (i.e., noble and ideal or brutal and violent) contribute to societal cohesion and bind past and future memory and obligation. These and other issues (e.g., morality may demand sacrifice but sacrificial acts do not necessarily create legitimacy) are succinctly introduced and analyzed from historical, cultural, and psychological perspectives and in the fullness of Jewish sacred texts, halakhic jurisdiction, and non-Jewish sources. In sum, Halberthal presents an exacting and lucidly written narrative about the sense and essence of sacrifice from religious biblical injunction of animal sacrifices to patriotic ideas such as self-sacrifice in war.

KORBAN

The key to unlocking Halbertal's intent with this recent work is understanding the meaning and application of *korban* (sacrifice), which is spelled out in his Introduction in terms of religion, ethics, and politics. This, in turn, implies the binary division of the book into sacrifice as a religious ritual and commitment of "Man to a Higher Being" and sacrifice motivated by obligation entailing "giving for" as an idea, a cause, etc. Part One, "Sacrificing To," suggests that *korban* in biblical, rabbinic, and liturgical texts is divided across grateful expression and a course of action, method, or instrument by which an act can be accomplished or an end achieved. Religion-related issues are primarily discussed. Primarily animal sacrifices but also human sacrifices are depicted as obligated fulfillment of the command of God. Contrary to contemporary expectation, no reciprocal benefit is guaranteed or received, since God as God is beyond mortality and powers thereof. The divine-human contract is uneven. Required obligation of man to God does not equate to a God restricted to the whims of man. Thus, bringing sacrificial animal offerings to secure some health, happiness, victory in battle, wealth, and so on is wishful vanity. Additionally, sacrificial offerings portrayed as a gift to God is weighed by Halbertal, who also acknowledges the Semitist William Robertson Smith's cogent point that the act of sacrifice is an expiation of sins.

Part Two, "Sacrifice For," deals in moral and political usage, which emboldens self-sacrifice, martyrdom, and acts of brutality and violence.

Halbertal views his sections as independent fields of inquiry, but he acknowledges that in various cultures and languages, the categories are interdependent and, in the end, "encompass rich and diverse realms of human life."

GIFT TO GOD

Part One, "Sacrificing To," raises issues specifically related to sacrificial offerings: acceptance, and rejection, substitutes (charity, suffering, prayer), exchanges, and love. Torah and other biblical references are coherently viewed through the lenses of revelation, rabbinics, and reason (deductive). Haberthal grasps the differences between theoretical and practical constructs of sacrifice, that is to say, meaning and acceptance (or rejection). Against the canvas of ancient Mediterranean religions, Greek Hellenistic and Roman thought, and a nod to the early Church leaders, or Church fathers, the author conjectures biblical narrative, Second Temple Judaism, and rabbinic thought as reenactments of God's sacrificial design on humanity's terms. He uses liturgical selections to underscore specific Jewish parallels and departure.

Part One discusses at length that sacrifice is a gift to God but the reward is the giver's and not the receiver's. God as God is the creator of light and life, the provider of the good and peace, and is in no need of mortal accolades, which function as tokens of submission and gratitude, and are driven toward an end to wars. Sacrifice plays a purification role suggested by the link between animal sacrifice, divine expiation, and violence. Namely, the purport of animal sacrifice emboldened by true contrition per divine dicta notably diminishes the spread of violence and the dominance of war. How so? A chosen victim (animal or human), as substitute for the participants in the atonement ritual, is offered to placate God, to annul self and group punishment, and to halt violence by one's foe. The lesson taught here is that sacrifice leads to the atonement of sin. Noteworthy is the language of natal origin of Israel, first-born Son of the Lord, and (in Christian context) Jesus, the son of God. The former is birthed in slavery and traverses to freedom, and the latter is crucified to attain atonement for others.

Tzedakah

Part One discusses other acts of divine atonement. *Tzedakah* (from the Hebrew root Ṣ*dq*, meaning justice and encompassing righteousness and fairness) refers to the responsibility to assist the poor, to sustain the needy, and to provide support for worthwhile causes. Believing in *tzedakah* is doing *tzedakah*, conscientiously contributing to a moral society and worldview. Practice of the doctrine of *tiqqun 'olam* (repair of the world/construction for eternity) is incumbent on Jew and Gentile to restore the earth and all therein to receive a fair and just share of the world's resources. Gleanings reflect the role of *tzedakah* in Jewish theological and ethical thought; cited sources on the subject of charitable giving and receiving are also noted.

Tzedakah donations are a central part of the Jewish way of life. The norm of giving to charity is 10 percent of one's income though many who are able might give more. *Tzedakah* boxes adorn homes and synagogues. They are filled regularly for a variety of reasons, both personal and communal. Take prayer time, for example: worship attendees donate at the end of a weekday service (not on Shabbat or at festivals where currency is prohibited); mourners contribute on days of mourning and *yahrzeit* (customarily, a year after burial); both donate in memory of the deceased. Traditionally, women's private prayer and petition are before *licht bentshen*, domestic candle lighting ushering in holy time, Shabbat, and festivals, and so forth. The purport of animal sacrifice (biblical and rabbinic), in the main for petition, forgiveness, and thanksgiving is universally replaced today by acts of *tzedakah*. Indeed, according to Jewish law, the poorest of the poor is obligated to participate in this beneficiary *mitzvah*, which some sages claim is the highest of all commandments.

Indeed, it is counted with *tefilah* (prayer) and *teshuvah* (repentance) in helping divert the divine punishment of individual sin (see *m. Pe'ah* 1:1, recited in Rosh Hashanah and Yom Kippur *musaf* service according to the *Ashkenazi* rite). To live in the image of God-the-Protector is the blueprint of *korbanot* and *tzedakah*. The evidence is in the doing. Also, in lieu of animal sacrifices, post-Second Temple rabbinic adaptation of suffering as a substitute for punishment and daily prayers of appeal, intervention, requests, and thanksgiving are enactments of atonement.

METHODOLOGY

Halberthal's meditative philosophical approach *sans* biblical criticism or academic reading may explain some impropriety in biblical understanding. For example, Halbertal sees no *peshat* explanation in Genesis 4 regarding differences in the sacrificial offerings of Abel and Cain. Yet, the former is accepted and the reward is murder. To wit, Halbertal extracts/interprets (*drash*) a sacrificial fallout; that is, non-acceptable divine offerings may cause acts of violence and murder. Fair enough, but symbolically Cain (agriculture) and Abel (meat) represent contesting economic systems mirrored throughout the ages. We, thus, find an academic, etiological explanation to Halbertal's observation that rejected sacrifices seed traumatic after-effects. Similarly, he questions what would Father Abraham have gained by sacrificing his beloved son, Isaac, in response to a divine decree? Here, a close examination of rabbinic notions of attributes, associated with the names Elokim (Justice) and HaShem (Mercy), may decipher the deeper structure of Genesis 22. Elokim requests the filial offering and the *malakh HaShem* rescinds it. 'atah yad 'ati (now I know) exonerates the willingness of Abraham to obey God's command. What was the test of Abraham?—Unquestionable *moral* obedience (Gen. 22:11–12).

Sacrifice Dilemma: Preserving Life and *Kiddush HaShem*

Preserving life is a core teaching of Judaism. While Scripture contains no specific injunction against suicide, based on Genesis 9:5 ("For your lifeblood I will surely require a reckoning"), the sages taught that suicide is wrong and punishable by divine decree. In the community, it meant burial outside the sacred precincts of the cemetery and suspension of mourning laws and customs.

This strong edict was intended to discourage Jews who contemplated suicide, but it caused great grief and embarrassment for the family of those who did commit suicide. To mitigate this problem, the sages ruled that for a death to be treated as suicide under the law, it must be both voluntary and premeditated. The rabbinical presumption was that people who kill themselves—axiomatic in cases of child suicide—do so without the premeditation. So their death is not considered a suicide at all. This idea is founded on the suicide of King Saul, who is described as having been in great mental distress "lest these uncircumcised (Philistines) come and thrust me through and make a mock of me" (1 Sam. 3:14). His death by his own sword is used by many rabbis as a precedent for not stigmatizing a person who, in a situation of anguish, stress, and despair, takes his or her own life.

Thus, while in normal times, acts of suicide may be blameworthy, in stressful times—Masada, the Bar-Kokhba rebellion, the Crusades, Inquisitions, pogroms—letting oneself be killed or even killing oneself for "the sanctification of God's name" is deemed by many to be praiseworthy. Maimonides, who codified Jewish attitudes toward martyrdom, taught that a Jew forced or intimidated to transgress the commandments in public or in a time of great religious persecution is expected to suffer death instead (*Mishneh Torah, Yesode Ha-Torah* 5.3). On the other hand, Maimonides made clear that a person who unnecessarily suffers death—for example, in circumstances under which Jewish law should be set aside in the interest of saving a life—is an ordinary suicide. But medieval French and German commentators opposed this decision. They felt that all people who sacrificed themselves, even when not strictly required to do so, are worthy of admiration and respect.

Persecution and destruction of Jews and Jewish communities over the centuries have contributed to the importance in the Jewish tradition of the concept of *kiddush ha-Shem*, sanctification of God's name through martyrdom. The talmudic dictum "be killed and do not transgress" has been the unyielding spine of a martyred Jewish people whose limbs were torn in nearly every historical time and place. In the medieval period, many Sephardim responded to acts of isolation, vilification, and expulsion by a policy of outward adaptation to the host culture and belief, coupled with an inward turning to a messianic Jewish ideology. To combat relentless terror and forced apostasy, Ashkenazi Jews, on the other hand, demonstrated a very strong belief in resurrection of the dead. Whole communities of Ashkenazim, thus, embraced martyrdom, and accounts of righteous martyrs of the past became part of the everyday teaching and veneration of Central and Eastern European Jews. Indeed, a central focus on the commandment of martyrdom—to be preceded by its own benediction: "Blessed are you, Lord our God, King of the universe, who has commanded us to sanctify His name publicly"—is found in the famous work *Shenei Lukot ha-Berit*, known by the acronym Shelah, or SHeLaH, written by the Prague-born and Polish-educated legal decisor and mystic Isaiah ben Abraham ha-Levi Horowitz (*circa* 1565–1630), published in Amsterdam in 1649.

Nevertheless, the pietistic, quietistic, and pacifistic way to heaven represented by the traditional approach to martyrdom was challenged by individual religious Zionist rabbis and Hasidic *rebbes* alike, who responded to the unparalleled horrors of the Shoah by advocating spontaneous as well as planned acts of sanctifying life (*kiddush ha-hayyim*) *even to death*. The pattern of spiritual resistance falls into three categories, each responding to a different stimulus but united by the intention to combat the enemy's determined goal of total annihilation of the Jewish people: the Jew's obligation (1) to fight and resist in order to preserve life (Rabbis Isaac Nissenbaum and Menahem Zemba, Warsaw Ghetto); (2) to observe Jewish belief, faith, rites of passage, and the sacred calendar, however minimally and symbolically (for they contribute to reconstruction [*tiqqun*] in the midst of Shoah (Rabbi Kaloni Kalmush Shapiro, Piaseczno); and (3) to return to Zion, rebuilding the Land of Promise so the souls in burnt bodies can be restored to life by a people reborn (Rabbi Issachar Schlomo Teechthal, from Piestany, in present-day Slovakia, murdered after the war in 1945 by Ukrainians).

CONTEMPORARY "SACRIFICE FOR"

Halbertal's volume confronts the "sacrifice idea" on two fronts. The first discusses ancient and traditional understandings of sacrifice as a religious concept and the second delves into the political and moral aspects of "sacrifice for" as a cause but at a price. To fulfill an obligation, in Kantian terms, Halberthal hypothesizes misguided self-love/self-transcendence and violence, resulting in immeasurable moral conflict. Self-interest, however self-honorable, does not justify unjust undertakings. His exegesis on the morality and immorality of war reflects well on issues facing the contemporary state in times of war and peace. Turning self-sacrifice into justification for immorality is an insightful oxymoron. On the other hand, acts of self-sacrifice for the common good, prosperity, peace, and justice for all is acceptable and admirable.

REFERENCES

1. Moshe Halbertal is Gruss Professor of Law at New York University Law School, New York, and Professor of Jewish Thought and Philosophy at Hebrew University, Jerusalem.